Internationalizing the Academy

Internationalizing the Academy

Lessons of Leadership in Higher Education

Edited by

GILBERT W. MERKX
RIALL W. NOLAN

HARVARD EDUCATION PRESS
CAMBRIDGE, MASSACHUSETTS

Library of Congress Control Number 2015938036

Paperback ISBN 978-1-61250-866-5
Library Edition ISBN 978-1-61250-867-2

Published by Harvard Education Press,
an imprint of the Harvard Education Publishing Group
Harvard Education Press
8 Story Street
Cambridge, MA 02138

Cover Design: Ciano Design
Cover Image: DrAfter123/Digital Vision Vectors/Getty Images

The typefaces used in this book are Adobe Garamond Pro for text and Corbel for display.

To the late Senator J. William Fulbright,
who sponsored the 1946 legislation that led to
the largest educational exchange program in history;
to the late Senator Paul Simon,
passionate supporter of study abroad;
and to Professor Richard D. Lambert,
advocate and analyst of foreign language
and area studies programs.

Contents

Foreword   ix
David Ward

INTRODUCTION
The International Education Landscape   1
Riall W. Nolan and Gilbert W. Merkx

CHAPTER 1
International Education in the United States   9
Gilbert W. Merkx

CHAPTER 2
The Senior International Officer—an Advocate for Change   23
Riall W. Nolan

CHAPTER 3
International Education Leadership: Reflections on Experience   37
Jack Van de Water

CHAPTER 4
The Senior International Officer as Itinerant Professional   53
John D. Heyl

CHAPTER 5
Atlas, Sisyphus, or Odysseus? An SIO Career   65
Gilbert W. Merkx

CHAPTER 6
An Unconventional Path to International Education Leadership   87
Howard Rollins

CHAPTER 7
The Senior International Officer—a Modern Proteus?   111
Maria Carmen Sada Krane

CHAPTER 8
Nine Pretty Hard Lessons from Twenty-five Years as a
Senior International Officer   127
   Uliana Gabara

CHAPTER 9
Reflection on International Education Leadership
Experience at a Small Liberal Arts College   151
   Joseph Tullbane

CHAPTER 10
SIO—the Hardest Job You'll Ever Love   169
   Riall W. Nolan

CHAPTER 11
A Contemporary Odyssey to Senior International Leadership   183
   William Lacy

CHAPTER 12
Whole Person Education in a Whole World Context:
International Education and the Liberal Arts   199
   Joseph L. Brockington

CONCLUSION
The Challenge of Internationalization   213
   Gilbert W. Merkx and Riall W. Nolan

Notes   225

Acknowledgments   229

About the Editors   231

About the Contributors   233

Index   235

Foreword

In the quarter-century since the end of the Cold War, American colleges and universities have become increasingly engaged in international curricula and relationships along a variety of dimensions. Following the collapse of the Soviet Union, the rapid rise of transnational exchange networks of all types, often called *globalization,* brought a new set of challenges to the United States and its institutions of higher education. Growing numbers of foreign students are enrolled on US campuses, and growing numbers of American students are participating in study abroad programs. The faculty of our colleges and universities are increasingly international both in their countries of origin and their research specializations. Interdisciplinary centers dedicated to foreign language and area studies, international relations, and global issues are well established. The STEM fields are increasingly international not just in personnel but also in the scope of research collaborations. Professional fields such as management and medicine, which once were US-centered, now conceive their missions in global terms.

These developments have been well received, but not without anxious reservations. Academic institutions are communities with deep traditions and strongly held commitments. Presidents and provosts have learned from experience that innovation in academic communities, to be successful, must be a consensual participatory process. Thus, the process of internationalizing a college or university requires visionary leadership for planning, building consensus, and dealing with management issues that cross disciplinary boundaries. The emerging challenges of internationalization have necessitated new senior administrative positions to sustain challenging innovations.

Despite the diversity of leadership roles delegated to international strategies, there are now well-developed initiatives at many national higher education associations designed to promote appropriate public policies and to foster interuniversity collaborations. Currently we do not have a consensus on an optimal institutional structure for international studies, nor do we have a well integrated set of national practices. Nevertheless, much progress has been made, and there is a growing awareness of best practices.

In this book, ten former senior international officers provide accounts of their careers in a variety of college and universities. Collectively, their narratives offer insider views of how their institutions developed international programs. The reader will be impressed by the frankness of these narratives and by the realism of their portrayal of the politics of internationalization. These are not just success stories but are also unvarnished accounts of stalemates and even failures.

Academic leaders—chancellors, presidents, provosts, deans, and directors—will find these experiences both familiar and decisive for making their institutions more international. As a former chancellor, I was struck by one theme that emerged over and over again in these accounts: namely, the importance of support and commitment from the highest leadership. When that leadership was present, the senior international officer was able to serve as a successful change agent. But when that connection was broken, usually due a change in leadership, the internationalization effort often stalled.

Another theme presented here that resonates with my experience as a former chancellor is the scale and complexity of internationalization initiatives and programs. We have long recognized that the university is enriched intellectually by international teaching, research, and service and by the diversity of cultures and languages brought to the campus by international students and faculty. However, each new layer of international activity also challenges established organizational structures, For example, how should inoculations and medical advice be provided to those about to travel (assessing overseas risk, finding insurance for overseas activities), how can we ensure compliance with federal export controls (including restrictions on the content of laptop computers taken abroad), how do we withhold taxes and make payments to foreign residents, and how should we assist foreigners in confronting the exigencies of campus life in the United States?

It makes no sense for each school or college of a university to devise its own ad hoc solutions to such administrative challenges. The initiation of and coordination among such service activities should be led by the core campus leadership, which is one of the reasons that so many institutions have appointed senior international officers. To be effective in overcoming the bureaucratic obstacles endemic to any large organization, these officers need support from the top. Once the international support mechanisms are in place, they tend to function smoothly. But putting them in place is not a simple process.

Internationalizing the Academy does not merely offer a deep look into the ongoing process of making US higher education more international in scope and content. Nor is it a cautionary tale about how hard it is to bring about change in higher education. In the final analysis, it paints an optimistic picture of a variety of colleges and universities in the midst of change, each finding its own path with the assistance of deeply committed senior international officers. While the journey is hardly complete, American higher education is well on the way to coping with the challenges of globalization.

—*David Ward*
Chancellor Emeritus, University of Wisconsin–Madison
President, American Council on Education, 2001–2008

The International Education Landscape

Riall W. Nolan and Gilbert W. Merkx

INTERNATIONALIZATION is increasingly seen as a strategic imperative for American colleges and universities. There is, however, some confusion about what internationalization means for an institution and how to go about achieving it. There are a number of different routes that institutions have taken to become more international. These include recruiting more international students and more international faculty, sending American students to study abroad programs, participating in international development and technology-transfer programs, developing on-campus centers for international and foreign area studies, expanding foreign language offerings, and introducing new courses in fields such as comparative history, international political economy, and cultural anthropology.

These core activities are not mutually exclusive; in fact, they are mutually reinforcing. Any route that an institution chooses to begin its internationalization will create a demand for other activities. Students returning from study abroad programs may want more courses about the places where they've studied and the languages spoken there. International faculty may want to start study abroad programs in their countries of origin. Technology-transfer programs stimulate more applications from foreign students. The introduction of more courses on international topics leads to more interest in study abroad programs. And so on. This virtuous cycle leads not only to more activities of an international character but a growing need for administrative coordination—not just of the international activities themselves but of the interface between international programs and the more traditional units of the college or university.

The administrative requirements of the internationalization process have led many US colleges and universities to appoint a senior international officer (SIO) charged with coordinating, planning, and developing their international initiatives. The first positions of this kind emerged in the 1980s, began to multiply in the 1990s, and now are commonly found in all types of higher education institution in the United States. Similar administrative positions are now emerging in Europe and around the world. The emergence of this new profession has, in turn, stimulated the rise of new professional associations for international educators, one of which is the Association of International Education Administrators (AIEA).

We coeditors are active in AIEA. We met at a time when we were both senior international officers, Riall Nolan at Purdue University (as associate provost for International Programs) and Gil Merkx at Duke University (as vice provost for International Affairs). Nolan chaired the task force that developed AIEA's first strategic plan, and Merkx served on that task force and later as AIEA president. Both of us are social scientists, Nolan an anthropologist and Merkx a sociologist, and have spent much of our earlier careers doing overseas field research.

The commonalities drew us together as colleagues. Our ensuing conversations led us to reflect on what we were hearing at the AIEA annual meetings. We were both struck by the disjuncture between the success stories recounted in the panels at the AIEA annual conference and the conversations about woe and disaster that took place in the corridors between the panel sessions. We decided that a more complete picture of the emerging SIO position could be provided by first-person accounts of both successes and failures. Recognizing that sitting SIOs were unlikely to speak as frankly as those no longer serving in such a role, we decided to invite a group of distinguished senior colleagues, largely retired, or about to be, to tell their stories.

As the narratives came in, we read and reflected on them. We gradually came to realize that these accounts of efforts to make the academy more international raised larger issues about the culture of American higher education, its institutional characteristics, and the challenges posed by globalization. These issues are the subject of our two opening chapters.

In chapter 1, Merkx discusses the history of international activities in US colleges and universities from an institutional perspective. He traces the development of the Western concepts of a university from its religious roots but emphasizes how the US higher education system eventually grew to become quite different from that of Europe. He shows how international education in the United States grew from the experiences of World War II and the American expansion that followed, and the Cold War. Merkx concludes by showing how the differential responses of US colleges and universities to these new opportunities and pressures helped structure and define the roles played by SIOs on our campuses.

Nolan examines in chapter 2 the contemporary issues that characterize the field of international education from the perspective of the SIO. He begins by noting that the ability to understand and work with the contemporary world's diversity has become an essential skill for virtually all US college graduates and that, despite the clear need for international education, few of our institutions are doing a particularly good job with it. He discusses some of the main ways in which internationalization happens on our campuses, highlighting the role of the SIO. Nolan draws particular attention to the difficulties with identifying and hiring good SIOs, largely stemming from the unique aspects of the job. He concludes by underscoring the importance of strategic conversations regarding the goals and mechanisms of internationalization and the importance of stakeholder involvement in these conversations.

In the chapters that follow, each author provides an account of his or her career and draws lessons from these experiences. The colleges and universities featured in these accounts are Agnes Scott, Cincinnati, Creighton, Cornell, Duke, Emery, Georgia Tech, Golden Gate, Illinois Wesleyan, Kentucky, Kalamazoo, Missouri, Nebraska Wesleyan, New Mexico, Old Dominion, Oregon State, Pittsburgh, Purdue, Richmond, St. Norbert, Syracuse, and UC Davis. This list includes both public and private institutions, large and small campuses, teaching-oriented and research-oriented institutions, and a geographic diversity that represents every quadrant of the United States.

Jack Van de Water, after starting his career at Syracuse University, assumed leadership of the newly created Office of International Programs at Oregon State University in 1976, becoming its first SIO. In chapter 3 he analyzes the key tasks awaiting an SIO on an internationalizing campus, from the recruitment and training of staff to the development of strong creative links with faculty and upper leadership. He stresses an understanding campus culture and the need for networks of support inside and outside the university. Van de Water reminds us, however, that administrative support for international education will ebb and flow over the years.

Jon Heyl began his career as a tenured professor of history at Illinois Wesleyan University, and he eventually moved to the University of Missouri–Columbia as the administrator in charge of international programs. Twelve years later, in the wake of turbulent events at Missouri, Heyl moved to Old Dominion University and then on to a senior position at a private study abroad provider. In chapter 4 Heyl describes in detail the risks and rewards of close associations with campus leaders at all three of his universities. He provides a host of details about how an SIO "leads from the side" even under uncertain, shifting, or adverse conditions. His account reminds us of how vulnerable most SIO positions actually are.

Gilbert Merkx weaves place, change, and circumstance into his account in chapter 5. He describes how growing up in a multilingual environment led him into sociology and Latin American studies prior to his work as an SIO first at the University of New Mexico and then at Duke University. He describes in detail some of the key aspects of SIO work, including getting involved in—or avoiding—local campus politics, lobbying at the state and national levels for support, and building alliances. He also highlights the role of turnover, turmoil, and instability in campus life and the roles of power and politics in enabling and constraining what an SIO is able to do.

Howard Rollins, a professor of developmental psychology, describes in chapter 6 his experiences at Emory University and Georgia Tech. His early academic experiences overseas set him on a course to become Emory's first SIO. He describes how Emory's international programs grew and how he approached key issues such as finance, faculty involvement, and policy, as well as how elements of university culture and politics impeded this effort. Rollins describes his move to Georgia Tech and his involvement in the design and introduction of a comprehensive set of international initiatives. He concludes with insightful observations on the role of top leadership in setting the course of internationalization and on when and why SIOs should change institutions.

Maria Carmen Sada Krane, who holds degrees in linguistics and education, discusses her career as SIO at three different institutions, first at Nebraska Wesleyan, then Agnes Scott College, and finally Creighton University. In chapter 7 she describes how in each institution she worked to expand and develop international opportunities for faculty and students, in ways consonant with each intuition's goals, background, and character. She provides valuable detail about her work in developing English as a second language (ESL) programs and strategies for increasing the number of international partners. Krane thoughtfully analyzes the variety of pressures and constraints that SIOs must work under, many of which are beyond their control.

Uliana Gabara, a specialist in Russian language and literature, provides in chapter 8 a detailed account of her experience as the founding SIO at the University of Richmond. She also emphasizes the importance of a thorough understanding of institutional character and strong relationships with the faculty. Gabara describes how she recruited faculty through an innovative program that took faculty overseas to meet potential partners. She views internationalization as requiring a comprehensive campus effort that promotes collaboration, synergy, and creativity. Her account provides a wealth of practical detail about how to conceptualize, set up, and manage a program that touches virtually every aspect of the university.

Joseph Tulbane, after a career as an army officer specializing in Russian and eastern European affairs, became the first SIO at St. Norbert, a small liberal arts institution in the upper Midwest. Tullbane describes in chapter 9 how his previous internationalization experience helped him to approach the challenges and opportunities of this new position at a time of significant restructuring and financial constraint. He brought a largely independent international operation more fully into the academic mainstream, while at the same time building a dedicated staff and achieving financial success for the college. Foreign student enrollments and study abroad participation increased significantly during his tenure. However, these accomplishments were taken for granted by a new central administration, which undid much of what he had achieved.

In chapter 10 Riall Nolan provides an account of how he got involved in international education as an international development specialist. He describes his decision to leave development work for higher education and then to leave teaching for international education administration. As he moved through four different institutions, he came to understand and appreciate the immense role that institutional culture plays in enabling—and at times constraining—internationalization. He emphasizes the role and importance of motivation in international work, the narratives people use to frame their situations, and high-level support and continuity in order to sustain accomplishments.

William Lacy, a sociologist, became the first SIO at the University of California, Davis, after a career at half a dozen other institutions. In chapter 11 he describes how he established himself and his office within the Davis academic community and how he began the work of consolidation and expansion of international programs. Through patient work with a variety of stakeholders across the campus, Lacy succeeded in developing a campuswide conversation about internationalization and a strong agenda for action. Faculty involvement, coupled with sound finances, permitted internationalization to grow and diversify. Equally important was securing the involvement of upper campus leadership—the chancellor, provost, and deans.

Joseph Brockington arrived at Kalamazoo College in Michigan in 1972 as a professor of German. Brockington describes in chapter 12 the process by which he became progressively more involved with international activities at a liberal arts institution with a distinctive and highly original learning model and how, in 1992, he became the college's SIO. He describes his patient, strategic, and quietly relentless efforts, in concert with others at Kalamazoo, to transform the institution's idea of "internationalization" from study abroad to something much more comprehensive and transformational. His account underscores the role of faculty involvement, the fundamental importance of connection to the campus mission, and the need for high-level support. He also draws attention to the catalytic role played by outside networks and organizations, and in particular the American Council on Education's (ACE) Internationalization Collaborative, in supporting change.

Despite the varied character of these colleges and universities, the same issues emerge again and again. The overseas activities that are part of international education and the internal challenges of institutional politics recur in these narratives, as do the techniques for dealing with such issues. These chapters also raise the issue of the career trajectories that the narrators have experienced. Many of our authors describe this as a kind of arc: first a period of ascendance, then a period of frustration. For some, the second phase led them to change institutions.

These accounts are also about the rise of this new administrative specialty in American higher education, the senior international officer. At the start of our careers, the SIO position did not exist. Now it is common at many institutions in the United States. Similarly, in 1982 AIEA was established as the first professional association devoted exclusively to SIOs and had an initial membership of forty. By 2015 AIEA had a membership of nearly one thousand.

The founders of AIEA broke away from a larger organization founded in 1948, the National Association of Foreign Student Administrators. This organization also grew from modest beginnings, reaching a membership of ten thousand by 2015. Its mission expanded to include people staffing every aspect of international education, from study abroad to visa services, and its name changed in 1990 to NAFSA: Association of International Educators. AIEA's founders viewed NAFSA as an organization that focused on the nuts-and-bolts issues facing staffers rather than on the leadership concerns facing the emerging community of senior officers charged with coordinating a diverse set of issues.

The growth of international education in the United States also led to a variety of other professional associations and organizations. The Council on Student Travel, founded in 1947 by the study abroad community, changed its name in 1967 to the Council for International Education and Exchange. The European Association for International Education was established in 1989. And the Forum on Education Abroad, another breakaway from the original NAFSA, was founded in in 2001. These organizations are not the subject of this book, but their very existence attests to the rise of international education and its complexity. Their growth also demonstrates the need for senior administrative leadership to coordinate institutional strategy.

The narratives that make up *Internationalizing the Academy* reveal how internationalization actually takes place. The chapter authors provide richly contextualized accounts of how they addressed the challenges of bringing about change on their campuses, accounts that illuminate not only the strategies and tactics that they employed but also the patterns, constraints and possibilities that shape internationalization efforts in US higher education.

CHAPTER ONE

International Education in the United States

Gilbert W. Merkx

ACTIVITIES ASSOCIATED with international education emerged in the second half of the twentieth century. These activities gained increasing significance with the acceleration of global interactions that followed the end of the Cold War. However, they must be understood in terms of the historically grounded mission, curriculum, and organization of American higher education, which provide the context for understanding the role of the senior international officer of a US college or university.

THE EXCEPTIONALISM OF US HIGHER EDUCATION

Higher education in the United States is unlike that of any other country in several key respects. First, it is not a unified government system, as it is in most other countries. Second, it is a heterogeneous mix of various types of colleges and universities. And third, its undergraduate curriculum is unlike that of most other nations. These fundamental differences are the sources of endless misunderstandings. When university leaders from around the world come together in international meetings, they often talk at cross purposes because they assume, quite incorrectly, that all universities bear a generic resemblance to one another.

Western higher education emerged from the crucible of the Middle Ages as a product of two different Christian institutions: the cathedral and the monastery. In 1179 the Third Lateran Council decreed that all cathedrals should have a master whose task was to teach clerks and poor scholars, and from this decree cathedral schools developed.[1]

The deans of the cathedrals were responsible for the schools, which focused originally on theology and then gradually on fields like philosophy and medicine. Eventually these schools aspired to universal knowledge and adopted the title of "university." Students attended lectures until they could pass the periodic examinations, but the cathedral provided no support other than the lecturer and the venue. Thus arose the "student quarter" in the cathedral town. The cathedral towns grew rapidly in the High Middle Ages as marketing centers. Some towns prospered more than others, such as Bologna, Salamanca, and Paris; their cathedrals prospered and their universities grew in prestige.

The economies of northern Europe took off in the modern period, and universities in the north became the most prestigious. Science and scientific research became increasingly important. The mission of the university now included not just the transmission of knowledge but the generation of new knowledge. First the Netherlands and then the German states took the leadership in building and funding these research institutions.

The monastic orders offered a different model of learning. Monasteries were repositories of sacred and classical texts, largely in the classical languages, and where these texts were reproduced. Other dimensions of monastic life included instruction in and the practice of agriculture, animal husbandry, physical education, classical languages, mathematics, rhetoric, and similar pursuits. The mission of a monastic order was not just to transmit knowledge but to educate, or transform, the whole person in a residential community based on Christian principles.

The British Isles proved especially welcoming for the monastic movement, which flourished in both England and Ireland, which were less urban and less centralized than the Continent. The landed gentry developed the practice of sending their sons to live in monasteries to learn to read and write and also to receive also a well-rounded education that included civic and Christian virtues. In England, these monastic institutions evolved into residential colleges that began to cluster in towns like Cambridge and Oxford. While Cambridge and Oxford nominally became known as universities, both were actually collections of colleges, each aspiring to provide a unique education to its residents.

The British colonists in North America brought with them the British model of the residential college offering a well-rounded education, not the continental model of a nonresidential center dedicated to the pursuit of knowledge. The first six colleges were sponsored by churches: Harvard (1636, Puritan), William and Mary (1693, Church of England), Yale (1701, Puritan), Princeton (1746, Presbyterian), Columbia (1754, Church of England), and Pennsylvania (1755, Church of England). The number of such residential colleges grew rapidly throughout the last half of the eighteenth century and into the first half of the nineteenth century; still, North America had no universities.

By the mid–nineteenth century, American elites were traveling to Europe, and there they discovered the research university. Particularly inspired by German institutions, Americans imported the German model and tried to impose it on the college system. The result was a uniquely American hybrid institution that combined the functions of both the British college and the continental university. The original colleges survived, but universities were established around them in the form of graduate and professional schools. Thus, Harvard College and Yale College continued to exist but were subsumed into Harvard University and Yale University. The colleges offered a liberal education, and the universities offered specialization and research. In any given institution, the balance between these two missions was not easy to maintain and often lead to arguments over the relative merits of teaching versus research. Many colleges, of course, refused to become part of a university. These independent colleges, such as Colby, Haverford, and Grinnell, continue to be an important sector of American higher education.

Thus, whether in a college or a university, higher education in the United States begins with four years of a "college education," which means a broad liberal education and well as a modest degree of specialization. In contrast, in most higher education systems around the world, based on the European or continental model, there are no colleges providing a liberal education. Students graduating from secondary school enter different university faculties, such as law and medicine, and are trained in those fields alone. If they decide to change fields, they must start from the beginning in a new faculty.

In the United States, students seeking the specialized knowledge found in the continental university must, after graduating from college, seek admission to a graduate or professional school.

The implications for international education are significant. The four years of liberal education in a college allow not only for study abroad but for the study of foreign languages and literature and of disciplines like history, geography, politics, and economics, which are useful for understanding international issues. In contrast, the lockstep, professionally oriented curriculum of the continental model is not conducive to developing international competence.

Most of the world, however, adopted the continental model, thanks to the influence of the European colonial powers and the Soviet Union. Students in such countries do not have time to study abroad for a semester once they are enrolled in university, whereas American undergraduates have the flexibility to study abroad. On graduation, American students apply to graduate and professional schools, while European students graduate at the same age with professional degrees. Hence, there are few foreign students in US law and medical schools unless they have been undergraduates in an American college.

THE TRANSFORMATION OF THE AMERICAN CURRICULUM

At the start of the nineteenth century, American colleges, without exception, offered what was known as the classical curriculum. This curriculum focused on the study of Latin, Greek, and Hebrew; the history of Greek and Roman civilization; the literature of the Greece and Rome; Greek and Roman philosophy and political theory; and classical mathematics, such as plane geometry. The century's first decades saw a proliferation of such colleges and the continued domination of the classical curriculum, despite calls for reform by educators such as George Ticknor of Harvard and James Marsh of Vermont. In 1826 the faculty of Amherst delivered a report to the Amherst trustees calling for modernization of the curriculum. This came to the attention of the Yale trustees, who asked the Yale faculty for their views. The faculty response was the famous Yale Report of 1828, which defended the classical curriculum and, for half a century, was the most influential document in American higher education.

Yet, by the end of the nineteenth century the higher education curriculum was entirely different, having undergone a hard-fought change of paradigm. The "new" curriculum of the late nineteenth century is instantly recognizable to anyone who graduated from an American college or university in the twentieth century. This curriculum focused on European languages, such as French, German, and Italian. Classical history was replaced by European and American history, Greek and Roman literature was replaced by European and American literature, and philosophy and political theory became European and American in focus. Classical mathematics became a stepping stone to the natural sciences and applied fields like engineering. The classics remained, but only as electives, not requirements, and as an interdisciplinary field within the larger university.

The ascendancy of the new curriculum was due to many factors, but the primary cause was suggested by Frederick Rudolph in his magisterial *The American College and University: A History*.[2] He contended that students preferred the new curriculum, and they voted with their feet. Rudolph noted that more than seven hundred colleges closed in the two decades before 1860, even as many new ones were being founded. Most of the colleges that failed were wedded to the classical curriculum and died for want of enrollment.

In the context of the twenty-first century, the curriculum that triumphed in the late nineteenth century seems remarkably Eurocentric, reflecting the Euro-American flow of commerce and culture of the Gilded Age. Today, however, commerce and culture are global. Students will be better prepared to be citizens of a globalized world if they learn the history, politics, economics, sociology, literatures, and philosophies of the world rather than just those of Europe and the United States. Students seem to have gotten this message as well. Enrollment in European language courses is declining while enrollment in Asian languages is rising. The database of the Modern Language Association shows that college enrollments in French and German have fallen by half since 1980, while Chinese and Arabic enrollments have grown exponentially. Within other academic disciplines, courses that offer international and comparative perspectives are increasing their enrollments. Colleges that stress study abroad programs and international education have seen enrollment growth at the same time that other colleges are facing enrollment declines. At some point these trends may lead to a restructuring of the curriculum, much like that of the nineteenth century, and for the same reasons.

Internationalization of the undergraduate curriculum is therefore one of the major challenges facing senior international officers on US campuses. Unfortunately, curriculum reform is a process so fraught with difficulty that it could be termed the "third rail" of academic politics. Departments and faculty whose courses are required by an existing curriculum will fight tooth and nail to keep those requirements in place. Overcoming such vested interests requires careful strategy, key alliances, and support from the top.

SIMILARITY AND DIFFERENCE IN INSTITUTIONS OF AMERICAN HIGHER EDUCATION

In 2011 there were 4,706 degree-granting institutions of higher education in the United States, enrolling 18.1 million students. About one-third of these institutions was public and two-thirds private. The privates were more or less equally divided between not-for-profit and for-profit institutions.[3] Despite the preponderance of private institutions, the public institutions enroll more than half of all students. The various institutions fall into several types: public community colleges, private small colleges, public and private four-year universities primarily focused on teaching, public research-intensive universities, and private research intensive universities.

Each distinct type of institution has its own particular set of challenges, and institutions within each category tend to resemble one another more than institutions of the other types. Within each category there are subtypes, such as religious versus nonsectarian colleges and land grant versus non–land grant research intensive institutions. The boundaries between all the types are somewhat permeable, inasmuch as institutions can aspire to change their missions, to be absorbed into the public sector, or to privatize.

Despite these differences, undergraduate education is conceived in very similar terms by all US higher education institutions. The international challenges of undergraduate education are also similar across institutions, consisting of curriculum issues (basically foreign language and international-content courses), study abroad programs, and recruiting and supporting foreign students. These challenges are shared by every senior international officer regardless of the nature of the institution.

An additional set of challenges emerges when an institution is research intensive. Such research is associated with the graduate and professional schools found at comprehensive universities. The international education challenges at such institutions may include research partnerships with foreign universities, short-term exchanges of graduate students, the management of overseas technical assistance programs, visa and counseling services for foreign postdocs and visiting faculty, export controls, and overseas risk management. Dealing with these issues involves addressing not just the needs of a student clientele but those of a large number of administrative offices in the university and in its graduate and professional schools.

The international education challenges of undergraduate-oriented and of research-intensive institutions are relatively new to American higher education since the second half of the twentieth century. The rise of international education as a specific endeavor within the academy was a consequence of the participation of the United States in World War II and of American efforts at postwar reconstruction.

WORLD WAR II AND THE INTERNATIONALIZATION OF AMERICAN HIGHER EDUCATION

In 1941 the Japanese attacked Pearl Harbor, forcing the United States into a two-front war with the Axis powers. The American military, however, lacked the foreign area competence needed for such an effort, and so the new Office of Strategic Services (OSS) recruited university faculty for their language and area expertise and put them to work as intelligence analysts. The OSS commissioned studies of national character for every country on both fronts.[4]

At the same time, the US Army established the Army Specialized Training Program (ASTP), which sent officers to institutions of higher education for crash courses in needed skills, including foreign languages and area studies. At its high point in 1944 the ASTP had 150,000 officers enrolled in fifty-five colleges and universities. In 1943 the US Navy set up a similar program, the V-12 Navy College Training Program, which enrolled more than 125,000 officers before it was terminated in 1946. The success of these ventures led the army to establish in 1945 an American-style university in Biarritz, France, complete with faculty, college credit courses, and several thousand GI students, for the purpose of maintaining its capacity to function globally.[5] Unfortunately, this experiment fell victim to postwar budget cuts.

The ASTP and V-12 programs were highly effective and established a model of university-government collaboration that was to be the inspiration for Title VI of the National Defense Education Act (NDEA) of 1958. Other postwar spinoff programs include the Fulbright Act of 1946, the Marshall Plan of 1947, the Point Four Program of 1949, the Foreign Assistance Act of 1961, and the Title XII overseas agriculture assistance program of the Board for Food and International Development (BIFAD), passed in 1975.

World War II veterans, who become internationalists because of their overseas service, were the promoters of these federal programs. Frederick Wakeman, a China specialist who served as president of the Social Science Research Council, called attention to this generational effect in 1996. Speaking to the Council of Directors of National Resource Centers, federally funded foreign language and area centers, Wakeman argued that after World War II an elite network of influential veterans emerged that was committed to maintaining the United States' role as a world power. Members of this network worked in the major foundations, universities, and government agencies at various times in their careers and used their contacts to promote US international competence. McGeorge Bundy, for example, worked in army intelligence during World War II and after the war served as an assistant to Secretary of War Henry Stimson, went to work for the Council on Foreign Relations, became a professor at and then dean at Harvard, returned to the government as a national security adviser to Presidents Kennedy and Johnson, and then, toward the end of his career, became president of the Ford Foundation.

A major accomplishment of the internationalist network was the Fulbright Act of 1946 (later replaced by the Fulbright-Hays Act of 1961), conceived as a way of spending down lend-lease loans owed to the United States by World War II allies whose weak currencies could not be converted into dollars. By sending faculty and graduate students to foreign countries, and receiving faculty and students from those same countries, the Fulbright Program established personal networks and stimulated interest in overseas research. It also familiarized Americans with foreign universities and foreigners with American universities.

It was not long before foreign faculty began to use their US connections to place their students in American universities. Foreign student enrollments in the United States had been virtually nonexistent before World War II. After the passage of the Fulbright Act, enrollments of foreign students began to grow, at first slowly and then exponentially. In 1959 there were 48,000 foreign students in American colleges and universities; by 2006 there were 582,000 such students.

Another effect of the Fulbright Program was that American faculty began to use their foreign connections to establish study abroad programs for their own students. Before 1950, only 6 US academic year study abroad programs existed, a number that grew to 103 in 1962 and 208 in 1965. Summer study abroad programs grew from 63 in 1962 to 97 in 1965.[6] The Institute for International Education reported 18,000 Americans studying abroad in 1965, 49,000 in 1985, and 224,000 in 2005.

Another push toward internationalization came from the Soviet Union's 1957 success in launching *Sputnik,* the first orbiting satellite, led to a wave of public hysteria in the United States, comparable to reactions to attack on Pearl Harbor and the destruction of the World Trade Towers on September 11, 2001. The Eisenhower administration was suddenly on the political defensive, accused of letting the Soviets get ahead of the United States. In response, Eisenhower proposed a new federal program to support science, engineering, language, and area studies in higher education, the National Defense Education Act (NDEA).[7] The NDEA included Title VI, a new version of the Army Specialized Training Program, authorizing partnerships between government and higher education to train foreign language and area experts. NDEA was passed in 1958 and signed by President Eisenhower. In response, dozens of universities established foreign area centers. Over the next decades new Title VI missions were added, such as outreach, citizen education, internationalizing the undergraduate curriculum, international business education, minority recruitment, language research, and support for overseas research centers.[8]

Another international innovation was dealing with postwar global food shortages by applying overseas the agricultural extension programs developed for domestic use by the Roosevelt administration. Technical cooperation for agricultural development was one of the components of the 1949 Point Four Program and later legislation, most notably the 1961 Foreign Assistance Act. In 1975 these agricultural assistance programs were consolidated in Title XII of the legislation authorizing the establishment of the Board for Food and International Development.[9] The government entered into long-term contracts with major land grant universities to enable them to participate in overseas AID agricultural projects. These universities often had dozens, or even hundreds, of faculty, staff, and students working overseas on agricultural development.

In sum, the postwar overseas government programs led to four different kinds of campus activities: study abroad, foreign student enrollments, foreign language and area studies, and overseas technical assistance. These types of campus-based international education activity had several defining characteristics: each was constituency driven; each was mission specific, devoted to a particular function; and each tended to be organizationally discrete, housed in a functional unit designed to carry out the mission. As a result, international education was organizationally fragmented. Many institutions engaged in only one or two of these activities; and even if an institution did offer all four types of programs, they were housed in different offices and often under different deans.

Four modal patterns of organizational response to internationalization can be identified. At some institutions, primarily the more prestigious liberal arts colleges, international education became synonymous with study abroad programs, and the official in charge of such programs became the chief international education administrator.[10]

In another set of institutions, enrollments of undergraduate foreign students came to be important at some research universities, such as Columbia and Pennsylvania, as well as at public universities and colleges with relatively low tuitions, where study abroad programs were small but where enrollment-based formula funding gave foreign student enrollments considerable importance.[11] Miami-Dade Community College, with the largest number of foreign students of any US college or university, is one such example. The increasing number of foreign students at these sorts of institutions required offices to deal with recruitment, visa issues, housing, and advising. At many of these institutions the head of the foreign student services office became the chief international education administrator.

At land grant public universities with strong agriculture and engineering schools, the driving factor was federal funding for international agricultural extension and development programs. Internationalization at these institutions involved overseas development projects, and so the official in charge of these development projects became the chief international administrator.[12]

Faculty interest in international, foreign area, and foreign language studies, stimulated by the 1958 enactment of NDEA Title VI, was found largely at non–land grant research universities.[13] International programs were generally housed in interdisciplinary centers or institutes headed by senior scholars and often had significant impact on undergraduate and graduate teaching.[14] The chief international administrator at these universities was usually drawn from the ranks of the international and foreign area center directors.

The initial wave of internationalization of US higher education had several dimensions that were experienced differentially by diverse types of colleges and universities. Divergent understandings emerged as to what constituted the internationalization of higher education, or, as it came to be known, international education.[15] These differences in perspective were reinforced by differences in organizational loci and by the recruitment of administrators from different professional backgrounds. On campuses where one or more types of internationalization existed simultaneously, conflict and competition among the various constituencies, or among their leaders, were not uncommon.

INSTITUTIONAL POLITICS

Colleges and universities are quite unlike other social organizations in American society. The various communities that constitute a university often have strikingly different views of what that university ought to be. For the faculty, the ideal university would be a Greek republic of which they are the citizens. The students prefer to see the university as a democracy that serves the needs of the people. Deans of schools and colleges would like a feudal system in which their fiefdoms are unmolested by central authority. The administrative personnel who cope with records, payroll, and personnel think that the university should be a rational bureaucracy. The trustees see the university as an absolute monarchy in which they can impose or depose the king, or, in modern terminology, as a corporation in which they select the chief executive officer.

These intersecting visions lead to a complex social order characterized by frequent, if usually discreet, struggles over procedure, authority, policy, and resources. The roles of the key central administrators, the president and provost, are ambiguous and often contested by other parties. Moreover, while there is considerable turnover among presidents and provosts, it is rare that any of the other players are forced out the institution, even if they lose a fight.

In Max Weber's classic formulation, social institutions are shaped by the interaction of wealth, power, and prestige.[16] In a unique institution such as the research university, the referents of these terms have specialized analogues. Wealth in the university can be operationally defined as a function of the size of the budget over which an actor has discretionary, as opposed to formal, authority. Power in the university is a function both of the extent of authority to make decisions that influence subordinates and of the scale of that authority as measured in numbers of subordinates. Prestige in a university is of two different types. Vertical prestige is a function of hierarchy or rank in the administrative structure. Academic prestige is a function of scholarly achievement and is usually measured by research and publications. There are very few positions in the research university that combine the three dimensions of wealth, power, and prestige.[17]

Faculty members can gain high academic prestige but lack wealth and power.[18] The president has high vertical prestige and a sizable number of subordinates but often a small discretionary budget and limited discretionary power, since the critical funding and personnel decisions are exercised at lower levels.[19] Some of the administrative officials who report to the president, such as the vice president for business, the director of the physical plant, the director of human resources, and the athletic director, have significant budgetary discretion and numerous subordinates but lack academic prestige, and in some cases, vertical prestige.[20] At the other end of the administrative chain, the department chair may have academic prestige but low vertical prestige, little or no discretionary budget, and limited authority.[21]

The provost, the dean of the college of arts and sciences (A&S), and the deans of the major professional schools, such as medicine, engineering, law, and business, all enjoy a combination of vertical and academic prestige, control large budgets, and exercise real discretionary authority over large numbers of subordinates. [22] Collectively, the deans have more budgetary discretion and control over hiring than the provost. However, they usually serve at the pleasure of the provost and must exhibit a suitable amount of deference, just as the provost serves at the pleasure of the president. Thus, no one official, and no one set of similar officials, can have sufficient leverage to dominate the others. Moreover, the decentralized nature of authority creates many veto points. Organizational change in such an institution requires negotiation and consensus building, so it is necessarily gradual. This gradualism makes innovation difficult but also prevents the abrupt transformations that can result from the winner-take-all decision making of the business corporation.

THE SENIOR INTERNATIONAL OFFICER

As campuses have expanded their international activities, central administrators have begun to name a single person to oversee all the international activities on behalf of the central administration. These senior international officers enjoy titles such as dean, vice provost, or associate provost for international affairs, global education, or international strategy. While the titles are impressive and the access to senior administrators is good, in practice the role is limited by the overall decentralization of authority and often by a lack of discretionary funds and personnel. As a result, these administrators have relatively little power and serve primarily as advocates or emissaries rather than authority figures,

In four-year colleges, international education activities began with study abroad programs and the admission of foreign students. Accordingly, the SIO is usually an associate dean or director in the college of arts and sciences. However, this placement is less than ideal for addressing the needs of the professional schools, if they exist, or for mediating university-to-university relations with foreign institutions. Placement under the A&S dean is also less than helpful for securing support from the president and provost for international initiatives.

In comprehensive and research intensive universities, a more common outcome is the naming of a SIO who reports directly to the provost. This involves the provost in the internationalization process, facilitates working with the professional schools, and increases the vertical prestige of the new position. Whether the international officer is effective, however, is also determined by the discretionary budget and line authority that are assigned to her and whether the deans have an interest in internationalization.

The optimal case would be a vice provost with line authority over the personnel and budgets of study abroad, foreign student services, technical assistance programs, and international and area studies programs, as well as a substantial discretionary budget to provide incentives for cooperation with the central administration's internationalization agenda. Establishing such an office requires overcoming a natural resistance on the part of the deans to granting significant resources to the new office. In consequence, only a few SIOs have such authority.

The SIO reporting to the provost is unquestionably an agent of the central administration in its constant struggle to impose central direction and coordination on the complex social system of the university. As a result, relationships with the academic deans are necessarily problematic. The major challenge for the international officer is to mediate the relationship between the deans and the central administration to create patterns of cooperation rather than conflict over international activities. This requires rewarding the deans for their support of the administration's international initiatives and helping them achieve their own international agendas. The senior international officer has two significant advantages: a strategic position with access to all the key academic administrators and a mandate that can be perceived as timely and of broad potential benefit. However, internationalization is not the first priority of any other academic administrator. Overcoming this challenge requires dedication, energy, techniques of advocacy, the ability to forge alliances, the power of persuasion, and the ability to define issues in a way that leads to win-win outcomes.

CHAPTER TWO

The Senior International Officer—an Advocate for Change

Riall W. Nolan

INTERNATIONALIZING our higher education system is probably one of the most important tasks facing American society today. As Julia Chang Bloch, the former US ambassador to Nepal, once noted, "How people of different backgrounds learn to work together is probably the prime human resource challenge of the 21st century."[1] As we move further into the twenty-first century, it becomes increasingly important not just to understand the world beyond the shoreline but to know how to engage meaningfully and constructively with it. On graduation, every one of today's students will be involved internationally, working with diverse others across the globe on a variety of pressing and important problems, not all of which are even clearly defined at present. To do this, they will need more than technical understanding; they will need skill at understanding and working with people who think as well as they do but who think differently.

There are some very specific reasons why a deeper understanding of the world's "others" is important. Nearly thirty years ago, noted anthropologist Sue Estroff said, "The next decades will present us with choices we have avoided making explicitly and with intention for a very long time. The fabric and values of our culture will be stretched and revealed in many ways. Who is deserving? What will we value most? Will we choose to be comfortable or comforting? None of these agonizing choices can be made humanely without an understanding of these 'different others' and their worlds."[2]

Those next decades have now arrived, accompanied by a host of what we have come to call "grand challenges." These challenges—climate change, poverty, hunger, insecurity, violence, and environmental deterioration, to name just a few—are intricate, perplexing, and multifaceted. Their resolution is uncertain, complex, and contested and, most certainly, not purely technical in nature. Ignoring them is not an option. The spread of global commerce, communication, and transport has brought many of these problems into high relief and, in the view of some, may actually have made them worse.

Whatever else we may think the purposes of our higher education institutions ought to be, surely one of these is preparing the next generation to think about and engage with these pressing issues in concert with other concerned citizens around the globe. We cannot sustain our own way of life and work constructively with others without a globally aware and multiculturally competent citizenry. Internationalizing our institutions is one of the most important ways to ensure that our own citizens are prepared for the challenges that lie ahead.

WHAT IS INTERNATIONALIZATION?

What does it mean for a university to be *internationalized?* It depends on who you ask. Generally speaking, however, we can use international education expert Jane Knight's useful definition as a guide: "Internationalization at the national, sector, and institutional levels is defined as the process of integrating an international, intercultural, or global dimension into the purpose, functions or delivery of postsecondary education."[3]

Operationalizing this concept takes a number of forms on our campuses, including:

- *Moving students and faculty out into the world.* The "export" side of internationalization makes it possible for students and faculty at various levels to spend part of their academic career learning about another culture.
- *Bringing the world to the campus.* The "import" side attracts students and faculty to an institution from somewhere else and involves them in a range of educational activities.

- *Outward engagement through partnerships.* More complex than the simple movement of people, this involves the university undertaking long-term activities somewhere overseas. These are done in collaboration with overseas partners and include such things as the establishment of research programs, study abroad centers, and/or branch campuses.
- *Curriculum reform.* Promoting internal changes to the curriculum to better address international aspects of the subjects or disciplines being taught.
- *Improving policy support.* Aligning campus policy to support international efforts of different kinds. This might include policies on promotion and tenure, funding, credit and tuition transfer, and risk and safety.

For most institutions engaged in internationalization, the campus dialogue usually revolves around some combination of these.

If internationalization has a clear set of components, this does not mean that every university does all of these things or does them in the same way. Far from it. And so it becomes important to look at a university's character (its "organizational culture," as an anthropologist might say) and its capabilities to understand how and why internationalization has taken the shape that it has and, more particularly for the SIO, how this might change and develop in the future.

LEVELS OF INTERNATIONALIZATION

Internationalization occurs at several different levels. At the *individual* level it may involve a faculty member embarking on a research collaboration with a colleague overseas, exchanges of individual scholars or students, or individual faculty members or students spending a semester or year abroad. At the *departmental* level it may involve the creation of a new major, a permanent study abroad program integrated into the core curriculum, or the establishment of a long-term research project. Although the internationalization activities that occur at the individual or the departmental level can be innovative, exciting, and important, they may directly affect only a few faculty or students—or, indeed, only one person. These arrangements, although in some ways complex, generally leave the rest of the institution more or less intact.

At the *university*, or campuswide, level, however, internationalization can be a transformative opportunity. Significant, multiunit, long-term changes occur, involving shifts in activity as well as changes in time and resource allocation. Because of the transformative nature of these, the collaboration and support of a great many stakeholders, not just the faculty, is required. Indeed, faculty by themselves are unlikely to be able to marshal the resources and sustained effort required to make such transformations effective.

INDICATORS OF INTERNATIONALIZATION

What would a successfully internationalized university look like? Although it is true that in outward respects all universities may look remarkably similar, internally they are as distinctive as the personalities in a crowd. When internationalization is successful, however, it generally presents itself in one or more of the following ways:

- Internationalization is an integral part of the university's self-definition, supported by adequate internal and external resources and a facilitating policy environment.
- Both faculty and domestic students are highly involved in a variety of international activities on and off campus, which contribute to building capacity for understanding and action.
- A supportive and diverse environment exists for overseas students and scholars to enhance both their learning and their contribution to campus life.
- International activities, topics, and connections, and the learning they generate, have found their way into many, if not most, levels of the curriculum.
- International educational programming is strategic, interdisciplinary, issue centered, and theme based.
- Off-campus constituencies such as alumni and donors are part of the internationalization effort.

HOW WELL HAVE WE DONE SO FAR?

Although there are numerous success stories, overall our universities haven't done very well with most of the points listed above. Few institutions will have internationalization as a key point in its mission statement, few will have a comprehensive strategic plan for making the place more international, and only a very few will explicitly recognize and reward international effort by the faculty.

Study abroad numbers—a clear, simple indicator of one small aspect of internationalization—tell the tale well. The American Council on Education polled entering college students on their interest in international education and found that "fifty-five percent [of those polled] indicated that they are certain or fairly certain they will participate in study abroad, with another 26 percent indicating a strong desire to study abroad."[4]

The sad reality, however, is that less than 5 percent of US students ever study abroad. And in those programs many only experience a foreign culture in relatively brief periods of four weeks or less. In far too many of these study abroad programs, American students are clumped together and live, eat, and drink together experiencing the foreign culture, if at all, only through the windows of classrooms and tour buses. Far too few students manage to have sustained contact with members of the local culture. They interact with them mainly as consumers and tourists and come away from their experience with very little understanding of the ways in which these others are similar to, and different from, themselves. Majors on many of our campuses make little or no allowance for study abroad, overseas research or internships, or, indeed, any substantial experience of an other-cultural sort. This is particularly true for the STEM disciplines, which have recently come to be seen as a priority in the United States. For example, in a typical classroom in one of our top-ranked engineering programs, we might see three students—one a Chinese, one an Indian, and one an American—sitting side by side. All three are bright and hard working. All three are receiving a world-class education in engineering. On graduation, each will receive a highly respected diploma from a top-ranked school. Two of the three students, however, will speak more than one language (in addition to English), will have a passport, will have lived in a foreign country for a substantial period of time, and, most importantly, will understand a great deal about how another culture thinks. The third student, alas, will probably not have any of these attributes. Guess which nationality the third student is?

Of course, most of our US-born students will eventually graduate despite this lack of opportunity. They will go on to become voters, taxpayers, and parents—people who will be making key decisions about our country's relationship to the rest of the world. They may, however, be doing these things with a very inadequate understanding of what the rest of the world is like.

HOW INTERNATIONALIZATION HAPPENS

On any campus, the faculty and the upper administration, and the relationships between them, are the key to successful internationalization. Whatever strategy or plan for internationalization eventually emerges, it must fit with, and be an asset for, the priorities of the upper administration while at the same time serving the needs of the faculty.

Perhaps the fundamental point—and it is a simple one—is that internationalization (of whatever sort) will involve changes in what people in the institution do, how they allocate resources, and how they assess their performance and that of others. An institution unwilling or unable to change is unlikely to internationalize successfully.

This can be a difficult and sensitive point to raise with university people, particularly with the faculty. As budgets shrink and programs expand, there is a great temptation to opt for international programs which "pay for themselves," thus avoiding reallocation decisions. Even better are international programs designed to actually turn a profit for the institution. And of course there is always the equal temptation to set up programs and activities that take place in isolation from other university activities, thus avoiding decisions about curriculum change.

The essential building blocks of successful internationalization are planning, funding, and incentives.

Strategic Planning

Some institutions (or at least some upper administrators) do not believe in strategic planning. At other institutions people may not know much about how strategic planning is actually done. But conducted carefully and thoughtfully, and with the essential character of the institution always in mind, strategic planning can be of enormous benefit to an institution.

It's not easy, however. Successful planning requires commitment from the top, engagement from all sides, sustained effort, and sincere input. All too often strategic plans wind up consisting of faculty wish lists, with no real indication of how or when, if ever, the hoped-for results will materialize. In other cases, commitment to the plan erodes as individual stakeholders begin to perceive that the changes embodied in the plan are likely to become real for them. In still other cases, individuals or groups within the institution will attempt to derail the entire effort, or major parts of it, in order to "send messages" to other groups on campus. "Strategic plans," as one of my mentors once pointed out to me, "are often about preventing things from happening rather than encouraging change."

Funding

Most internationalization costs money. Where the money for international activity comes from, who gets it, and how it is spent become key issues at most institutions. If one is operating in a zero-sum environment, where an increase in funding in one area results in a decrease in another, then there are going to be some very difficult conversations around this point. In most cases, of course, efforts are made to increase the size of the pie through some form of outside fund-raising, and this introduces additional issues of its own.

International units at whatever level that are obligated to seek their own funds have a very limited set of options at their disposal. They can, for example, write grants to various donor agencies, and at some institutions there is considerable institutional support for such activities, such as a team of grant writers or researchers made available to them. At other places, the unit is on its own. Dependence on outside funding usually also involves dependence on what an external donor thinks is important, and this may or may not mesh with institutional needs and priorities. Grants and contracts are particularly donor driven.

The better alternative is often targeted fund-raising through the university. Most institutions have an office whose role is to raise money from alumni and others. At many larger universities these offices are substantial. Getting internationalization "on the list" for fund-raising, however, may be a sensitive matter and therefore difficult to achieve.

Incentives

The issues of reward and recognition are probably the most difficult for institutions as they internationalize. This has been made worse in recent years as a result of the many changes now happening in higher education that affect faculty, including the decline in tenure-track positions, the steady raising of the bar for tenure in many disciplines, the increasing use of adjunct or part-time faculty, the generalized "audit culture" taking hold on many campuses, and the generally negative effects of budgetary systems which force individual academic units to "pay their own way."

University faculty work hard, for the most part, and are generally highly motivated. But they respond, as most people do, to signals from their institution about what activities and accomplishments "count" and which do not. At most US universities, faculty are not recruited based on their international skills, abilities, or accomplishments. Nor are they, as a rule, tenured or promoted on the basis of their international work once inside the university. It is a sad and inconvenient fact that at the present time, and at the overwhelming majority of our institutions, international activity simply doesn't count for very much. Indeed, it may be actively discouraged for junior, tenure-track faculty.

HIRING SIOS

The senior international officer is not a ready-made "profession" in the ordinary sense of the word. Because there is not a clearly established pipeline for SIOs, identifying and hiring suitable candidates becomes very important. SIOs have traditionally come mainly from the ranks of the faculty but increasingly are coming from the outside as well, from the private and non-profit sectors, the diplomatic corps, and even the military. Their career paths are bewilderingly diverse, as is the range of their core skills.

There is, however, general agreement on what SIOs need to know and be able to do, and this was defined quite clearly in a Delphi study of thirty-odd successful and senior SIOs at US institutions.[5] What emerged was a complex picture of knowledge, skills, and attitudes necessary for success, some very general and some quite specific (see figure 2.1). Of particular importance were things like cross-cultural skills; skill in communication, budgeting, and planning; and a good understanding of academic institutions and how they work. Although a great deal remains to be known about how SIOs actually work, this preliminary study has been helpful to both campus committees and recruiting firms as they search for SIOs.

FIGURE 2.1   Attributes of a successful SIO

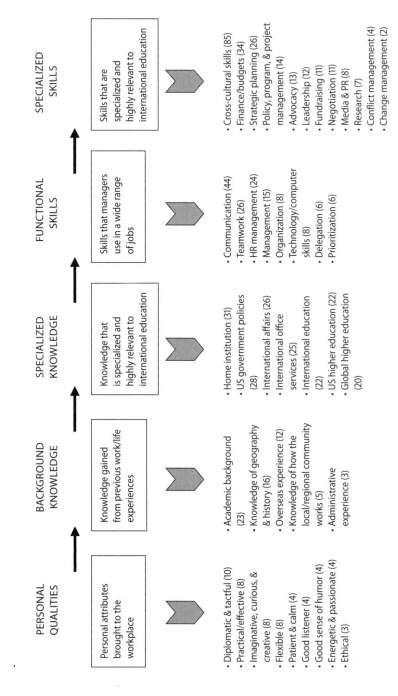

PERSONAL QUALITIES

Personal attributes brought to the workplace

- Diplomatic & tactful (10)
- Practical/effective (8)
- Imaginative, curious, & creative (8)
- Flexible (8)
- Patient & calm (4)
- Good listener (4)
- Good sense of humor (4)
- Energetic & passionate (4)
- Ethical (3)

BACKGROUND KNOWLEDGE

Knowledge gained from previous work/life experiences

- Academic background (23)
- Knowledge of geography & history (16)
- Overseas experience (12)
- Knowledge of how the local/regional community works (5)
- Administrative experience (3)

SPECIALIZED KNOWLEDGE

Knowledge that is specialized and highly relevant to international education

- Home institution (31)
- US government policies (28)
- International affairs (26)
- International office services (25)
- International education (22)
- US higher education (22)
- Global higher education (20)

FUNCTIONAL SKILLS

Skills that managers use in a wide range of jobs

- Communication (44)
- Teamwork (26)
- HR management (24)
- Management (15)
- Organization (8)
- Technology/computer skills (8)
- Delegation (6)
- Prioritization (6)

SPECIALIZED SKILLS

Skills that are specialized and highly relevant to international education

- Cross-cultural skills (85)
- Finance/budgets (34)
- Strategic planning (26)
- Policy, program, & project management (14)
- Advocacy (13)
- Leadership (12)
- Fundraising (11)
- Negotiation (11)
- Media & PR (8)
- Research (7)
- Conflict management (4)
- Change management (2)

But the process by which SIOs are hired leaves a great deal to be desired. When faculty are recruited, there is usually a high degree of consensus on two points: what sort of candidate one wants to hire and what the criteria are for determining the outstanding candidates in the pool. If a university is searching, for example, for a professor of chemistry, the chemistry department will have already decided what sort of candidate would best fit their needs. Chemistry professors write the job ad and serve on the search committee, where they take the lead in scanning and evaluating applications. Once a short list has emerged, generally accepted disciplinary standards and criteria are applied to help choose a finalist. Once hired, the successful candidate is relatively quickly and smoothly integrated into an ongoing departmental operation. None of this necessarily applies to hiring an SIO. There are no advanced degree programs which specifically prepare one for the job of chief international officer. There are no standards of certification and no outward measures of rank or quality. Candidates will likely have come from across the academic spectrum or from the public, private, or nonprofit sectors.

There is usually only one SIO on each campus. On a campus hiring an SIO for the first time, there may be no SIO on the search committee, no one with any substantial experience of having done the job. The other members of the search committee, often representing a broad range of campus stakeholders, are typically diverse and somewhat fragmented in terms of their past experience with, and approach to, internationalization. Some have a "big picture" focus, while others are much more parochial and narrow in their view. They are likely united, however, in one respect: all consider themselves to some degree to be knowledgeable in the international field.

This last point deserves some elaboration. In the case of the chemistry department's search, the search committee is almost certainly composed of a mix of chemists and non-chemists. But the non-chemists are not there because of their expertise in the discipline and would not have much to say about how chemistry should be taught. In international education the situation is quite different. Almost anyone who has ever been overseas has some claim to an expert opinion, and it is easy for faculty and administrators to consider themselves highly experienced in this area, albeit on the basis of a few trips, conferences, or vacations. If almost anyone can claim expertise—or at least substantial experience—no one's opinion is necessarily worth more or less than anyone else's. SIO candidates have to be alert to the sensitivities this situation creates as they attempt to talk their way into the job.

Moreover, there are few universal criteria for evaluating one candidate over another. This is not an altogether bad thing, for it allows each campus to search for and identify candidates who are likely to be a close fit with the institution's overall culture, character, and aspirations. But search committees may lack an appreciation for all of the different skills and competencies available in the candidate pool and required at nearly all institutions.

The intelligent candidate will be aware of all of this, of course, and during the recruitment process will attempt to elicit from the search committee the institution's goals and priorities for internationalization in order to address these in constructive ways. Unfortunately, what all too often results is little more than recitation of a wish list, wherein each committee member advances a request for whatever seems desirable in their own unit. Often, sadly, these may boil down to little more than requests for more money. While it is certainly legitimate, and at times smart strategy, to use the search process as a way to get what you want in other areas, such an approach often reveals the fragmented and self-interested character of the institution's current international posture.

Finding and hiring an appropriate person to lead internationalization on any US campus is a formidable task, akin to playing blind man's bluff in a dark room.

THE SIO'S ROLE IN CAMPUS INTERNATIONALIZATION

SIOs play an interesting and important role in internationalizing US campuses. Although not the only internationally minded and internationally informed members of a university community, SIOs are a catalyst for change. They provide encouragement and support to faculty and students and strategic advice to senior administrators. They are upwardly responsible and laterally supportive. And while they often cannot direct activities, they can instead encourage others to act.

Opinions about what internationalization actually consists of for a specific institution, and how best to get there, vary across a campus. Indeed, there are probably as many opinions as there are individuals. In such an environment, it is very important for the SIO to tread carefully, to develop consensus, and to be able to bring diverse viewpoints together and, from them, forge a common consensus about how to move forward.

SIOs thus face two key tasks: the development of good working relationships with faculty on the campus and a strategic partnership with the top leadership of the institution, typically the president and the provost. It goes without saying, perhaps, that on campuses where the senior leadership and the faculty are at odds, this job becomes particularly difficult.

Successful SIOs begin by getting the measure of the institution by developing a good sense of its culture, key players, strengths and weaknesses, hopes and dreams. Building effective relationships with those key stakeholders is the next step. Through conversations, shared understandings and meanings emerge. As a result, eventually a strategic vision—and later a plan—can emerge.

An internationalization plan or strategy is hardly ever a blueprint; it's more of a developing conversation, an iterative process of meaning-making where creative solutions emerge over time from a series of significant and intentional conversations. This is what environmentalist Wendell Berry has termed "solving for pattern": situating a solution within its overall context in such a way that change does not ignore or disregard the larger connections of which it is a part.[6]

SIOs often begin these conversations with the institution's leaders, for without their support very little of importance will happen. In addition to the provost and president, other members of the senior administrative staff will usually be involved, most notably the chief financial officer, the head of research, and the director(s) of outreach and fund-raising.

At the same time, however, conversations also need to take place with members of the faculty, and across as wide a spread of programs and disciplines as possible. The SIO must identify and work with faculty opinion leaders who have the ability to communicate with and influence others. This is particularly important on large campuses with hundreds or even thousands of faculty.

These conversations are not always easy, and they are often complicated by cultural narratives, the frames or belief structures held by various constituents. In one such narrative faculty view the administration and its activities as "the dark side." For their part, the administrators' narratives liken dealing with faculty as akin to "herding cats."

Another narrative, sometimes found within our larger research universities, sees the institution as existing principally to serve and support the interests of faculty "free agents." These free agents, in turn, are under no particular obligation to think or act in terms of the common good. One sometimes hears statements like, "I'm a tenured senior professor with a fully funded research agenda. Why should I care about internationalization?" Still another narrative sounds like this: "I've been to conferences overseas dozens of times. I don't think I have much to learn about international matters. In any event, what I don't know probably isn't worth knowing." And finally, of course, there is the narrative that comes from hubris: "We're one of the top institutions in the richest and most powerful nation on Earth. What do we have to learn from others?"

These kinds of statements are often merely irritating; but if they emanate from campus opinion leaders, they can prove to be a formidable obstacle.

WHAT WE ARE LEARNING

What, then, might we have to learn by looking at the work of SIOs on our campuses today?

- *Approaches to internationalization.* As noted, there are many paths to internationalization. Each institution is, in a sense, a unique culture, and for this reason alone visions of a more internationalized campus will reflect each college's or university's history, character, and capabilities. How have SIOs incorporated a campus's "personality" into their work, and how does this limit or enable what is possible?
- *Artistry.* Although each university is different, the basic building blocks required for internationalization are fairly similar across institutions, and the SIOs leading such efforts have developed a set of highly specific skills that travel well from one place to another. Almost no one, however, begins his career with all of these skills in place, and skill sets developed at one institution cannot simply be "plugged in" at a new one. Success in the SIO job requires performing a delicate balancing act: meeting the needs of

both the upper administration and the faculty and bringing them together in a variety of ways to promote change. How, then, do SIOs learn their trade in the first place, and how do they practice it under a range of different circumstances?

- *Institutional learning.* Institutions approach the task of internationalization from different angles, but they also develop fuller and more nuanced collective understandings of what they are doing as time goes on. Thus, the issue of how, why, and what institutions—as opposed to the individuals working within them—learn is a major point of interest.

Looking at the work of SIOs will help in our understanding of how to accomplish the long-awaited and much-needed transformation of our higher education structures into truly global institutions. What we manage—or fail—to achieve will help set America's course in the twenty-first century. Better international education will not necessarily give our students the answers they seek, but it will certainly help acquaint them with what some of the more significant questions are. For, as Louis Pasteur reminded us, chance favors the prepared mind.

CHAPTER THREE

International Education Leadership

Reflections on Experience

Jack Van de Water

PROVIDING LEADERSHIP to the international agenda of a university is a complex process. It can take years to acquire a thorough understanding of campus dynamics, decision making, and institutional change. A senior international officer must have a clear administrative philosophy that guides decision making, goal setting, and prioritizing. The quicker the SIO gains this understanding and develops a clear focus, the more successful her career will be. My goal is to help others avoid mistakes I made and thereby benefit from my thirty years' experience as an international education administrator.

I was one of the first people to be appointed as an international education administrator in a central university office, accepting the position of director of International Education at Oregon State University in 1976. In this chapter I reflect on how my thinking evolved as I gained experience, acquired new ideas, learned from my colleagues, and took on additional roles and responsibilities. I also trace the growth of the international mission and goals of a major land grant university and provide examples from my career to illustrate major turning points and significant changes in my university as well as my own thinking.

GETTING STARTED

I was a graduate student at Syracuse University in the late 1960s studying international development and the role of education in that process. I had a National Defense Education Act (NDEA) fellowship that, along with the GI Bill, funded most of my studies. The fellowship ended when I completed my coursework. In need of income, I found a part-time position in the Division of International Programs Abroad (DIPA) on campus. I interviewed hundreds of undergraduate applicants for study abroad, coordinated a number of summer programs, and conducted evaluations of the study abroad experience. These evaluations opened my eyes. Hundreds of students were responding with the same message: the study abroad programs provided the most important educational and personal experience they had ever had. In many cases, these programs were life changing in their impact.

I shifted gears and decided to write a dissertation on the impact of study abroad, comparing three Syracuse programs. This experience made me a true believer in the importance of an international dimension to higher education. It also left me questioning why universities were so underdeveloped in this regard. I became convinced there was a future for me in international education as a career and that I might contribute to the expansion of international programs.

On finishing my PhD, Syracuse asked me to assume the resident director position for its study abroad center in Amsterdam. Soon I had eighty undergraduates to advise, a small faculty and staff to oversee, and a challenging course to teach. It was all I could handle. After eighteen months I returned to Syracuse to become acting director of DIPA while the director ran the large program in Florence. This was my first experience interacting with deans and vice presidents as a colleague. They were, for the most part, supportive and tolerant of my inexperience. We developed a proposal for a new center in London, and I directed the implementation of that large program. After a challenging year, I returned to Syracuse and the acting directorship.

This period provided the foundation for my professional future, but only in a limited sense. I was embedded in the study abroad subculture, and that curtailed my teaching experience, my research interests, and my involvement with other international dimensions of the university. I acquired a thorough knowledge of a particular study abroad model, but my initial attempts to persuade Syracuse to expand beyond this model did not succeed. There was little interest in the reciprocal exchange model or in building new programs in the developing world.

In 1976 I moved my family of five to Corvallis, Oregon, to take the directorship of the Office of International Education at Oregon State University (OSU). OSU was a traditional land grant university with strong programs in agriculture, forestry, oceanography, and environmental sciences. It did not have any distinct international agenda, but it was involved internationally in many ways. This involvement was a major reason OSU created the Office of International Education, with the director reporting to the dean of Undergraduate Studies. This first step recognized OSU's potential for developing a stronger international dimension and coordinating its diverse international interests. There were no precedents for how this would happen, but there was support from the central administration.

When I arrived, the Office of International Education had three major components: international students and scholars, study abroad programs, and the English Language Institute. It was made clear to me in the interview process that OSU wanted to strengthen and expand this office.

Looking back, I can see that I had limited experience and skills to bring to this new position. An immediate challenge I faced was an office staff that needed upgrading—which, I learned quickly, was more difficult to do in the public sector than the private. But within a year the weak links had been strengthened.

Adapting to a new campus culture and new superiors proved to be a major challenge. I had good mentors in that regard, but they had limited international experience and little vision. And the same was true for me at first. My first efforts reflected my limited background. I did what I knew: developed study abroad programs.

OSU had responsibility for administering a network of exchange programs on behalf of the Oregon University System, and in my position I worked on a statewide basis to expand this network and add new components to it. There was tension between my campus and my system roles and responsibilities, but my staff and I were able to develop several large exchange programs and an ambitious international internship program.

There are several lessons to be learned during this early stage of your career development. Taking a new position at an unfamiliar university means many risks and a steep learning curve. And so it is important to evaluate your prospective employer. What is its stage of international development? How does that match your goals, experience, and credentials? In my case, my new employer was in an early stage of development, as was I. So it was not such a bad fit. Everyone had a lot to learn.

It is also important to evaluate your administrative philosophy and its compatibility with your new institution and with your immediate superiors. This requires that you have an administrative philosophy. Do you prefer public or private higher education? Do you believe in the merits of a strong central office? Do you favor the reciprocal exchange program model to the study abroad model? Do you prefer the top-down to the bottom-up approach to decision making? The answers to these questions will have much to say about how compatible you are with your new environment and how well you adjust to your new position and the people with whom you work. On arriving in Oregon, I was just beginning to form my philosophy. But because there were so few policies and practices in place, there was little chance of major conflict.

THE BEGINNING YEARS

Thinking back on my first years at Oregon State, I realize that I had much to learn and that I took too long to learn it. I had little understanding of both public higher education and the land grant mission. I did not understand the campus power structure and how it was based on the major colleges. I did too little to learn about the international interests of the colleges and how I could support them. I needed a senior colleague with relevant experience, a professional association to join, or *a book* that addressed my situation and challenges. I had none of these. But, fortunately, I had tolerant superiors who were patient and willing to hope I would grow into my job.

I did learn, and I did slowly acquire a philosophy as I listened to my senior colleagues. I began to grasp the potential for providing leadership across the campus and for raising my sights beyond those parts of my position with which I was comfortable. The lesson here is to see the big picture and to learn how to contribute to the major goals of the institution. Too often an SIO is content to play a secondary role and to impact programs of marginal importance. Becoming a mainstream player requires growing into (or perhaps out of) a new position; acquiring a good knowledge of the campus culture; building a competent staff; learning how and why decisions are made and priorities are set; and reaching out to peers to understand their interests and how you can influence their thinking. This stage of learning is accelerated by cultivating the support and confidence of senior colleagues. It is also enhanced by networking with more experienced colleagues at other universities.

A key part of this process is to figure out what you are trying to accomplish. Are you seeking to build a strong central international office that controls the major international programs and services? Or do you want to limit your goals to providing relevant services to the academic units? How do you define success? What can you learn from other SIOs?

The starting point is focusing on the fundamental goal of contributing to and accelerating the process of helping your institution become truly international in its primary functions of teaching, research, and service. That means becoming involved with developing a mission statement that has an international perspective. It also means working to have the general education requirements reflect the mission statement and acting as a change agent in developing promotion and tenure policies that reward faculty for their international efforts. It means taking any initiative possible to address the fundamental changes required for *all* students to have a significant international dimension to their higher education. These are ambitious goals that require the SIO to have a clear administrative philosophy regarding how to provide leadership and how to relate to the major campus units. It took me several years to bring these goals into focus and to develop my philosophy, years in which I was far too involved with marginal programs and activities. I had to learn to think like an SIO and to act accordingly.

How does the SIO acquire a strong leadership role? Leadership does not come from aggressive efforts to control as many international programs and services as possible. That only impedes the process of institutional change. Gaining control encourages colleges across campus to ignore the international dimensions of their disciplines and administrative offices. Consider the rapid expansion of study abroad programs. Professional schools are developing programs, internships are popular, and new sites are being developed around the world. If an SIO tries to retain or gain control of this expanding network, the result is the loss of an opportunity to make the university a more international institution. If a central office works with and supports a college or department to develop and implement a new program, it succeeds in involving that department or college in a way that will contribute to the fundamental goal of becoming an international university. This example is true for all parts of the university. The central office does not want to control and administer international alumni affairs; it wants to support the Alumni Office in doing so and thereby becoming more international.

The key point is that the SIO needs to be a partner in the process and not someone seeking to control it. A second point is to figure out how the SIO can acquire the ability to influence the international agenda without controlling it. Both points are critical to defining your administrative philosophy. Influence should flow out from the central office from three primary sources: ideas, funds, and services.

A major objective of the SIO and the central international office should be generating ideas which lead to new initiatives that move the institution's agenda to the next level. The central office is the point on campus where people whose first priorities are international matters congregate. The SIO and the international office need to generate ideas that are relevant to the academic units and other administrative units, ideas that deal with the curriculum, study abroad and exchange programs, recruitment, and research. Leading this process is preferable to receiving, and having to react to, ideas from colleagues for whom international matters may be a secondary priority.

Good ideas generate opportunities for change; they also often create funding challenges. However, proposals for new programs and services that are linked to possible new funding sources will be met with a more positive response than a proposal that competes for existing resources. The SIO is a fund-raiser for new ideas and programs. The ability to track new funding and compete for it is a major source of influence. Going to an important meeting with a good idea or proposal relevant to your colleagues and with funds to put on the table virtually guarantees that the SIO will influence the outcome of the discussion.

Services are an essential part of every international office, and the quality of those services is a major factor in the ability of the SIO to influence decisions. The services are a major point of intersection between it and the academic and administrative units. Therefore, the SIO must lead a strong professional staff and ensure that it understands the main goals of the office and the importance of influence as opposed to control.

The early years of an SIO career need to lead to the development of a clear administrative philosophy and the ability to answer the question, "What am I trying to accomplish?" That provides the foundation for the future. The less time this takes the better.

THE NEXT PHASE

This next phase of my career as an SIO started with being selected as an American Council on Education Fellow in Academic Administration. An ACE Fellow has the wonderful opportunity of spending an academic year being instructed by experts in the various dimensions of university administration, interacting with other fellows who are full of ideas and energy, spending time observing and interacting with university presidents and provosts, and taking an active part in discussions and presentations relevant to his interests. The experience broadened my perspective, improved my understanding of senior administrative positions, elevated my professional goals, and gave me more confidence that I could be an effective campuswide change agent and a leader in strengthening the international dimensions of education in Oregon.

Not everyone has the ACE Fellow opportunity, but it is possible to pursue relevant professional development experiences through seminars and workshops, informal networking, and active participation in professional associations, such as the Association of International Education Administrators. I was involved at the beginning of AIEA and have found it to be an excellent network for meeting colleagues, acquiring new ideas, learning about current trends, and keeping up with federal government programs.

Soon after my ACE Fellow year (1982–1983), Oregon State changed significantly, with a new president and provost and several new deans. The campus culture became more receptive to change and became more engaged internationally. The administration wrote a new mission statement and strategic plan that gave the international dimensions of OSU a higher priority.

This was the beginning of a long run of innovative ideas, new program development, curricular change, and external funding opportunities.

A major challenge was to change the general education requirements, or core curriculum, which was outdated and did not reflect the realities of the rapidly changing international environment. I served on the committee charged with preparing the new requirements. This was an assignment that would have been impossible without my earlier learning experiences. I advocated for a strong international dimension to the core curriculum. Some of my senior colleagues also believed in the importance of international content and supported my case. We were able to add two requirements to the general education of all undergraduates. One required students to take courses dealing with cultural diversity; the other required them to take courses concerned with global issues. This was an important change; it impacted all students and most of the faculty. Courses needed to be developed or revised to meet these new requirements.

This example demonstrates how important it is for the SIO to be in a position to influence mainstream activities. It also illustrates how necessary it is for the SIO to be able to adjust to new institutional leadership. The campus culture is constantly changing as it responds to external forces and internal events. No change is more important than a new president and/or provost. The SIO must recognize that this is a time when priorities shift and new ideas are introduced. This change may signal new opportunities for the SIO, or it may indicate a lower priority for the international agenda. The SIO needs to figure this out quickly. In my case, the changes at OSU were very positive, and it was clear that new international ideas were welcome.

While the committee discussion which led to the new general education requirements had positive results, several participants felt that the university needed to respond with additional changes. Since my title had been changed to University Dean for International Programs, that made it easier for me to engage my colleagues on the Dean's Council. Three of us, along with the chair of foreign languages and a senior staff member from the Office of International Education, developed the idea of a new degree program. This International Degree proposed that undergraduate students in any degree program could work toward a second degree in their discipline. In addition to the traditional degree requirements, the International Degree had four requirements:

- Study abroad for at least one term
- Complete four years of foreign language study
- Take additional coursework in your degree field that is primarily international in content
- Complete a senior thesis and defend it in a public presentation.

This proposal attracted strong support and strong opposition. It required the active support of two powerful deans plus the provost and president as well as outstanding staff work by one committee member. The proposal was accepted. It attracted significant external funding that allowed for curriculum development, student scholarships, and staff support. The International Degree, which now enrolls more than one hundred students annually, attracted considerable attention across the country, but, despite its success, it has not been replicated elsewhere.

State support for higher education during this period, 1986–1996, was declining steadily. Implementing new programs was a budget challenge: if the SIO won a budget struggle for internal resources, it might mean a colleague lost a program or a position. This is a situation that creates tension for an SIO who is dependent on campuswide support for the international agenda. There is no ideal solution. In my case, our office took several steps to minimize the problem. One was to create split appointments with academic departments. This built good bridges and a shared sense of coping with budget problems. We also became more aggressive in attracting external funding. This was only a short-term success, however; the funding issues remained and became increasingly problematic.

During this period, we also initiated or expanded several other programs out of the Office of International Programs (formerly the Office of International Education). We expanded the International Cultural Service Program (ICSP), which provided partial tuition support to outstanding international students who were willing to serve as an educational and cultural resource for the university, the community, and the surrounding region. A large federal grant enabled us to start an ambitious systemwide international internship program, and a major USAID grant funded the English Language Institute's development and administration of the new Yemen-American Language Institute. Another grant funded an international research program for undergraduates. A major factor was the success of the Office of International Research and Development (OIRD), which received several USAID grants that funded OSU faculty's involvement overseas; this in no small measure contributed to the growth of the OSU international agenda.

During this period Office of International Programs had many outstanding and effective staff members worked across the campus and the state. The combination of high-level support, excellent staff, good ideas, and new funding produced significant institutional change and excellent new opportunities for students and faculty. This period was the high-water mark of my career as an SIO. I had developed an administrative philosophy, come to understand the campus culture, assembled an excellent staff, and learned how to be an effective change agent, and I also had the benefit of supportive colleagues at all levels.

THE YEARS OF SHIFTING SANDS

An SIO must expect frequent changes in the senior administration and in reporting lines. These changes are critical to the international agenda and to the ability of the SIO to develop and/or sustain momentum. As such, an SIO should lobby to be a member of search committees for high-level positions, or to have a strong ally on them.

As SIO, you should expect an ebb and flow of administrative support and funding and be prepared to adjust to it. When a new president or provost takes office, remember that your best advocates are your senior colleagues who value your ideas, funds, and services. These are the people who should join you in briefing your new superior. Without them you are just another "special interest group."

Also, realize that a new president or provost wants to make her mark, to put her stamp on the institution. This could mean that there is little support for sustaining the programs of her predecessor. As SIO, you have to be ready to shift gears to become aligned with the changing priorities—which may be positive or negative, depending on the new leadership's commitment to the international agenda. In my case it was a negative.

In 1995 a new president and provost took office, and major changes followed. I had grown accustomed to high-level cooperation and had come to expect it as part of the institutional culture. So it was a painful process coming to terms with the reality of declining support and the complete satisfaction with the status quo. After years of progress and growth, not only of my unit but of my capabilities, I now faced the discouraging results of a new strategic plan, budget cuts, benign neglect, and competing priorities and interests. I was frustrated with my inability to sustain momentum for the international agenda. I knew how to go about it and had some strong allies, but I had to recognize that any additional development or advances would be accomplished with minimal support from my superiors.

The recent history of US higher education is one of declining budgets and increasing competition for available resources. In public higher education there has been a dramatic decline in state funding. In Oregon, as budgets were cut, I became more and more a fund-raiser and grant writer. A major step backward came when I was told that my unit would not receive any part of new state funds because I had demonstrated the ability to attract external funding. My staff and I were able to cope with reduced funding in this manner, but it introduced new issues.

Short-term grants and contracts make it very hard to sustain programs and to plan for the future. They also encourage the SIO to become opportunistic and to respond to funding opportunities that may not be completely consistent with institutional priorities. The more external funding awarded, the more fixed-term staff and faculty are vulnerable to being cut back or terminated when the grant period ends and the institution is not willing or able to provide support. The result is increasing pressure on the SIO to identify new funding and repeat the cycle. Becoming more dependent on external funding is not a good formula for progress.

A senior administration that finds the international status quo acceptable is not easy to work with. The SIO needs to be ready to make the case for the international agenda and to rally support for it. Support networks, on and off campus, are important in this process. A smart SIO will develop a network of external champions—business leaders and others with influence who believe in the international agenda and will support it—who can help you deliver your message to a reluctant president or provost. And in addition to continued advocating and rallying of support, be prepared to be patient or, as I did, do some serious retirement planning. An SIO cannot swim upstream for very long before feeling battered by the prevailing currents.

It is a mistake to try to counter shifting institutional priorities by seeking to accomplish your own agenda. The bottom line is that the SIO is part of the university and, as such, must find a way to contribute to it, even if that is not very rewarding.

A career in higher education in the United States is an excellent and rewarding one, regardless of the pros and cons of any particular discipline, administrative area, or institution. Interacting with intelligent students, faculty, and administrators is stimulating and energizing. An SIO should never underestimate the importance of influencing the values and worldview of the next generation of leaders. I have very few regrets.

ADVICE FOR A NEW GENERATION OF SIOS

Here I make some generalizations based on my years of experience as an SIO that are intended to be of assistance to my younger colleagues and to university leaders who serve as mentors to these new SIOs.

It is fundamental to recognize the central role of faculty and academic departments in the process of growing a university internationally. The curriculum is at the heart of the educational process. Therefore, the SIO position needs to be defined in a way that permits some influence to be exerted with deans and academic departments. A seat at the Deans' Council table, or equivalent committee, provides the setting for exercising influence. What is to be avoided is an SIO position that primarily provides administrative services and has only secondary, or marginal, responsibilities in academic affairs. A university needs a strong SIO who is capable of influencing the mainstream academic life and of serving as a catalyst for change with ideas, funds, and services.

Networking is another key ingredient for success. The SIO cannot be content to work in an office and expect positive results. An SIO must be assertive in meeting colleagues, both at home and abroad. Networking starts at the campus level through actively developing relationships with deans, administrators, and faculty at all levels. Department heads are especially important, as they are making decisions about curriculum, hiring, promotion, and student advising. An institution-wide international committee, preferably linked to the Faculty Senate, is an important component of good communication and support building for the international agenda. The SIO must network off campus as well. State agencies, business organizations, and professional associations are all potential allies that have international interests which overlap with the institution's agenda. Also, the SIO needs to know the economic development agenda of the state and how university international programs might complement and support it. It is also essential to connecting with counterparts abroad and in this country. Staying in regular contact with overseas colleagues ensures good communication, improved understanding of perspectives, and stronger personal connections and working relationships. A worldwide network of exchange programs will operate much more smoothly if the key people involved have good rapport. Contact with colleagues serving as SIOs in other US universities is a vital source of new ideas, of help evaluating problems, and of broader perspectives on major issues and trends. I am proud of the development of AIEA as the primary professional association for SIOs. Every SIO should be a member and take advantage of its programs.

Technology is changing the whole environment within which universities function and how students and faculty interact on campus and around the world. The SIO should stay ahead of the technology curve and be alert to applying new technologies to support the international agenda. The traditional role of the SIO has been as a catalyst for change; to move away from the provincial roles of the university to make it more international. There is exciting potential in new ideas for linking students from different countries through degree programs, course projects, and online face-to-face interactions. Nearly every student will graduate to start a career that has international dimensions and that requires interacting with other cultures and countries. New technologies can provide the education needed to help prepare students for these careers.

Promotion and tenure are central to the career of most faculty members. A university seeking to become a strong international institution needs to examine its promotion and tenure policy to see what message it is sending to faculty. If the policy provides no rewards for international initiatives and ignores contributions to the international agenda, the faculty will find it very difficult to become more engaged with the international dimensions of their disciplines. It is surprisingly difficult to find a US university with a promotion and tenure policy that explicitly signals faculty that their international efforts will be recognized and, if appropriate, rewarded. This is an aspect of the internationalization process that deserves considerably more attention, and the SIO should be a leader in bringing this issue into focus.

Study abroad has become an important part of most universities' international programs. There are increasing numbers of US undergraduates who now have the opportunity to live in and study another culture. Study abroad programs remains Eurocentric, and short-term non-language-intensive programs are the most popular. However, this does not reverse a positive trend. One must crawl before walking and walk before running. A university needs a menu of study abroad opportunities, with programs in every part of the world. Yearlong programs are ideal for language development and cultural immersion. I strongly prefer the direct exchange model based on reciprocity between the partner universities. Direct exchange reduces costs to students, the primary reason for nonparticipation in overseas study. In a direct exchange, each partner wants to make the student experience as rewarding as possible in order to maintain a positive balance in the partnership. The SIO should be a central figure in helping develop new programs and should serve as a key resource in the process of proposing, approving, implementing, and evaluating study abroad programs.

The question of where the SIO should be located within the administrative structure arises frequently. The position of a central international officer is quite new to higher education, and there have been a wide range of reporting lines as positions were established. It has become clear to me based on my experience at Oregon State University and from several visits to other US campuses, that the SIO is best positioned within the academic affairs structure. The ideal reporting line is to the provost, or vice president for Academic Affairs. This sends the message across campus that the SIO is a major player in the academic life of the institution. It also places the SIO near the power center of campus decision making and close to sources of discretionary funding. (During my "productive years" at OSU I reported to the vice president for Research, Graduate Studies, and International Programs, a reporting line that worked very well.) The SIO position I describe here could not operate effectively from a Student Affairs base.

An SIO has the important task of hiring and developing staff. This presents some interesting challenges. An open position in the international office tends to attract a surplus of well-qualified applicants with impressive experience. These applicants tend to be idealistic and ambitious individuals aspiring to gain experience that will lead to an SIO appointment. The normal career path is to first be a tenured faculty member before transitioning into an administrative position, one that perhaps leads to an SIO appointment. An excellent staff member with a master's degree has little chance of becoming an SIO, despite their outstanding work. This should be explained to the applicant at the end of the hiring process, so that the new hire might then begin work toward a PhD, become an assistant professor, gain tenure, and eventually transition into an SIO position. The point is to give the prospective or new hire a realistic understanding of how most careers in international education develop.

The SIO needs to be serious about professional development opportunities for younger colleagues. We need to mentor junior staff and faculty members to encourage them to expand their knowledge and open their eyes to the full scope of internationalization. It is often the case that a new staff member is attracted to a single dimension of an international office and has little understanding of the other components of international education. This represents an opportunity to cross-train and to jobshare in creative ways, for it is important that all staff members understand how the various sections are complementary and form part of a whole with a common mission. Understanding the big picture is a critical component of professional development.

My perspective has been greatly influenced by the era in which I gained my professional knowledge of the field. My career started during the Vietnam War, and it ended with wars in Iraq and Afghanistan. Each of these wars was spawned by a lack of cultural understanding, sustained by an arrogance based on militaristic values, and marked by an ignorance of history, religion, politics, and languages. Now we have the added dimension of increasing terrorism, much of it generated by our own foreign policy.

So with wars as bookends of a career dedicated to promoting cultural understanding and knowledge of other peoples and places, I feel qualified to assert that the next generation of SIOs needs to be more effective. The challenge to the incoming generation of international officers is to provide educational opportunities that produce citizens who understand *more than* how to compete in the global marketplace. We need citizens who also understand foreign policy issues so that they can vote intelligently on matters important to the nation.

My generation of SIOs has seen considerable progress. Today there are more positive than negative long-term trends in international education. However, my generation of leaders in politics, business, and education has failed in many respects. As a nation, we need to accelerate the process of change whereby universities infuse a stronger international and global dimension within the curriculum. We need to change basic policies so that faculty is rewarded for their international efforts. We need to shift institutional priorities so that future graduates provide the quality of leadership now lacking in education, business, and politics. We cannot afford to be timid in pursuing more ambitious international goals for our universities. We need strong leadership in international education in the next thirty years—even more so than in the past.

CHAPTER FOUR

The Senior International Officer as Itinerant Professional

John D. Heyl

SENIOR INTERNATIONAL OFFICERS follow many different professional paths into and out of the position, serving at one or more institutions. Some SIOs are established faculty at a college or university who serve in that role for a relatively long period, basically having made a career shift away from most of their teaching and research and toward academic administration. This includes several of the authors in this volume (Van de Water, Gabara, Tullbane, Brockington, Nolan). Some are faculty who serve for a shorter period with the expectation of returning to a (tenured) faculty role at some point, maybe after only a few years as SIO.

But there is a larger group of SIOs: those administrators who actually manage international affairs full time (not like some at the vice provost or vice president level who manage several areas that may include international) who may have had a faculty appointment at one time and may have given it up (and possibly tenure) or who may never have had a faculty appointment at all. For these SIOs there is no safety net. There is no retreat to the faculty. These SIOs often become itinerant professionals, part of a class of itinerant academic administrators holding unique middle manager roles on campuses across the nation. I belonged to this large group of SIOs.

I came into international education the way that many of my generation did. I studied abroad as a sophomore at Stanford University when it offered only three program options: France, Italy, and Germany. My study in Germany in an "island" program outside Stuttgart led to a career as a German historian and two years of Fulbright-sponsored doctoral study in Bonn in the late 1960s. By the time I took my first teaching position, at Illinois Wesleyan University ((IWU) in 1969, I had acquired personal experience of international education but had no idea what kind of professional field it might hold for me. I was trying to finish my dissertation, earn tenure, survive the early years of teaching, support a spouse earning her doctoral degree, and help raise young children. Even after leading student groups on short-term programs to Soviet Russia and Western Europe, I didn't really know how the field might be organized. Only when a colleague and I succeeded in starting an international studies program (a degree minor at the time) did I begin to realize that a more comprehensive approach to international education might be possible. I was still thinking as an academic, focusing on an internationalized curriculum with a possible study abroad dimension.

My first encounter with a professional in international education was in 1986. I met Jack Van de Water (see chapter 3) at a meeting of faculty from independent colleges interested in developing more international options for their students. I was a forty-four-year-old tenured professor with a modest record of scholarship and already an established middle manager as history department chair and social science division director at a small private university. Although I didn't know it at the time, I was a classic case of a stalled midcareer academic who was exploring a new career path. Jack helped chart my first steps on that path.

THE TRANSITION INTO THE WORLD OF THE SIO

As I was venturing into international education, another, independent, development played a key role in my first professional transition. Within a period of twenty-four months, I sat on a presidential search committee, served the new president as a kind of special adviser for international affairs, and then joined a cabal to force him out, as he had lost the support of key constituencies on campus. In the course of this process, I felt I had lost what credibility I had built over twenty years at IWU and immediately began looking for a full-time position elsewhere in international education administration. Although this painful departure led to my first real SIO position (without tenure but with a significantly higher salary), I promised myself I'd never again get too close to the president. I told myself, That way lies high risk and professional vulnerability. As it turned out, this was a promise I failed to keep.

My move to the University of Missouri–Columbia (MU) in 1988 involved moving into what was, to me, a new feature of a new field: grant seeking and management. While at IWU I had collaborated with Jeff Chinn, a colleague at nearby Illinois State University, on a US Department of Education Title VI grant to internationalize the curriculum at both universities. When Chinn took a position at Missouri, I included MU among the targets in my job search. After considering another option at a small private college a lot like IWU, I accepted the MU position. I was moving into a higher education world I did not know.

Thus, my transition from a long-time faculty position to an academic administrative position at a new (and very different) institution featured several of the factors that often come together when one is deciding to stay in or leave a job in international higher education.[1] Both push factors—personal issues (an impending divorce) and loss of credibility with current campus colleagues—and pull factors—a more prestigious role at a larger institution, a higher salary, and a friend at the new position—played their parts in my decision to leave IWU.

Within a year after taking the position of director of the Center for International Programs and Studies at MU, I attended my first conference of the fledgling Association of International Education Administrators (AIEA). Now, having given up tenure and put aside further scholarly projects in my academic specialization, I dove into the world of the SIO, which included aggressive grant seeking, consolidating international services, supporting faculty international development, and presenting at annual conferences in the field. Although I did not know it at the time, my itinerant career had begun.

A SECOND TRANSITION

My twelve years at MU focused on a process of centralization that ultimately saw the creation of the comprehensive International Center (IC) that brought together study abroad, international student and scholar services, faculty development, partnership management, and grant seeking and administration. This was a first for MU, and it wasn't without its stresses and conflicts. The visibility of the IC grew as millions of grant dollars flowed through it and as a specially designed space in the heart of campus was inaugurated in 1996. Managing the merging of office cultures was a labor-intensive activity, and it was coupled with an unexpected change in campus leadership. It was continuous process of adjustment to and reeducation of those to whom I reported and those who reported to me. One might say that, for the middle manager, this was the perfect storm.

The firing of MU chancellor Charles Kiesler in July 1996 came when I was traveling in Russia with the dean of MU's renowned School of Journalism (and a Russia expert). It came as a huge shock to me personally because I had traveled with Kiesler to the Balkans the year before and had become increasingly convinced that he was the right leader for MU in what were difficult budget times for the campus and higher education in general.

When Kiesler was fired in a 5-4 vote by the University of Missouri (UM) Board of Curators for "insubordination" (he refused to plan for staff and budget cutbacks), the entire campus community was hurt and angered. There were protest meetings; but the decision stood. The truth is, I and many other middle managers at MU would have gone through hell for Charles Kiesler. We trusted him; we respected him; we believed in his sense of the institution's mission. (Perhaps his most important legacy was to have very significantly expanded the number of minority faculty and staff.) Among other things, he knew that MU had to grow, not shrink, to overcome its budgetary woes, a course that was subsequently proven correct by his successors.) He was not always pleasant to be around—he admitted to being "gruff" with the board and other UM System leaders—but he exhibited the qualities of leadership that mattered most. He was a persistent and intelligent visionary, key qualities of a good leader. One could say, therefore, that Charles Kiesler had failed with integrity.

I became resentful of those at the UM System level who forced him out and felt that MU, and its international agenda, would be treading water for some time under his successor. Clearly, I had forgotten the lesson from my departure from Illinois Wesleyan: I had again become too emotionally connected to my boss. I immediately went on the job market.

As it turned out, I did not leave MU until 2000, and the intervening years were turbulent ones for me and for the IC. A succession of events led to a substantial diminution of the standing of the IC. A major external grant in the first round of competition for European Centers in the United States sponsored by the European Union was spearheaded at MU *outside* the IC— interestingly, by the vice chancellor for development. Development was the third major player—in addition to the College of Agriculture and the School of Journalism—to seek autonomous standing in the international arena at MU. This was part of a long process of decentralizing international activity and management at MU, and one that should be celebrated. But as much as I tried to follow many colleagues' advice to welcome additional campus players and support them, instead I felt that the leadership role of the IC was being diluted.

Meanwhile, several key IC staff departures in the late 1990s and a series of wage freezes hit the campus. In the midst of these stressful developments, a personnel issue became highly disruptive, both for morale and for the IC's standing on campus. There were student petitions, negative local newspaper coverage, faculty protests, an external consultant (interestingly, the consultant selected was Jack Van de Water), and confidential HR meetings. At one campus gathering, a faculty member stood up and recommended that the IC be shut down.

While campus developments were heading toward some kind of crisis as the 1999–2000 year opened, I went on the job market since September, and by the winter I had several promising interviews and offers. I could see that my tenure at MU had followed a familiar arc: from early innovation, successful staffing, expanded external funding, and greater campus visibility in the first eight years to a dilution of IC prominence and, finally, internal crisis in the last years. I was eager to move on.

A THIRD TRANSITION (AND "RETIREMENT")

My career in international education had already been marked by two arcs of achievement followed by abrupt crisis and exit. I was confident I had learned from the past thirty years—with the help of some therapy!—and was eager to apply those lessons in a very different setting. Old Dominion

University (ODU) was a striking departure, moving me from the midwestern college town atmospheres of Bloomington-Normal and Columbia to the urban commuter, upper South environment of Hampton Roads, Virginia.

I inherited many advantages at ODU's Dragas Center and the Office of International Programs (OIP). As head of the Dragas Center I had a campuswide role in promoting internationalization, and as director of the OIP I managed the unit that administered Study Abroad, International Student and Scholar Services, International Admissions, and the English Language Center. In effect, what I had built at MU in terms of a centralized leadership office in international affairs, JoAnn McCarthy had built at ODU. And I had learned at MU how important area director positions are and so was fortunate in being able to name three outstanding directors in my first three years at ODU. I also was lucky that Steve Johnson, the long-term study abroad director, remained during my entire tenure at ODU and continued to provide both continuity and valued advice.

My main goal was to raise the visibility of ODU within national circles (which my AIEA presidency at the time facilitated) and, simultaneously, raise the global expectations of ODU students and faculty. This meant setting three main priorities: (1) making study abroad more accessible by expanding short-term programs; (2) mobilizing faculty support by elevating campuswide recognition of international engagement and managing funded international graduate students; and (3) supporting the synergy between multicultural and international programming on campus.

But senior leadership changes again undercut both the international agenda and its institutional coherence. I was hired in 2000 by Provost Jo Ann Gora. We had good rapport from the beginning, and we immediately began to craft an institutional international vision, beginning with appointing the Council on International Initiatives (CII), which I was to chair. The next year, however, Gora left for the University of Massachusetts in Boston. Her successor had strong international credentials, so despite the change at the top, the prospects for ODU's international agenda appeared to be good.

In my six years at ODU, I reported to four different bosses: first the provost who hired me, then the interim provost who succeeded her, then the next provost named by the new president, and finally the vice provost for Graduate Studies, as the provost tried to shed direct reports. I no longer met with the provost, and my various proposals were no longer heard at the senior level—that is, until one caught the attention of the president.

With the help of the CII, I developed a proposal to establish an external advisory body to advise on (and perhaps help fund) ODU's global initiatives. I based the framework for this group on a similar and very successful body in the College of Business. I discussed potential members with a vice president, and he was helpful and encouraging. But when the president became aware of the proposal, she notified me that I was trying to "poach" her prized (and personal) university benefactors and needed to drop the idea immediately.

In my final two years at ODU, the Dragas Center was dismantled. International Student and Scholar Services was moved to Student Services, and International Admissions was transferred to the Admissions Office. The Dragas Center was now little more than a study abroad office with some additional administrative staffing, a shell of what I had inherited five years earlier. Once again I had gotten too close to a president—or at least to the president's special turf. I started planning my early retirement from university life.

Interestingly, the key international units have recently been recentralized at ODU under a new president, after the demolition of the old Dragas Center to make way for a football stadium parking garage.

GOING TO "THE DARK SIDE"

When I retired from ODU in June 2006, the only international project I was still involved in was a short-term Holocaust study abroad program in Berlin and Krakow. I ran one more program out of ODU and then another in 2008 out of the University of Arizona, as my wife and I had moved to Tucson. I also conducted consultancies with several universities. Then, quite unexpectedly, I learned of a senior academic position at the for-profit, private study abroad company CEA Global Education (now CEA Study Abroad), based in Phoenix, less than a two-hour drive up Interstate 10. In June 2009 I was hired full time by CEA. A year later I transitioned into a consultant role but remained actively involved in CEA's academic affairs.

Some colleagues, aware of my long career on nonprofit campuses, commented that I had "gone to the dark side." I'm sure this was meant (and taken) as humor in our field. But the truth is that I had entered a quite new environment, unlike any of the diverse institutions I had served over the years. Now lead conversion, return on investment, margins, seasonality, and bandwidth were critical terms in our hallway conversations and conference calls. I became aware of the services that a provider organization could offer campuses large and small, internationalized and only beginning the journey to a global vision. But I also became aware that providers are increasingly competing with institutions that are turning their study abroad offices into profit centers—that is, turning themselves into provider organizations.

Finally, in 2014 I launched www.IELeaders.net, a website focusing on SIO and leadership issues in international education. IELeaders provides a platform for sharing both my experiences and interests, as well as those of other SIOs, through interviews, articles, and inspirational commentary. Full "retirement" from international education continues to elude me. Such is the pull of a multidisciplinary field with multiple dimensions, multiple voices, and multiple levers for leadership and change.

LESSONS LEARNED

Opportunities and Contexts

SIOs, as middle managers, do not determine who their bosses will be or how long they will remain in place and provide a sustained base of support. Therefore, it is difficult to identify what one's legacy will be since so much is determined by opportunities seized at a particular time and place. Context matters. Even for the SIO who is long-tenured at a single institution, the specific setting and the momentary opportunity is really all the SIO has to work with. In my case, my legacy at each institution was different, and each was shaped by the confluence of setting and opportunity.

At IWU my legacy is the international studies major, one of the most popular interdisciplinary majors on the campus today. SIOs, as middle managers, can have a substantial impact in terms of leading a "center of excellence," as Jim Collins writes, in providing key international services, advice, and vision to the campus.[2] My legacy at MU is the International Center— a centrally located, comprehensive, highly professional service unit to the campus. The IC also provided aggressive support for successful Fulbright applications from across campus. The IC leader, although one among many international players on a diverse and complex campus, remains a major actor in discussions on a global vision for MU. At ODU my legacy may well be the institutional commitment to study abroad, which includes an expansion of faculty-led study abroad, to meet the needs of first-generation, working, and commuter students. Or it may be the master's program in international higher education leadership in the Darden College of Education. At CEA my legacy is the heightened professional activity of its academic staff and the renewed commitment to elevate academic leadership within the company. These various legacies reflect the diverse contexts in which I have worked. Although SIOs are sometimes hired to institute a signature program, I think more common is an institution's search for expertise, vision, and management skills to develop and implement a new global outlook—with the resources available at that institution at that time.

CEO Relations

Although it's critical that the SIO have a good relationship with his immediate boss, usually a vice provost or provost, very little of lasting institutional importance can be achieved without the support of the president or chancellor. I envied SIOs who appeared to have a close working relationship with the CEO, such as John Hudzik with Peter McPherson at Michigan State University or Joel Glassman with Blanche Touhill at the University of Missouri–St. Louis. However, there is plenty of evidence that a strong, supportive partnership between CEO and SIO can be followed by a negative relationship, or benign neglect. This has certainly been my experience. My response to negative changes in campus leadership has been to change institutions, or at least to test the job market. The truth is, I was actively applying for other positions on a regular basis over the last twenty years of my university career. Others with longer tenure at a single institution have shown more persistence and waited for more favorable developments. That a better opportunity always presented itself to me following a crisis at my previous institution suggests that the itinerant SIO will always be an important feature of the profession.

Leading from the Side

Although I occasionally entered a president's inner circle during the course of my career, I was always more suited to what Maurice Harrari once called "leading from the side."[3] For me, the outstanding example of this approach was the development of MU's Global Scholars program, now in its twentieth year, which began as an idea from a colleague in the College of Agriculture, was shaped into a successful Title VI grant proposal by the International Center, and was then funded by the provost. In 2002 it won the Heiskell Award for Faculty Programs. I suspect the MU chancellor at the time was scarcely aware of this program, as it was initially nurtured in the IC.

I could cite other cases of this kind of "stealth management"—an international living-learning unit, external funding for international graduate students, free passports for incoming freshmen, a master's program in international education leadership—that involved gaining support for an idea from key campus constituencies, mobilizing a team to implement the idea, and pooling funding to make the project feasible and, if possible, self-sustaining. Needless to say, this approach was not always successful, but the process suited my personality and leadership style. I preferred to create small engines of change across the campus landscape, hoping for cumulative internationalization over time, even after my departure.

The Itinerant SIO

Although careers in international education certainly exhibit many shapes and contours, there appears to be something to the observation that the SIO often occupies a vulnerable role on a US campus, which makes it more often a career with several stops and sharp turns. Three factors play a role in such situations. First, the very role of SIO is still relatively new. Most of those who've contributed to this volume were the first to hold this position, often the first at more than one institution. Second, the notion of what properly belongs to the internationalization process is still highly variable depending on the campus context. The curriculum belongs to the faculty and fundraising belongs to the president; so as middle managers, SIOs have limited opportunities to make transformative change happen. Third, fiscal pressures, especially at public universities, make the SIO's salary an easy target for reducing administrative costs. This is often the case when administrative realignment moves the SIO role under a unit focused on other priorities, such as extended education or graduate studies, or eliminates the SIO position altogether.

The other case studies of SIO careers in this volume offer something of a test of this hypothesis. Is the SIO role inherently vulnerable for some of the reasons I indicate? Or can individual SIOs create a base of support that allows them to articulate and implement a sustainable strategic vision for an institution? And, perhaps most importantly, what distinguishes the first pattern from the second?

CHAPTER FIVE

Atlas, Sisyphus, or Odysseus?

An SIO Career

Gilbert W. Merkx

IN GREEK MYTHOLOGY, Atlas bore the world on his shoulders. Sisyphus was condemned to roll a heavy stone up a hill only to have it roll down again. Odysseus, following the Trojan War, set forth on a long voyage home during which he faced challenge after challenge. Each of these mythological characters embodies an aspect of the story that follows.

This narrative is a cautionary tale about responsibility (like Atlas), labor (like Sisyphus), and a journey with challenges (like Odysseus). Certain underlying themes emerge and reemerge. One theme is the importance of *place,* or unique social spaces bounded by language and culture. For this reason the headings refer to places. Another theme is the challenge of moving to new places. A third theme is the effort to bring about change within the academy, reflected in the strategy and tactics of issue identification, coalition building, and mobilization for collective action. Throughout the story, the question of power within the academy appears and reappears. Senior international officers strive to innovate, but our success is always contingent on the larger context and the structure of power.

VENEZUELA

This story begins in Maracaibo, Venezuela, where I was born in 1939. My mother was a schoolteacher from the small town of Chadron, Nebraska; she had gone to teach in an American school established by US oil companies, the Escuela Bella Vista. My father was a captain in the Royal Dutch Shell tanker fleet; he was in charge of tanker traffic between Lake Maracaibo and the Dutch West Indies. We lived in a Shell camp, the Colonia Bella Vista. The vista was not bella, but the place was definitely colonial. Our neighbors were mostly Dutch, with a few English and Venezuelans among them.

Thus I began life in a trilingual, neocolonial environment in which people spoke English, Dutch, and Spanish. This seemed perfectly normal to me. My parents had agreed that their children would be raised to be Americans, so I spoke English with them, Dutch with the kids in the neighborhood, Spanish with the Venezuelans, and both English and Spanish at school. All three cultures seemed totally distinct, each one a kind of separate reality. When I read Rudyard Kipling's *Kim,* I recognized a childhood like my own.

Once a year we would visit my grandparents in Nebraska and my aunts and uncles in Chicago and Detroit, but because of World War II we could not visit my relatives in the Netherlands. In 1948 my mother began to worry that I was going native and that my Spanish was better than my English. So she rented a house in the tiny Appalachian town of Blowing Rock, North Carolina, and moved there in time for me to start third grade. My father came up for Christmas and spent his three months of foreign leave with us. That was my first taste of life in the United States. I quite enjoyed this new reality, especially the autumn leaves and the snow, which I had not seen before. At the end of the school year we returned to Maracaibo.

OKLAHOMA

Two years later my rather idyllic neocolonial childhood came to a screeching halt. My father retired from Shell. He bought into a small business owned by an oil company acquaintance in the small town of Chickasha, Oklahoma. We moved there in the summer of 1951 in time for me to start junior high school. This was a tremendous culture shock for me. Instead of the tolerant multilingual and multiracial environment of Maracaibo, I was now in a highly segregated, racist, and fundamentalist town in Oklahoma's cotton belt, marked by considerable poverty and a declining economy. Chickasha is about sixty miles north of Archer City, Texas, where the movie *The Last*

Picture Show was filmed. Years later when I watched that film it seemed like a documentary of my high school years.

If those teenage years in the 1950s were not always enjoyable, they were at least an education in American popular culture: cars, proms, baseball, football, rodeos, dragging Main, country music, rock and roll, and rituals such as the Fourth of July, Halloween, Thanksgiving, and Christmas. My secret ambition, however, was to get as far away from Chickasha as I could. In my limited imagination that meant Harvard. I applied there, and only there, in my senior year of high school. Miraculously, I was not only accepted but given a scholarship.

HARVARD

The mystique of Harvard in the 1950s was intact. I was sure that all my professors were the best in the world and that all my fellow students were smarter than I was. I loved the atmosphere of commitment to knowledge for its own sake and the many small quirks of Harvard culture. I also loved the cultural complexity of Boston, with its gritty Irish, Italian, and African American neighborhoods and aloof Beacon Hill elite. I waited tables for spending money, sang in the choir of an Episcopal church in racially mixed Roxbury, and did volunteer social work in a reform school and with an African American gang in Roxbury called the El Supremos (none of whom spoke Spanish). I also managed to develop solid study habits and get grades good enough to finally persuade me that I was not actually the dumbest kid in my class.

After four marvelous years at Harvard studying social relations (a mixture of anthropology, sociology, and psychology), I was a graduating senior and had not the slightest idea of what do next. So I did the usual evasive maneuvers: I applied to the Foreign Service, to Law School, and for a Fulbright to Peru (that year Peru was offering a large number of Fulbright scholarships). All three options came through. I decided not to go to law school because I didn't really know what lawyers did. I asked the Foreign Service if I could delay entering to take advantage of the Fulbright, and they said yes. The Fulbright looked like a way to postpone a career choice, so I took it and flew off to Peru, a decision that was to change my life.

PERU

The Peruvian Fulbright Commission placed me at the University of San Cristóbal de Huamanga in the southern Andes town of Ayacucho. According to the 1960 Peruvian census, Ayacucho had 24,000 inhabitants, of whom about 500 spoke only Spanish, about 3,500 spoke only Quechua, and the other 20,000 were bilingual. It was a colonial town, little changed from the eighteenth century, and it seemed to be in a fascinating time warp. Little did I know that shortly after my departure in 1962, Ayacucho became the focal point of the Sendero Luminoso guerrilla movement that eventually traumatized all of Peru.

The University of Huamanga was a colonial university that closed in the nineteenth century. It was reopened again in 1959 with a young and talented faculty mostly from coastal Peru, many of whom later had illustrious careers. I studied anthropology with an outstanding group of ethnographers, archeologists, and linguists. My childhood Spanish improved rapidly and soon was comparable to that of the other students, most of whom were native Quechua speakers for whom Spanish also was a second language. During breaks I traveled around Peru by bus or rail, visiting places like Huancayo, Cuzco, Puno, Arequipa, and Lima.

The Fulbright professor in residence at Huamanga was a human geographer from the University of Nebraska named Norman Stewart. He became my mentor and friend. Stewart asked me one day what I wanted to do with my life, and I answered that I wanted do something to alleviate the poverty and inequality that surrounded us. Stewart laughed and said. "So why do you want to be a diplomat? You will just be an agent of American foreign policy. If you want to change the world, you need to get a PhD and have something to offer. Then people will pay attention to you."

Stewart persuaded me to apply to graduate school. While I liked anthropology, in those days the field was mostly focused on indigenous peoples. Urban anthropology had yet to be established. Because I was interested in underdevelopment and modernization, I decided to study sociology. I was fortunate enough to be admitted to the PhD program at Yale. When the Fulbright was up, I left Ayacucho and headed to New Haven.

YALE

Sociology proved to be intellectually satisfying, giving me the theoretical and methodological tools that I was hoping for. I trained in several subfields, among them epidemiology and medical sociology. After I passed my qualifying exams, the chair asked me if I would like to teach half-time for the department in the Culture and Behavior special major, in which faculty from biology, psychology, sociology, and anthropology taught a year-long double seminar that met twice a week. I accepted. A year later I was given a tenure-track appointment; I continued to teach half-time in Culture and Behavior and half-time in the Department of Epidemiology and Public Health of the Yale Medical School.

Shortly after arriving at Yale I joined the Yale Russian Chorus, because I found out that they would be touring Europe the following summer. After auditioning and learning the Russian repertoire, I was able to travel to Europe with the YRC. That trip enabled me to visit Sweden. Sweden fascinated me because at the time it had about the same geographic size and population as Peru, but there seemed to be little or no poverty. I decided that to study development I needed to understand how a formerly poor country like Sweden had achieved prosperity. On my return I enrolled in a class in Swedish at Yale. I visited Sweden regularly for several years and eventually taught there.

Teaching at Yale was rewarding because the students were so talented. Most of my spare time was spent writing my dissertation, a study of economic, social, and political changes in Argentina over the previous century, based on extensive use of historical sources and time series analysis. I had never been to Argentina, but I chose it because there were better data sources for Argentina in the nineteenth century than for any other country in Latin America. Later I visited Argentina many times and fell in love with the country.

With the dissertation almost finished, I went on the job market. I was happy at Yale, but I wanted to go to a place where I could teach and do research on Latin America. Latin America wasn't much on the radar at Yale. In 1968, with the dissertation finished, I accepted a job at the University of New Mexico (UNM), where they wanted me precisely for my expertise on Latin America.

NEW MEXICO

In 1968 the University of New Mexico had about twelve thousand students and four hundred faculty. It was beginning a period of rapid growth that would double in size within ten years. In the late 1930s UNM had established a School of Inter-American Affairs, which was the third Latin American studies program to be established in the United States, and offered both BA and MA degrees. In the 1950s that school was folded into Arts and Sciences as the Division of Inter-American Affairs (DIAA). When I arrived there was also a Latin American Center (LAC), which was funded by Title VI of the National Defense Education Act (NDEA) and offered a PhD in Ibero-American Studies. Part of my salary was initially paid by the LAC. The third international program was a fledgling unit called the Office of International Program Services (OIPS), headed by a recent graduate of the Ibero-American program. This office handled visa requests and counseled foreign students and faculty. It also was in the process of starting study abroad programs, initially in Latin America.

Once I had arrived, it soon became apparent the relationship among the DIAA, LAC, and OIPS was not just problematic but dysfunctional. Each of the three directors ran their units as personal fiefdoms, and they were constantly wrangling over turf. I did my best to stay out of this conflict and tried to focus on teaching, research, and publication. Another issue that confronted me was the student protest movement against the Vietnam War, which was highly active at UNM. I made the mistake of agreeing to be the faculty adviser for one of the antiwar student groups. The activities of these groups led to enormous local controversy, and I ended up having to testify before an investigative committee of the state legislature.

SWEDEN

In the spring of 1971 I was given tenure at UNM and decided to take a leave of absence to escape the increasingly violent polarization resulting from the protest movement. I applied for a job opening in sociology at Göteborg University in Sweden and was hired there, also with tenure, starting in 1972. My classes at Göteborg were mostly bilingual. Although my Swedish was fairly good, I felt more comfortable teaching in English. My students spoke fairly good English but were more comfortable speaking and writing in Swedish. My Swedish colleagues were excellent, and I made some good friends both in Gothenburg and in Stockholm, where I frequently visited the Latinamerika Institut at the University of Stockholm. Among these friends were sociologist Göran Therborn, who is now a professor of sociology at Uppsala University, and journalist Sigfrid Leijonhufvud, who became editor of Sweden's largest newspaper.

Despite the relief of having escaped the polarized atmosphere of the United States, I found that I missed the multicultural environment of New Mexico. Sweden in the early 1970s was still a culturally and socially homogeneous Scandinavian society. Compared to the hurly-burly of American society, it was rather staid. I decided to take leave of my Swedish friends and return to the University of New Mexico. That was a fortunate decision, because shortly thereafter I met my future wife, Karen Remmer, a political scientist newly recruited by UNM.

NEW MEXICO, AGAIN

At this point my career took an unexpected turn. In 1974 the UNM Latin American Center failed to win renewal of its Title VI NDEA grant. There was a sense among the faculty that the central administration had lost interest in the Latin American program, perhaps as a consequence of the infighting among the various program leaders. In 1975 UNM president Ferrell Heady retired and was replaced by William E. "Bud" Davis. The Latin Americanist faculty requested a meeting with President Davis to ask for his support. Davis responded by naming a task force and charging it with bringing specific recommendations to him.

After a year the task force presented Davis with a report that recommended consolidating the Latin American Center and the Division of Inter-American Affairs into a new unit to be called the Latin American Institute (LAI), which would have a university-wide mission and report to the provost rather than the dean of Arts and Sciences. Davis liked the report and acted on it. The LAI was established and Davis announced that there would be a nationwide search for a director for the new unit. He called me into his office, told me that he did not want the unit to be headed by any of the directors of the former units, and asked me to chair the search committee.

A two-year-long search resulted in a sequence of three offers to outside applicants. All three turned down the position for various reasons. At that point Davis called me back into his office and astonished me by announcing that he wanted me to be the new director. Having invested so much time on the task force and the search process, I felt that I had to try to make the new institute a success, so I accepted. I became the director in 1980, starting with a staff of three people and a budget of $70,000.

I brought to this role some sociological observations that proved to be helpful. I observed that the directors of the LAC, DIAA, and OIPS had all run their units as top-down operations. As a result, none of the units had much faculty participation. I resolved to involve faculty in the Latin American Institute as much as possible by transferring to faculty committees much of the decision-making authority of the director. Different committees set the policies and priorities of the LAI, determined the procedures for support of faculty travel, decided which students got financial aid, and determined which faculty and students received research support. Once the faculty realized that these committees had real authority, they were happy to serve. Faculty participation increased, and the faculty became a source of energy, new ideas, and support.

The first problem I had to face was the closure of the UNM Andean Center. Established in 1968, this was a branch campus of UNM in Quito, Ecuador, that functioned primarily as a year-round study abroad program, gave UNM credits, and charged UNM tuition. It had a US academic director with a UNM faculty appointment and an Ecuadorian administrative director, and most of the teaching staff were locally contracted. It was essentially an "island" program for American students. The program had been self-sustaining until the oil shock of 1974 led to a sharp rise in airline fares and a rise of the Ecuadorian currency relative to the dollar. At that point enrollments dropped and the Andean Center began to lose increasing amounts of money. The UNM faculty had never been very supportive of the Quito campus. The administration asked me to shut it down. Extricating UNM from Ecuador proved to be a costly process, given local labor laws, and the task took several years to complete.

One of my key strategies as director of the LAI was to empower the faculty by seeking outside funding to put their good ideas into practice. Our most important proposal for the next Title VI competition met with success. The LAI was awarded the status of an NDEA National Resource Center for Latin America.

Then a new threat emerged. The same semester I became director of the LAI, Ronald Reagan was elected president of the United States. The Republicans also took control of the Senate. Reagan's first budget message to Congress in January 1981 called for the elimination of all funding for Title VI programs. I flew to Washington to meet with my two Republican senators, Pete Domenici and Jack Schmitt, to plead for their help in saving Title VI funding. That was my introduction to lobbying.

I soon was in contact with others trying to save Title VI and became a part of a network of advocates for area studies in particular and international education in general. One problem that we faced was competition among the different area studies fields for federal funding. To alleviate this issue, I teamed with David Wiley, the director of the Center for African Studies at Michigan State, to organize all the Title VI centers into a single association, the Council of National Resource Center Directors (CNRC). CNRC made it possible for the area studies centers to speak with one voice.

At this time I was interested in Venn diagrams. I realized that the overlapping sets of actors at UNM I was trying to cultivate to build the Latin American Institute, such as area studies faculty, language teachers, librarians, and the professional schools, all had counterparts in Washington in the form of national, or peak, associations. So I set out to cultivate people in these peak organizations as the first step in establishing the same alliances in Washington as I'd built at UNM. One of these organizations was the newly founded Association of International Education Administrators (AIEA). In 1985 its second president, Jack Van de Water of Oregon State University, asked me to address the annual conference in Washington about the Title VI advocacy effort.

By 1992 the time seemed right to formalize an organization that would be a Venn diagram of associations interested in foreign language and area studies. A friend of mine, Cole Blasier, who was then the director of the Hispanic Division of the Library of Congress, agreed to host a foundational meeting. To our delight, every organization we invited accepted. And several organizations we had not invited found out about the meeting and asked to be included. More than twenty groups attended, including CNRC, AIEA, several language and foreign area studies associations, two library associations, six associations of colleges and universities, two associations of business schools, and peak organizations for the humanities, social sciences, and learned societies. Those present founded the Coalition for International Education. The Coalition was fortunate enough to be able to recruit the wonderful Miriam Kazanjian to be its consultant for federal relations. This organization, and Miriam, continues to play an important role in advocating for language and area studies.

My ability to lobby effectively was in large part contingent on two features of the New Mexico context. New Mexico had a very small population, so it was easy for me to get access to my senators and their staffs and to develop a relationship of trust with them. Senator Pete Domenici rose to become a powerful figure on both the Senate Appropriations Committee and the Senate Budget Committee. Also, during this entire period UNM had no federal relations officer or other presence in Washington, despite being a Carnegie 1 research institution. The UNM administration knew of my lobbying activities and viewed them with benign disinterest. Only later did I realize that my freedom to lobby without constraints was relatively uncommon for a flagship state university. In many other institutions I would not have had the same latitude.

In the following years, I spent my creative energy lobbying and writing funding proposals instead of research papers. I traveled to New York to meet with foundations and to Washington to meet with government funding agencies and lobby for Title VI. I also lobbied the New Mexico Legislature for earmarks, visiting some of the same legislators who had interrogated me a few years before. I was fortunate enough to have some of my first proposals funded by the Rockefeller, Mellon, and Tinker Foundations and by several government agencies, including the National Endowment for the Humanities and the Inter-American Foundation.

From its small beginnings, the LAI grew rapidly. Our MA program expanded from 13 graduate students in residence to a high of 135 students. The undergraduate major went from a handful of students to about 100 graduating seniors per year. The staff grew from 3 to about 40 employees and 10 student assistants. The hard-money UNM budget increased from $70,000 to $700,000 annually. Adding grants and contracts, the total LAI budget was well over $2 million a year when I left in 2001.

However, just as the LAI began to take off, an unexpected development took place at the top. A scandal erupted when it was discovered that the UNM basketball staff had been falsifying the grades of players. As a result, President Davis dismissed both the basketball coach and the athletic director. The latter, however, was a friend of the chair of the Board of Regents, an oilman named Calvin Horn. Horn forced Davis to resign in 1982. With that, the LAI lost its most influential supporter.

The departure of President Davis ushered in a long period of administrative instability and financial austerity at UNM. During my twenty-one years as director of the LAI, I served under six presidents and eight provosts. With each change of leadership, the LAI and its budget came under attack from rivals on campus. Moreover, each new leader wanted to have a new signature initiative and was not keen on prior initiatives.

With the constant administrative turnover at the top, I had to spend inordinate amounts of time defending the LAI internally and justifying its importance to the university. I learned not only that support from the top cannot be taken for granted but that it was a mistake to be too closely identified with any one president or provost given their short terms in office.

Given these internal challenges, I spent more and more time developing other forms of social capital through networking activities, such as serving on key faculty committees and chairing the Faculty Senate. External funding also was critical to maintaining both the operations and the credibility of the LAI.

However, the success of the LAI came at a personal price. I was devoting increasing time to faculty politics and university service. I was locked into writing a constant stream of grants to keep the soft money flowing. Also, I was beating paths back and forth to Washington and to the state legislature in Santa Fe. My research was suffering, and I was beginning to feel the symptoms of burnout.

In 1999 our youngest child went off to college. My wife, who had recently stepped down as chair of political science, told me she was tired of working at an institution in perpetual flux and wanted to finish her career at a first-rate university. Although I still loved New Mexico, it was hard to disagree. So we went on the academic market as a couple. After considering several alternatives, we accepted offers from Duke University. In 2001, some fifty years later, I was returning to North Carolina.

DUKE

The provost at Duke, Peter Lange, offered me a five-year renewable contract as vice provost for International Affairs, as well as a five-year renewable contract as Professor of the Practice of Sociology. I was giving up the tenure I had earned at the University of New Mexico. However, by this time I had become deeply immersed in international education advocacy and administration, and the chance to become Duke's chief international officer seemed more important than tenure. Other aspects of the new job were also persuasive. Duke's president, Nannerl Keohane, was a strong proponent of internationalization. The president and provost together offered me an annual. discretionary fund of $500,000 to be invested internally at Duke to promote internationalization. Instead of spending my time raising money, I would be able to make strategic investments. I was also offered the position of director of Duke's Center for International Studies, a Title VI–funded center, which meant that I could continue my advocacy for Title VI. Duke had five other Title VI centers, all of which would be under my purview.

In the 1990s Duke had made extraordinary progress in internationalizing, under the leadership of its first vice provost for International Affairs, who was now the provost (I was the third person in the position). Major investments had been made in staffing the visa office, international student and scholar services, and the study abroad office. Study abroad was a particular success: 45 percent of graduating seniors had studied abroad. The undergraduate curriculum included a foreign language requirement for all students, and there was even an undergraduate major called Comparative Area Studies.

When the provost was recruiting me, he said, "We internationalized Duke as a bootstrap operation, focusing on internal obstacles. We really had no idea what we were really doing, and we didn't know what other institutions were doing. Other institutions still don't know what we have done here. But you are an international education professional. You know the field and what other places are doing. I want you to raise our national profile and take us to the next level." It would have been hard to imagine a more attractive challenge.

I arrived with a great deal of enthusiasm and set to work to master the intricacies of my new job and the politics of Duke as an institution. I learned that the administrative politics were more complicated than I had foreseen. Five of the seven area centers reported to me, but two reported to the dean of Arts and Sciences. The Visa Office was located in the Duke Medical School. The foreign student and scholar services unit, known as International House, reported to the vice president for Student Affairs. The Study Abroad Office reported to the Arts and Sciences dean in charge of undergraduate education. International admissions were split between the dean of admissions and the graduate school. Alumni Affairs controlled access to alumni but did not communicate with international alumni (or even have a data base for them). Theoretically, I was a dotted line to each of these units, but in practice I had no authority over any unit that did not report directly to my office.

I set out to meet with the directors of these units and learn about their priorities. These directors all served on a committee that I inherited and chaired, the International Affairs Committee (IAC). The IAC also included representatives of the deans of Duke's seven schools, the directors of the foreign language and area centers, and representatives from the library and the foreign language faculty. At my first meeting with the IAC, I asked those present whether they thought the committee was worth their time. The answer was a resounding yes. One person said that it was the only place that they could find out what was happening in terms of internationalization at Duke, and others vigorously agreed.

I thus faced three institutional challenges. One was to raise Duke's profile as an institution committed to internationalization. A second was to reduce the administrative Balkanization of the various offices with international responsibilities. The third challenge was to further internationalize Duke as an educational institution. But, new to the university, I had additional challenges, such as learning the institutional culture, getting to know all the relevant actors, and winning the confidence of the provost, the deans and directors, the faculty and staff. To expand my networks I volunteered to serve on a variety of campus committees, including the equivalents of my UNM committees (library, university press, and buildings.) I also offered to teach a course or two, but the provost told me that I would be too busy to teach. He was right.

Not long after my arrival, I had another conversation with the provost, and he told me, "I want to plant the Duke flag overseas." I thought to myself, "That sounds rather colonialist"; but what I actually said was, "Why would you want to do that?" He said that Duke could gain international recognition by having overseas operations, such as branch campuses. I responded by saying that I thought Duke would get more recognition by forging partnerships with the leading universities of the world. This conversation turned out to be a harbinger of things to come.

To increase Duke's profile in international education, my staff and I developed a comprehensive website for all of Duke's international activities, including statistics documenting the university's many achievements in international education (such as the fact that nearly half of graduating seniors had studied abroad). I enrolled Duke as an institutional member of the Association of International Education Administrators. I arranged for Duke to host a national conference prior to the reauthorization of Title VI. I moved the secretariat of the Coalition of National Resources Centers from New Mexico to Duke and, shortly thereafter, brought the AIEA secretariat to Duke from SUNY-Buffalo, where it had previously been hosted. My unit also played a key role in forming the International Academic Collaboration of the Atlantic Coast Conference, and Duke hosted its first annual meeting. Duke received one of the first NAFSA Paul Simon awards for excellence in international education, as well as an award from the North Carolina Association of International Educators.

On the organizational front I had some successes, such as consolidating all the foreign language and area centers under my office. However, I was unable to do the same for the other key international operations, such as international student and scholar services, study abroad, and visa services, despite the desire of the directors of these units to move under my office. This consolidation would have had to be implemented by the provost, and he was unwilling to spend any political capital on it. I finally put reorganization on the back burner and focused on developing collegial relationships with various deans and vice presidents to whom these units reported.

The effort to make Duke more international was a see-saw struggle, with some successes and some failures. Shortly after I arrived, the provost asked me to develop a new internationalization plan to replace the previous plan that he had authored when he was the vice provost for International Education. I worked with the IAC on this plan, which incorporated some of the unmet objectives of the first plan. When the committee had approved the draft, I took it to the provost. After he read it we met, and he said, "There is a part of this plan I cannot support." I asked him what. He answered, "The recommendation that the tenure policy be changed to take account of international service." I replied, "I didn't draft that recommendation. You did. It was taken word-for-word from the plan that you wrote." He responded, "Well that was then and this is now. Now I am the provost." I responded, "Then we'll take it out. I won't advocate something that you don't support."

President Keohane retired from Duke in 2004. Her successor stopped contributing to the discretionary funds that my office managed, but the provost made up most of the difference. During this period I was able to help establish the Duke Center for Islamic Studies and then the Duke Center for Middle East Studies. We continued to hold our own in the competition for Title VI funding. And while our European and South Asian area centers lost their grants, we were able to win first-time Title VI funding for our East Asia and Middle East centers. I participated in the writing of two strategic plans for Duke University as a whole, and in both versions internationalization was a prominent goal. The second plan required that each school at Duke set its own internationalization targets, which was a significant step forward. I also was involved in the development of DukeEngage, an undergraduate service learning program in which most students served overseas.

As my first five-year contract as vice provost neared its end, a faculty committee evaluated my performance. The committee's report included the following: "We conclude that Dr. Merkx has not only done a spectacular job in this post locally and within the institution, but has taken Duke to a new level of visibility as a front runner in the internationalization process." Despite this accolade, I had become convinced that we were not addressing the most fundamental challenge facing Duke: providing *all,* not just some, Duke students with an education that would prepare them to be global citizens able to function in an internationalized world. This challenge could only be addressed by revising the core curriculum to make it less Eurocentric. I raised this issue with the provost several times. He had chaired the committee that pushed through the last revision of the curriculum in 2000 but was simply unwilling to reopen the issue. I understood, of course, that revising the core curriculum is always a contentious process. There was no way to start such a process without support from the top. I consider the lack of curricular reform to have been my greatest failure as vice provost.

As a vice provost, I not only served at the pleasure of the provost but was his agent. At the same time, I knew that for me to mobilize faculty and staff support for internationalization, it was important for me to be perceived as their advocate. For this reason, I worked hard to establish a sense of community among all the different players involved in one or another aspect of Duke's international activities. The IAC, comprised of directors of international units and faculty representing deans, was instrumental in this regard. My staff suggested that we establish a counterpart forum open to all staff working on international programs. We set this up and named it the International Affairs Group (IAG). The IAG was chaired by staff, met two to three times a year in different venues on campus, and invited speakers from different units to report on their efforts. The international staff across campus came know one another, and the sense of a campuswide community dedicated to internationalization became tangible.

Then IAG came up with the idea of back-to-school celebration sponsored by all the international units across campus, which I enthusiastically endorsed. It took place in the fall of 2008, the start of my seventh year as vice provost. We reserved a lovely venue, the Doris Duke Pavilion in the Duke Gardens. The sponsoring units included all nine area centers, the Office of Study Abroad, the International House, the Duke Visa Office, the International and Area Studies Department of the Duke Library, the Franklin Humanities Institute, the Duke Center for International Development and the international program staff of the Schools of Law, Business, Environment, Nursing, Public Policy, and Medicine. Some two hundred staff and faculty attended the event, which was initiated with much festivity and goodwill. As the event began, I felt a strong sense of pride in the community of which I was now a part.

Unfortunately, this event also marked the beginning of the end of that sense of community. We had invited the provost to address the celebration, in recognition of his key role in fostering Duke's internationalization. The provost began by thanking everyone for their contributions to making Duke more international. Then he said, "You have all been a part of the first phase of Duke's internationalization, which was to bring the world to Duke. We are now going to start the second phase of Duke's internationalization, by taking Duke to the world." He went on to say that Duke would be establishing a chain of sites, or campuses, overseas. As he spoke, the happy mood deflated. There was polite applause, and he left. Afterward several people came up to me and said things like, "Are we obsolete?" and "Did he just tell us that we are history?" I tried to minimize the damage, but I was equally taken aback.

THE DENOUEMENT

The issue of overseas sites for Duke remained active, partly because of the provost's aspirations and partly because Duke was constantly being approached by other countries. I was able to deflect a determined effort by a South Korean development agency that was building an industrial park and wanted a Duke campus to be its anchor tenant. Then an Indian land developer approached the provost and offered to provide Duke with a campus near Delhi as part of a major development he was planning. Several high-level meetings were held, which I attended, including one to which the developer himself came with a large entourage. I was skeptical; the provost was enthusiastic. Then some due diligence revealed that the land in question was still owned by farmers in Uttar Pradesh who would have to be evicted. A prominent Indian alumnus told us that the Duke brand name in India would never recover from being associated with this scheme. The project was dropped.

In my ninth year as vice provost, a third offer came, this time from the municipality of Kunshan, not far from Shanghai. Again Duke was promised a campus as part of a larger land development scheme on reclaimed marshland. Kunshan promised to pay for the construction if Duke would pay the architectural fees. This time I was not included in the planning meetings.

My Chinese friends on the faculty were very circumspect about the project, but privately they voiced grave concerns to me. I did not publicly oppose the project, but I did try to raise these issues with the provost.

One morning the provost came unexpectedly into my office. He said, "People are going to be mad at me, because they like you, but I want you to step down. You have done a great job and done everything I wanted you to do. But now I want to appoint a vice provost who makes the China project his top priority." I replied, "I'm happy to step down. You and I both know that China is not my thing. It's been a great ride for me, and I appreciate having had the chance to work for you." The provost seemed a little surprised at this response.

My replacement was the dean of the Divinity School, who was given the new title of vice president and vice provost for Global Strategy and Programs. He had no prior experience in the international education field. When I briefed him, I stressed the importance of the IAC and IAG as not only sources of good ideas but also essential to a sense of community for those who would be his natural constituents. My advice had little effect; he abolished both groups, and they never met again. The sense of a campuswide internationalization community quickly waned.

Much of the funding I had devoted to on-campus activities the new vice president/vice provost diverted to planning the China campus. He quickly built a large staff to help him plan the Kunshan project, which took more and more of his time. To reduce his burden, I took on the role of director of International and Area Studies, continued to serve as director of the Center for International Studies, and resumed teaching sociology. Teaching proved to be enormously rewarding.

LESSONS LEARNED

I did not begin my journey intending to have a career in international education. At various points I thought of myself an anthropologist, a sociologist, a Latin Americanist, a Scandinavianist, and a development specialist, among other things. However, everything that I had been doing throughout my career involved international education in some form or another. Then I finally became a senior international officer and had the chance to help advance the broad international agenda of a major research university. It was a welcome challenge that led to some accomplishments and, well, some frustrations.

From these experiences I draw six conclusions. First, *international experience* is extraordinarily important for an international administrator. The experience of living in the alternative universe of another culture and another language leads to an understanding of the value of international education that cannot be achieved in any other way, and certainly not by book learning. I was fortunate enough to have an international childhood, but my travels as an adult were equally important. Each immersion in a different national culture enriched my understanding not only of that culture but of the United States. These experiences made me a better researcher and teacher and also informed my goals as an international education administrator.

Second, *allies count*. Other people with international experience are natural allies, especially if their role in the university has an international dimension. Seek out and make into allies those faculty and staff whose work is international, whether that mission is area studies, study abroad, overseas research, international service learning, student and scholar services for non-nationals, curriculum reform, or something else. This involves framing the collective good in such a way as to emphasize the commonalities of interest that can motivate collaboration and thereby reduce the risk that the differences among these actors leads them to see one another as competitors. Mobilization requires not just identification of potential allies and framing the collective good but also creating venues that bring them together.

Third, *it's all about people*. Educational politics are as much about personalities as about intellectual issues. Overbearing, critical, or pushy treatment of colleagues quickly alienates them. In the business world, those who lose disputes are fired. In academia, they live to fight another day. Hence, it is sometimes more important to lose gracefully than to win unpleasantly. The inverse is also true. Successful interactions create good feelings that may prove valuable in unexpected ways. One can make observers into stakeholders by consulting them, taking their advice seriously, and, when possible, asking them to participate in decisions. Once they become stakeholders, they also become allies. This social capital can be translated into political support for the internationalization.

Fourth, *use a win-win strategy.* Promote internationalization not as a separate agenda but as a win-win strategy for all parts of the university—in other words, not as competitive with other agendas but as supportive of them. The objective is to treat every dean, every faculty member, every staffer, and every student not as a rival but as a potential stakeholder. This is not just a shift of rhetoric but a key change of stance. Universities are highly invidious and resource-limited environments in which actors are highly sensitive to the nuances of presentation. The win-win approach is disarming and creates space for dialogue.

Fifth, *contingency trumps agency.* No matter how effective one is as an agent, one always acts within a larger structure. The most important characteristics of that structure are contingent on factors that cannot be controlled or influenced by an international education administrator. The president or provost may become enamored with some new initiative and lose interest in internationalization. The president or provost may leave office and be replaced by leader with different priorities. The institution may run into unexpected financial problems leading to cuts in staffing or programming. Even without financial setbacks, a change agent may discover that the institution us unable or unwilling to make the strategic investments needed to advance internationalization, such as hiring the staff required to expand study abroad programs or the faculty to teach additional foreign languages. This can be offset to some extent by raising revenue from external sources, such as donations, grants, and contracts. However, there are natural limits to such fund-raising. If the fund-raising is not matched internally, the international administrator may end up in an endless cycle of grant writing simply to stay in place.

Sixth, there is always a *choice.* When structural contingencies reduce or limit agency, the change agent is confronted with a number of options, which might be described in poker terms as the "hold them or fold them" choice. A "hold them" option is to hunker down, run in place, and hope for a more positive context in the future. One "fold them" option is leave the international education field by returning to the faculty or seeking a different administrative job; the other "fold them" option is to stay in the field of international education by relocating to a different institution.

COMING FULL CIRCLE

This narrative documents the roles of both agency and contingency. When the contingences were positive at New Mexico during the Davis presidency, I was able to achieve some success in pushing the internationalization agenda. The same proved to be true of my lobbying activities in Washington during the Reagan, Bush, and Clinton administrations, thanks in large measure to the bipartisan congressional context. My initial experience at Duke, working under a supportive president and provost, was also a good opportunity to be a change agent. These were exhilarating periods.

In each of these three contexts, the same institutional contingencies that had at first empowered me ultimately came to limit my effectiveness. At New Mexico a supportive president was replaced by administrative instability. I hunkered down to wait for better times, which never came. Eventually, I folded my hand and relocated to Duke. At Duke I initially encountered a very positive environment. However, the supportive president retired and the provost developed a new set of priorities. When the time came to fold my hand, I decided not to relocate but to play a lesser administrative role and return to teaching. I continued to advocate for the federal role in supporting international education. However, in Washington bipartisanship was replaced by partisan gridlock that led to major setbacks for the funding of international education programs.

In some ways, my career went full circle. I began my administrative career with the challenge of shutting down a foreign campus, and I lost my job as a vice provost because I did not support opening a foreign campus. I started my career facing the elimination of federal support for international education, and despite all the successes of the intervening thirty years, the field is again threatened with the loss of federal support. I began my career teaching sociology, with a focus on area studies and international development, and once again I am back teaching sociology and am involved in area studies and development issues. It is tempting to sum all this up with Alphonse Karr's epigram, "*Plus ça change, c'est la même chose*" (The more things change, the more they stay the same). Yet, much has indeed changed in the international education, in the American university, and in American politics. Heraclitus offers a better summation: "No man ever steps in the same river twice."

CHAPTER SIX

An Unconventional Path to International Education Leadership

Howard Rollins

ALL THE INTERNATIONAL education leaders represented in this book had unique pathways to becoming leaders in the field. However, many studied or lived abroad as part of their early life experiences and/or chose academic careers involving international fields such as area studies (see chapters 4 and 5).

My own path was quite different. I grew up in a small North Carolina textile town. My college years were spent at Wake Forest University, where I got an excellent education, especially in psychology. However, the undergraduate population and the faculty there were mostly southern and Anglo-Saxon. My only experiences outside the South were my high school's senior class trip to New York City and a three-day cruise some college friends and I took to Nassau. This sheltered life ended when my faculty adviser in psychology suggested I get out of the South to earn a PhD in developmental psychology at UCLA.

My four years living in Los Angeles studying at UCLA were truly my first study abroad experience. I developed friendships with fellow students from all over the country and a few from outside the US, including from Canada, Mexico, and Israel. Of course, California was also culturally very different from the South. What a transformation! I even lost my southern accent, or softened it. One other important life event happened in Los Angeles. I met my future wife. She is a third-generation Canadian Catholic with roots in Poland and Ukraine who visited the States with friends and ended up in California. Indeed, my second study abroad experience occurred on the occasion of our marriage in Winnipeg, which bore no resemblance to the dry and boring marriage ceremonies in the South. As many readers with this unique experience will agree, living for years with a spouse from a different cultural background is also transforming.

My career began when I accepted an assistant professor position in psychology at Emory University. At the time, 1968, Emory was a small, private, liberal arts college, but it quickly grew into one of the top twenty US universities. While a leading institution now, in my early years at Emory it was clearly well behind top universities across the United States in terms of its interest in international education. There were a few summer study abroad programs, mostly run by the language departments, and four small area studies programs, again run out of larger academic departments with little or no college or university support or supervision. The presidents, provosts, and deans in those years were not particularly interested in international education, perhaps because of more important priorities as they focused on improving the national reputation of the university.

THE EMORY YEARS

How did a psychology professor move into an international education leadership position? Because one of my psychology colleagues had taken his sabbatical in England at University College London (UCL), which has an excellent psychology department, I decided to take my sabbatical there also. In 1975, my wife, two preschool sons, and I traveled through Europe for three weeks (the first visit for all of us) and then lived in London for five months. We developed strong friendships with colleagues at UCL and among our neighbors in the suburbs. This was the most important international experience for all of us to that date, and it clearly led to my growing interest in engaging the world beyond the United States.

One final set of experiences set the stage for my interest in international education. The chair of psychology had established a study abroad program for undergraduates related to clinical psychology. When, in the late 1970s, he decided to no longer run this program, he gave me the opportunity to establish a developmental psychology (my specialty) summer study abroad program. I lobbied for this program precisely because of my positive experience in London. The program had been designed so that Emory students interned at local elementary schools in Canterbury, England, for two weeks. While there they served as experimenters to collect psychologically interesting data on the children in their classrooms that could then be compared with date on children in the United States. The program leader and students then moved on to London, staying at UCL for three weeks and collating the data. Each student generated a research paper on the findings of the study. While the first group consisted of only 9 students, this program rapidly became very popular and thereafter had 25–45 students participating each summer.

I discovered that such study abroad programs have a significant impact not only on the students but on the faculty leaders as well. Students develop confidence, come to appreciate other cultures, better understand the United States, and often claim that it has been the best experience of their college years. Faculty study abroad leaders appreciate the closer relationships they establish with study abroad students and spending longer and more frequent periods overseas collaborating on research and becoming more familiar with the local cultures. This program continues to be popular today, some thirty-six years later. I was a faculty leader on this program as recently as the summer of 2012 and will participate again in 2015.

In the 1980s I was asked to serve as associate dean of Arts and Sciences in charge of faculty development and the budget. While unrelated to international education, this stint as an administrator provided me with invaluable leadership experience that came in handy later. After five years in this position, I returned to psychology, where I was appointed department chair, a position I held for eight years. During a much-needed second sabbatical, my wife and I returned to London, sans children. Sabbaticals are a good time to reflect and to consider what to do next in life and work. It was while in London that I got an email from the dean of Arts and Sciences, David Bright, asking if I would be interested in taking on the position of director of the Environmental Studies Program, which was just getting under way. Not being a particularly strong environmentalist, and having no experience in this field, I knew that this was not the right way forward. What I did know was how much I enjoyed establishing and leading the psychology study abroad program, it occurred to me that I might enjoy and be productive in a leadership role in study abroad in particular and perhaps in a broader international role if that became available. I emailed the dean in response and expressed instead in taking on a role in international education. His response was that this might be possible and to come to his office for a discussion when I returned.

I was subsequently appointed chair of an Arts and Sciences faculty committee to develop long-range plans for study abroad. At the time, the few summer study abroad programs were each run by the relevant academic department, but it was becoming clear that some higher-level supervision of these programs was necessary given the growth, the number of students participating, and the educational, legal, and ethical issues that might be involved. The committee recommended establishing a new organization called the Center for International Programs Abroad (CIPA) to oversee and set policies for all international programs. I was named the founding director of CIPA and began immediately to hire staff, including a secretary and an associate director, a young man who had just earned a PhD in history from Stanford and was looking for an academic job in Atlanta. One of the true pleasures of leadership in higher education is fostering the development of new faculty and staff. I am proud to say that Philip Wainwright became the director of CIPA after I moved to Georgia Tech and is now serving as vice provost for International Education at Emory.

CIPA expanded rapidly as we added study abroad advisers, additional secretarial help, and student interns. We not only increased the number of summer study abroad programs and range of countries involved, particularly outside Europe, but we also quickly established semester and year-long programs both of our own invention and in collaboration with other universities and various consortia. As a result, the number of study abroad students increased geometrically to the point where the dean and higher-ups began to ask whether there were limits on how many students could go abroad. The student housing leadership was getting nervous as well—about the high number of vacant dorm rooms. (In fact, the current rate is approximately 50 percent of each graduating class participating in some study abroad experience, and a relatively high percentage of these students study abroad for a semester or a year.) My response was that Emory could readily increase the size of the incoming classes both in the first year and, more importantly, in the second and third years (transfer students), which were the years during which many students studied abroad, in order to offset those students who were abroad for a semester or a year, which was usually in their junior or senior year. In fact, it does not take many new full-time students paying full tuition to cover the tuition revenue not paid by the students studying abroad for a summer or semester.

While I enjoyed immensely serving as the director of CIPA, there were significant issues that had to be addressed and a number of serious and difficult problems that arose as the programs grew and as students began studying in a wider range of locations. These issues primarily involved higher administration and faculty, especially leaders of study abroad programs but also chairs of academic departments. As CIPA director, I was responsible for dealing with all of these issues.

It is important to note that I had significant administrative experience prior to taking on the leadership of CIPA, having served both as the associate dean of Arts and Sciences and as the psychology chair. These positions gave me insight into the inner workings of the university at the department, college, and higher administration levels. This experience opened doors, showed me how the university as a whole worked, and gave me significant clout to persuade administrators and faculty about initiatives I wished to establish. It also gave me confidence in my ability to deal effectively with difficult situations and in obtaining support from the higher administration. Given the absence of strong international education programs at the time, and lukewarm administration interest, this experience turned out to be crucial.

One of the first issues I tackled was how to finance CIPA. Given that Emory is a private university with very high tuition rates, I made a strong proposal that, for the period of time a student studied abroad, CIPA should receive that student's tuition and that CIPA would operate without additional funds from the college or the university. CIPA would also cover student financial aid when students on aid studied abroad. To say the least, this proposal was not easy to get approved. I met with the dean, then with the appropriate vice provost, then with the vice president for Finance, and finally with the president. All were skeptical that this plan would work—which might mean subsidizing it—while at the same time they were also worried that we might generate far more income than we spent. Of course, a factor in our own thinking was that most study abroad programs, whether summer or semester, at a partner university cost less than Emory's tuition, so we were confident that the finances would work, and they did. After the first couple of years, CIPA begin to generate significant surpluses each year.

One of the lessons I learned in these early years creating an international education climate was that it is essential to involve the faculty and faculty leaders in the development process. A faculty committee participated in all aspects of development of CIPA and another faculty committee continued to be involved in management of study abroad programs. In addition, CIPA made efforts to encourage faculty to become involved in study abroad programs and to promote study abroad among their students. Clearly, the most important single factor for most undergraduates thinking about studying abroad is some encouragement from faculty advisers. We also met regularly with departmental directors of undergraduate studies and with department chairs to keep them informed of new initiatives and to seek new ideas for future study abroad initiatives.

While it is clearly important to have the central administration involved and on board in international education efforts, it is equally critical to have strong support from key members of the faculty. Yes, there are faculty who are committed to research and teaching and not interested in study abroad initiatives. However, many faculty are devoted to the academic quality of educational programming, and they can be highly suspicious of educational programs that take place overseas even when university faculty are involved but especially when students are allowed to earn credit at a partner university. These faculty concerns are understandable and must be addressed directly by the leader of international education. For example, CIPA encouraged faculty and department chairs with colleagues overseas to recommend universities that had good educational programs in their academic area and also involved them significantly in reviewing courses taken overseas to confirm their validity for Emory credit.

However, faculty and department chairs, while generally supportive of CIPA, were also unhappy with some of the policies we established. Faculty leaders of study abroad programs were upset on occasion when we established policies that meant they had to change the way their own study abroad program would operate (and *own* is the key word here). For example, one program used university funds to buy elaborate gifts for overseas faculty or staff who helped out in one way or another. (I recall gifts such as clothes, expensive underwear, pricey wine and liquor, and jewelry.) Faculty leaders and department chairs resented having to document in detail all expenses for their programs and the fact that surplus funds were to be kept by CIPA rather than going to departmental coffers. In addition, there were issues around the purchase of alcoholic beverages for students. As we all know, the drinking age in the United States is higher than it is in many other parts of the world. Some faculty leaders were buying beer and wine for study abroad students under age twenty-one. For many universities, this is a major issue, particularly if the overseas program is considered to be a part of the university campus. Emory was no exception.

Some lessons I learned regarding faculty leaders of study abroad programs is that training them and the faculty who teach in the programs is essential and that clear rules of appropriate action are needed and must be emphasized. Especially for faculty who wish to establish new study abroad programs, who have little or no experience overseas, and little or no experience having full responsibility for students while overseas, it is critical to develop some advising/training programs. An even better approach is to have such faculty go with an existing program to get some direct experience with study abroad before they lead a program themselves.

David Bright, dean and vice president of Arts and Sciences, stepped down several years after the establishment of CIPA, and Steve Sanderson took his place in 1997. Sanderson had extensive experience overseas and was very interested in international education. He approached me about establishing a broader and more comprehensive international education infrastructure. The key issue for him was to gain some higher-level management of all international programming, including not only study abroad but also area studies and other programs that had international elements. He asked that I establish a new faculty committee to explore how such an organization might be formed. I selected faculty who were involved with study abroad as well as faculty leaders of the various area studies programs. After several months of deliberation, which were often contentious, the committee recommended to

Sanderson that a new organization be formed, the Institute for Comparative and International Studies (ICIS). ICIS was to provide an overall umbrella organization for all international programs and thus be the home for study abroad and all area studies programs as well a public policy program that had an international emphasis. As chair of the committee recommending this new organization, I was asked to serve as its founding executive director. ICIS was first housed in in the library, with room for only the administration (me and a secretary) and study abroad and one area studies program. About a year later, ICIS moved into much larger space that accommodated the administration, all area studies programs, and study abroad. However, it is probably a reflection on the relative value of international education to Arts and Sciences that we were housed in a building at the very edge of campus.

After a few initial meetings with the area studies leaders, I came to understand why someone outside of area studies would be helpful as the leader of ICIS. The area studies leaders were very contentious with one another, having been in competition for limited resources for years. All the area studies programs were very small and received only modest funding to support a limited number of initiatives each year. Each of the leaders had strong, and incompatible, ideas about how ICIS should be structured. Moreover, they resisted all efforts to create collaborative programming that would to some degree integrate the area studies into a more comprehensive and, to my way of thinking, coherent and powerful group of programs that would generate higher financial support from the central administration. Each area study program had a very small number of undergraduates who took a few courses in that area and a small number of graduate students who could receive a PhD in that area in combination with an academic department.

The particular irony of the area studies leaders' resistance to collaborating with each other and with me was that substantial funding was likely available from the surplus funds generated by CIPA, that would far surpass the funding provided by the upper administration. I suggested the possibility of securing this extra funding as an incentive for collaboration among area studies leaders, but to no avail. One collaboration initiative I proposed was to establish a new international, Global Studies, degree for undergraduates. This would be a co-degree, occurring only in combination with a regular degree program within an academic department, so as not to compete directly with existing academic departments. Faculty in area studies would offer many of the courses in this program and thereby increase the number of students they teach and so enhance the value of area studies to the university.

As chair of psychology, I had learned that increasing the number of courses, the number of students taking these courses, and the number of students earning a degree within an academic department substantially increased resources made available to that department, including more faculty. However, this idea and the potential for growth and added resources that came with it went over like a lead balloon among the area studies directors. I did not realize it at the time, but the idea of more teaching was a disincentive for area studies. And while most academic departments were supportive of this idea, political science, which offered two bachelor's degrees (political science and comparative political science), opposed it. The chair told me that the Global Studies program would take place "over [his] dead body." With area studies opposed and one key department opposed, this new initiative went nowhere.

One of the lessons here is that parochial interests can trump attempts to create a new and more integrative approach to education, especially internationally focused initiatives. It is also possible that the area studies directors resented my involvement since I had no prior experience with these programs. This parochial attitude of faculty may be more prevalent in some universities than others, and it certainly provides a stark contrast between Emory and Georgia Tech.

After three years as executive director of ICIS, I decided to step down. Neither of the two subsequent executive directors—one out of anthropology and the other out of an area studies program—made much headway with area studies programs. ICIS was dissolved in 2009, twelve years after its founding, and Arts and Sciences abandoned efforts to integrate international programs under one umbrella organization.

In 1993 Emory created the position of vice provost of International Affairs, and Marion Creekmore, a former diplomat who served as ambassador to Sri Lanka and had several other overseas postings, was appointed to the position. The title of this position suggested a focus on international relations and diplomacy rather than international education. Creekmore had a PhD in political science but no experience in academia, and he knew very little about how universities work at the department, college, and university levels.

In fact, Creekmore spent his first three years at Emory almost exclusively at the Carter Center (a part of the Carter Presidential Library that was affiliated with university). This position was focused externally, primarily in arranging for Emory faculty to visit other countries, particularly India (where Creekmore had served in a diplomatic capacity) and Germany (the home country of a donor who funded the international initiatives), and inviting distinguished visitors to Emory to make presentations and interact with faculty and students. Creekmore did an excellent job given the mandate from the president and provost, but he made little progress on campuswide internal organization of international education, though he did try. In 2000, after seven years in this position, Creekmore retired. A new university award was established in Creekmore's name, and he was the first recipient on his retirement. The next year, in 2001, I was the second recipient of this award for my efforts to enhance international education.

Creekmore's retirement occurred in the early stages of my efforts to get ICIS under way. President William Chase and Provost Rebecca Chop decided to appoint an interim vice provost for International Affairs from among the Emory faculty. The provost asked me to assume the post for one or two years while the position and the office were discussed, fleshed out, and potentially restructured before hiring of a permanent new leader. Given that I felt an obligation to complete the development of ICIS, and knowing the real possibility that this position would terminate after two years, I turned down the interim vice provostship of International Affairs. A professor of the law school, Thomas Arthur, accepted this interim position and subsequently led a committee to develop a university-wide international affairs agenda that the new vice provost then implemented. I served on this committee.

As I look back on this period in my career, I have to wonder if I made a mistake by turning down the opportunity to serve as interim VP of International Affairs. Could I have had sufficient strength in the position to influence the direction of this unit so that internal support for international education would be significantly enhanced? I will never know, of course, but I doubt very seriously that this would have worked.

Two years later, when Tom Arthur stepped down as interim VP, I went to the new provost, Howard Hunter, formally dean of Law, to ask about the future of the position. He indicated that I would be welcome to apply but that the role of this position would not be changing significantly (it would continue to have an external focus), that the candidate would need to have significant international experience, and that the position would pay far less than my salary as executive director of ICIS.

In 2003, as his interim service as provost ended, Howard Hunter left Emory to become president of Singapore Management University. Later, when I visited Singapore on international education business, I met with Howard, and we discussed the challenge of moving higher in the hierarchy of university administration. He suspected that there might be a glass ceiling for faculty with long careers at a given university and that one might have better opportunities at another university. It is likely that Hunter resigned his position at Emory to take a higher-level position at another university because of his belief in this glass ceiling. As it turned out, I ended up doing the same thing.

I found myself in a difficult situation. I could stay on as executive director of ICIS or return to my tenured position in psychology. However, what I realized watching two outsiders fill the VP for International Affairs position is that I wanted to move up into a similar position, even if it meant leaving Emory. I decided to resign from the leadership position at ICIS and return to psychology as an interim step. But it quickly became clear to me that I was not happy in a straightforward academic position devoid of any international education leadership role. Yet, a major problem with looking elsewhere was a strong desire, especially from my wife, that we stay in or near Atlanta because we had one son living nearby, with marriage and children on the horizon. Nevertheless, I began to look at relevant websites for potential international education leadership positions. To my great surprise, I discovered that the Georgia Institute of Technology was just launching a search for a director of International Education who would have campuswide responsibility. I contacted Georgia Tech's vice provost for Academic Affairs to discuss this position, and the next day we met over coffee. We hit it off well, and he was receptive to my concerns related to the position, such as securing tenured appointment in psychology and some protection should there be a change at the vice provost, provost, or presidential levels. He indicated that they were looking for someone who could take International Education to the next level, which I assumed meant creating new initiatives. Everyone I met as part of the interview process was positive and excited about enhancing international education. While there was the issue of moving from a private to a public university, where funding might be smaller or unpredictable, I was very impressed, from the president and provost on down, with the intensity of interest and the willingness to consider new ideas. I was convinced that I would have the support of the central administration to move forward aggressively with new initiatives.

There are numerous lessons for future international education leaders to be gleaned from my experiences at Emory. First and foremost, one must be very sensitive to what motivates senior leadership of a university. The president and provost typically have an agenda that may be more or less transparent and more or less compatible with international education. Reading tea leaves, by taking into account informally gained information from colleagues and friends, is necessary. The Emory administration clearly wished to increase Emory's visibility nationally and internationally. At the same time, the administration was very sensitive about establishing a campuswide organization that might exert influence over all colleges and schools within the university, especially given the high degree of independence of the various colleges and schools at Emory and the likely backlash should central administration create an entity that would influence international initiatives within individual colleges. The net result was that international education languished while international affairs flourished, but in a limited way. The development of new international initiatives progressed within each college, especially in Arts and Sciences and the Business School, but there was little effort to bring these initiatives together to create a more coherent university-wide international educational process, and that remains true to this day. However, it is my hope that Emory's new VP for International Affairs, Philip Wainwright, as the first inside person and the first person to appreciate all aspects of international education to hold this position, will be able to bring the colleges together in some more coherent fashion.

THE GEORGIA TECH YEARS

The Georgia Institute of Technology, or Georgia Tech (GT), is a public university with six colleges: Liberal Arts, Sciences, Computing, Engineering,

Architecture, and Business. Georgia Tech is significantly larger than Emory (excluding Emory's Medical School and Healthcare System) both in terms of number of faculty and number of students. When I arrived at Georgia Tech in 2003 to take a leadership role in International Education, it was a well-established university with one of the top five engineering colleges in the country and very well-reputed programs in the other colleges. At the time, it had a centralized Office of International Education (OIE) driven primarily by problems arising from unsupervised faculty-led programs in the past. When I arrived, President Wayne Clough, Provost Jean-Lou Chameau, and Vice Provost for Academic Affairs Robert McMath were all very interested in enhancing international education and were willing to provide significant financial support for such enhancement.

When I accepted the position of director of the Office of International Education, I was quite concerned about the low level of the title, but I was assured that this could and would be elevated after I had been in the position for a year or so. Within two years I was promoted to associate vice provost of International Programming. Initially I was also concerned about the position's longevity. In the various positions I held at Emory, I witnessed a number of instances in which a person in an administrative appointment was asked to step down from that appointment sooner than expected. Often, such changes occurred at the hiring of a new president, provost, or dean who had different ideas about the direction of the university. For this reason, I insisted that my contract with Georgia Tech include the provision that I have an appointment as full professor of psychology with tenure and that should my appointment end as a result of a change in direction related to international education, I would be able to move back to psychology and receive two years of a twelve-month salary equivalent to my full administrative salary and thereafter the equivalent nine-month salary until retirement. This part of my contract eventually became very important.

From the start, I received tremendous support from higher administration, both financially and for initiatives we proposed with college deans. Within the first few months, I worked with the OIE staff to develop a five-year plan for the growth of international education that included new initiatives in study abroad as well as in international student support. The provost fully supported this plan and made a promise of significant funding.

In 2003, Georgia Tech, like many US universities, emphasized faculty-led study abroad programs mostly taking place in the summer. There was little emphasis on semester or year-long study abroad. There was also little effort to bring US students together in any meaningful way with incoming international students. International students, three thousand at the time, were scattered haphazardly among the various residents' halls.

In addition, just like at Emory, there had been little effort to bring coherence to international education. Faculty, colleges, and individual academic departments proposed new initiatives that were endorsed, or first modified and then endorsed, or turned down at the university level by a faculty committee. However, there was little effort to pull all the aspects of international education together and to make more obvious and clear to both faculty and students what international education programming was available. There was also little effort to connect international educational experiences with a student's academic interests particular to their major. However, the administration and faculty seemed prepared to consider the idea of an international education co-degree (which I had proposed and had been rejected at Emory) that might be connected to any and all undergraduate degrees in all the Georgia Tech colleges. For me, this prospect was the most exciting aspect of the new position.

Coming from a private university, I was suspicious of how public universities would operate, anticipating, for example, that there would be higher levels of bureaucracy and lots of hurdles for new initiatives. My suspicions were totally unfounded. I found instead that Georgia Tech administrators, both central and within each college, especially the college deans, were highly supportive of my efforts to enhance international education. The one admonition I received was from the dean of the College of Engineering, who said that his college was interested in international education initiatives as long as they added value for the students and that data supporting such added value would be an important component. (Surprisingly, support for new initiatives was most evident in the College of Engineering, which represented 60 percent of the students and faculty.) In fact, the zeitgeist at Georgia Tech was entrepreneurial with everyone hustling to create new initiatives and innovations on existing programs. A key factor here was that the advisory councils consisting of alumni and friends of each college in the university were making strong recommendations to increase students' international experiences, arguing that such experiences would be particularly helpful in securing and then performing jobs available at many companies. As a result, I was invited to attend and often to make presentations to meetings of the general faculty and meetings of faculty within each college, to members of the central administration, and to the President's Council, a collection of alumni and supporters of the university.

One of my concerns with the state of international education when I arrived at Georgia Tech was the sole emphasis on faculty-led, mostly summer programs. Such an island model approach, while better than no study abroad, does not provide students with a deeper and more culturally relevant overseas experience. From my perspective, longer-term programs involving immersion in the local cultures are needed to truly impact students' understanding of and appreciation for other cultures. I had seen the impact of this approach at Emory. Also, most of the study abroad programs at that time were organized by the humanities disciplines, in particular the School of Modern Languages and the School of International Affairs. While many of these programs were designed to make the programs meaningful to disciplines such as engineering, there were only a few study abroad programs operated by academic departments or colleges outside the humanities. I remained convinced, as I had been at Emory, that there should be central management and support for study abroad but also that each college and academic unit should be directly involved in the type and location of study abroad programs for its own students. This was particularly feasible at Georgia Tech, as compared to Emory, because of the genuine interest across all colleges for students to gain international experience.

It became clear to me in the first six months that there were four primary initiatives I wanted to try to implement. First, in this more receptive university, I wanted to implement a university-wide initiative to enable students to participate in robust international programs that would include study abroad as well as relevant courses at home involving international education and foreign language learning. This would enable individual academic departments to participate and to help choose where their students would study and what courses they would take outside the United States.

Second, I wanted US and incoming international students to interact in more meaningful ways. I thought it would be a win-win for both the international and the US students if some relatively powerful way could be found for deep and long-term interaction. This approach would be particularly important for US students who, for a variety of reasons, could not study abroad. It also would enhance the effects of international experiences if students could more fully interact with international students on their return from studying abroad.

Third, there was a strong interest at Georgia Tech in developing campuses overseas. GT Lorraine, which provided master's-level education for students in France and other nearby European countries, was already fifteen years old and was doing well. When I arrived, there was a growing movement at GT Lorraine to add an opportunity for engineering undergraduates to spend the summer or even a semester studying there. In addition, there was considerable interest in adding new overseas campuses similar to GT Lorraine. While I was not particularly a strong advocate for overseas campuses, I did want to play a significant role in their development, with the goal of making these campuses more likely to foster students' exposure to the local languages and cultures and not end up isolated on study abroad islands.

Finally, I wanted to encourage undergraduate students to study abroad for longer periods and to study in overseas partner universities where they would take classes directly with local students taught by local faculty, which some evidence shows produces higher levels of cultural understanding. Fortunately, my efforts to achieve these goals were enhanced by the fact that Georgia Tech was in the planning stages for its ten-year renewal of accreditation by the Southern Association of Colleges and Schools. A key component of this process is that the university must develop a Quality Enhancement Plan (QEP), which requires educational programming. QEPs are typically provided substantial funding from the university administration over a five-year period. I participated in planning sessions as one of a dozen or so others proposing ideas for the QEP.

In the fall of 2003, Vice Provost Jack Lowman and I met with the chairs of the School of International Affairs and the School of Modern Languages and the leader of the GT Lorraine program to discuss what form an international QEP proposal might take. There was considerable debate around the table. The head of GT Loraine (an engineer) pushed for a larger undergraduate program (both summer and semester) at GT Loraine. Modern Languages wanted the new QEP initiative to involve an emphasis on cultural immersion and learning a foreign language. And International Affairs supported the notion that any student going overseas needed some coursework (such as comparative politics) in that school. Despite the self-promotion, it was quite amazing how quickly we all arrived at a consensus.

We agreed that the QEP proposal should provide international education experiences for students in all colleges (and all schools within each college) with the overall goal of developing global competence. Some may recognize this program as the International Plan, which won several national awards for excellence in international education. This was designed to be the hallmark plan for students interested in international education, with about 10 percent of the student body participating. However, we anticipated that the impact of this program would expand beyond the students who participated to encourage other students to engage in international education, even if to a lesser degree. Clearly, the timing of the QEP, the support of the upper administration, and the eagerness of individual colleges and academic departments to participate in international education made this effort possible and successful.

How did we get from a consensus of four individuals to the campuswide approval of this new initiative? First, Jack Lohmann and I visited each of the six college deans to discuss these new initiatives. We asked for the deans' support (of course, the provost had already discussed, and expressed supported for, the program at a deans' meeting) and for them to recommend one or two academic departments that might be interested in participating in the planning of the program. All the deans were immediately on board, and so we ended up with twelve academic departments participating, including at least one department from each college. We established an International Plan Committee consisting of the directors of undergraduate studies in each of the twelve participating departments, and it began the arduous task of hashing out the fine details of the program. The selection of these directors was important, since they had the best knowledge of how undergraduate education worked. It took about eighteen months to reach the point where we had a complete plan with all the details determined.

The next step was to gain the approval of the university's Curriculum

Committee. Here we ran into significant problems. The chair of this important committee (an engineer) was strongly opposed to the idea that GT undergraduates would earn academic credit for courses taken at foreign universities. He believed that all foreign universities were inferior to Georgia Tech. Members of the committee raised other issues For example, why three international education courses? Too few for some, and too many for others. And why those particular international education courses? Who decided that Global Economics should be one of the three? It became clear that we needed additional support to get through this committee. We went back to the provost and asked for his support and help. Within a few days the committee informed us that our proposal had been approved. Provosts can work miracles sometimes.

In the next step, each college and school had to decide whether or not to participate. In the end, all the colleges and the vast majority (26 of 32) of academic disciplines did participate. Two reasons for the programs successes were that it was not required of all students and it was not mandatory for any college or school. We hoped it would attract 10–12 percent of each incoming class and that it would also stimulate interest in international education among a much wider range of students who might be convinced to do some components of the international plan even if they could not complete the whole program.

The International Plan was selected as one of two programs to participate in the QEP; the other program involved engaging undergraduates in research experiences with faculty. The International Plan resulted in a five-year effort to develop and implement this program and a substantial budget to support the plan. In the fall of 2005, the International Plan was implemented, with twelve schools participating. That first year, 125 students signed up. The International Plan Committee continued to manage the program and to make adjustments as necessary. In two short years we were able to implement a university-wide initiative to prepare at least a significant number of students to be globally competent. The number of students participating increased rapidly to approximately 300 first-year students per year and about 1,200–1,500 over the four or five years required to graduate. Today, ten years after the start of the program, it continues to be successful.

Of course, there have been problems—all handled successfully by the

International Plan Committee, a faculty committee. Should we keep the strict language requirement? No; some flexibility is allowed. Should we continue to insist that students spend six months in a single country? No; multiple countries have been deemed okay. It is important to note that the International Plan also increased interest more broadly in international education. The number of students studying abroad increased beyond the numbers participating in the International Plan, especially for semester/year abroad programs. And the number of students taking language courses and international affairs courses increased significantly. So did we address the admonition of the College of Engineering dean that we prove that value was added? The answer is a strong yes. Growth in global competence was significantly higher among International Plan students than other students who studied abroad (even for a semester or year) and higher than among students with no international experience.

I am proud of my role in making this remarkable program happen. It was clearly a team effort, which included administration at the highest level, the Office of International Education, the deans and department chairs, and individual faculty within each department that participated. How could this happen at Georgia Tech when it was virtually impossible to achieve at Emory? It was that entrepreneurial spirit that permeates the Georgia Tech campus. When proposals were made, the first answer was not "No" but "This sounds like a good idea; let's explore it further." There was also a collaborative spirit that bridged school and college boundaries. Humanities, Sciences, Engineering, Business, Computing, and Architecture were very comfortable working together and could see that there were common interests. No obvious in-fighting here.

Enacting my idea of bringing international students together with US students was surprisingly easy. The director of International Students and I met with a leader in the residence hall administration to propose that one floor of one residence hall be designated as I-House (International House). This idea was immediately embraced by campus housing. A residence hall close to the center of campus was selected, and one floor dedicated to I-House was scheduled to open the very next fall. We also recruited a faculty member from the School of International Affairs serving as adviser for the floor. The first year we promoted this opportunity, some sixty students (equally divided between international and US students) participated. The students participated in a weekly meeting and established a coffee hour, and these residents were invited to attend various international events around Atlanta. We now have approximately eighty to one hundred students participating annually. In terms of funding for this program, we asked the housing office to contribute, and our Office of International Education contributed a stipend to compensate the faculty member from International Affairs. Again, some eight years later this program continues to be successful.

As mentioned earlier, Georgia Tech wanted to expand overseas campuses beyond GT Lorraine, including efforts in Singapore, Shanghai, India, and, later, Panama. These initiatives were often driven by particular faculty, departments, or colleges. For example, many of the faculty in engineering and computing are originally from India or China, and some of these faculty and their academic departments wanted to develop opportunities for teaching and conducting research in their home countries. They particularly wanted to gain access to the outstanding top students in these countries. GT campuses in India and China offering graduate degrees in engineering and computing would provide satisfy both aims.

I was involved directly in initiatives to establish campuses in Singapore and India. The approach was for me to lead a delegation of interested faculty to visit each country to look at opportunities in key cities to create a campus. The visit to India, while promising, never resulted in a campus, despite much effort. Moreover, the trip itself was difficult. Eleven senior faculty accompanied me on this trip, and all had different agendas or different ideas about what type of campus we should build and where it should be located. We needed a more specific, detailed agenda and some clearer goals of what we wished to accomplish. The efforts in Singapore were more promising. Singapore had already helped to fund other university's campuses and had a campus being planned by a major university in Australia. The central administration in Singapore was very supportive of our proposal, so much so that we began to plan in earnest and with more detail about what the campus would look like, what academic programs would be involved, where the campus would be located, and how much such a campus would cost to build and operate. Provost Gary Schuster, the senior financial officer, and I visited to raise the level of discussion. Everything seemed ready to proceed.

However, suddenly, the Australian university backed out after the ground breaking for the campus had already taken place and after construction was under way. It turned out that there was turnover at that university's presidential level, and the new president decided to move in a different direction. To our surprise, the Singapore administration immediately decided to cancel our initiative as well. Thus, after substantial time, money, and effort on the part of many individuals at Georgia Tech, no new campuses were established in Singapore during my time in International Programs. More modest education and research-based initiatives are taking place in Beijing, Costa Rica, Ireland, Panama, Singapore, and Shanghai.

There were also efforts to bring more international students to study at Georgia Tech, especially at the undergraduate level. We were very successful in these efforts, with undergraduates from Singapore and Mexico integrated nicely through dual degree programs. This worked, too, with our effort to introduce GT students to students from other countries, and vice versa. The net effects of these new initiatives were substantial increases in the number of students studying abroad (to about 46 percent of a graduating class) and in the number of international undergraduates studying at Georgia Tech.

As is often said, all good things come to an end. For me, this happened when GT provost Jean-Lou Chameau left to become president of the California Institute of Technology. He was replaced by an internal candidate, Gary Schuster, who had been the dean of Science, and almost immediately changes began to take place. I was invited to a meeting with the senior vice provost for Academic Affairs, who informed me of changes in the hierarchy of the central administration. He showed me an organizational chart which indicated that a new position was being formed, the vice provost for International Initiatives. This position was to be above me, thereby weakening my own position and reducing my portfolio. It was clear at this meeting that there was going to be a search for someone to fill the position. While the senior VP told me that I could apply, it seemed clear that the administration could easily have appointed me to the position as a promotion, with no need for a search. Subsequently, I met with Schuster and pushed him for clarification of the nature of the position and whether this might be an opportunity for me. While his answer was not a definite no, it was pretty clear that they had someone else in mind (as it turned out, a member of the engineering faculty). It did not make sense to keep me in the high-level position I had with the salary I was making and also hire someone above me who would make an even higher salary. He asked me to stay on in my position until a replacement could be hired.

However, the contract I negotiated on arriving at Georgia Tech stated that I could move into psychology with my administrative twelve-month salary for two years and then receive the equivalent nine-month salary until I retired, should there be a change in direction in International Education. While I really wanted to stay on in International Education, I was upset that they were putting someone in a job above me and to whom I would report. So I decided to resign my position effective immediately. Had I stayed on, I might not have been able to use my contract to move to psychology at the higher salary.

After two years as a professor of psychology, I was informed by the department chair that the senior VP wanted to drop my salary well below what it should be as a nine-month version of my former twelve-month administrative salary. Fortunately, my original contract, and an agreement I signed when moving back to psychology, made it clear that my salary could not be dropped, and so I continued for four more years as a psychology professor until my retirement.

FINAL THOUGHTS

What do my experiences in international education suggest as lessons for present or future leaders in this field?

Remember that leadership of international education is not limited to faculty who have significant overseas experience and/or to those who have earned a degree in international fields. Organizing study abroad in just about any discipline can be the start of a path toward becoming an SIO.

Equally important, you must make the most of available opportunities while you have backing at the top. University leadership often changes at the dean, provost, and presidential levels. These changes in leadership often result in changes of direction that may jeopardize your own agenda and/or threaten your position. International Education is often not a top priority and so is expendable.

If you deem your international education career to be your primary interest, then be prepared to change institutions if you are being thwarted from carrying out your program at your current institution. And if your goals are blocked and you cannot change institutions right away, then have an escape hatch in your contract, such as tenure or some other way of maintaining your income until you can find a new position.

Finally, while the senior international officer must have support at the top to pave the way for new initiatives, this is not sufficient for success. You must also cultivate support from the deans, department chairs, and faculty. This is critical to your efforts to build and/or enhance international education on any campus. Without the backing of these individuals, your attempts to move forward may well be delayed or blocked.

CHAPTER SEVEN

The Senior International Officer—a Modern Proteus?

Maria Carmen Sada Krane

TWENTY-FOUR YEARS. Three institutions of higher learning. Eleven bosses. On the average, I reported to a different provost, vice president, or associate vice president every two years of my career as a senior international officer. Each one of them came with different views, perceptions, and priorities related to "international education," one of the many academic areas under their purview. Very early on I realized that change in command was just one of many uncontrollable variables the SIO faced. Like a modern Proteus, I had to be versatile, adapting to each new situation and staying in the revolving door long enough to advance the international agenda, somehow.

Challenging and exciting, international education is what I always wanted to do, even when I did not know exactly what it was.

Growing up in the two southernmost states in Brazil sparked my enthusiasm for foreign languages. In Santa Catarina, where I lived for nine years, I could hear German on the streets and at home. Although my mother's family had its roots in Portugal, she learned German and became a teacher of German as a foreign language at a local high school. From my father I heard Italian as he sang "Santa Lucia" and other traditional songs from *il bel paese.* Born in Brazil, he honored the traditions of his parents, who had hailed from Venice and Milan. In Rio Grande do Sul, my home state, I could hear radio stations from Montevideo and Buenos Aires sometimes more clearly than those from São Paulo and Rio. That is how I learned Spanish, or, more specifically, *castellano,* as the language is called in most South American countries, through the purely aural method. French I learned in school and from one of my sisters who came back from France speaking the language fluently. I loved all the languages that surrounded me, but when I heard English from a friend's mother who had lived in the United States, it was love at first sound. At the tender age of nine, I vowed to learn English and study in the US. I did not know how or when. I just knew what.

My high school and college years were dedicated to academics (especially languages), volleyball, and leadership in student government. The latter culminated in my election as president of the Centro Acadêmico Jacques Maritain of the Federal University of Santa Maria's School of Arts and Sciences (Faculdade de Ciências e Letras) during my senior year. As holder of that position, I was invited to participate in a US State Department–sponsored tour of the United States for Brazilian student government leaders. It was during this trip that I learned how and when to study in the US. After I graduated from the Federal University of Santa Maria with a BA in Germanic languages, I applied for a Fulbright grant to pursue graduate studies in the United States. I also enrolled in my alma mater's law school just in case my dream of studying in the US did not come true. . A year and a half later, things fell into place.

I received my master's degree in linguistics from Indiana University. On graduation, I taught Portuguese in the Department of Spanish, Italian, and Portuguese at the University of Illinois while pursuing additional graduate studies in linguistics. After returning to Brazil, I was hired by the Instituto Souza Leão in Rio de Janeiro to revamp their English as a foreign language (EFL) curriculum and to teach. So, I taught EFL at Souza Leão in the morning, and once a week, in the evening, I taught a graduate course in linguistics at the Universidade do Rio de Janeiro.

After getting married in Rio to a fellow Indiana University graduate, I returned to the States with my new husband. While he was completing his PhD requirements at the University of Minnesota, I took graduate courses in linguistics there and began working off campus. My responsibilities as director of market analysis data collection for Control Data Corporation introduced me to corporate America. It was a great opportunity to understand the business world, the supercomputer industry, and antitrust issues.

Trailing my husband, I found myself at the University of Wisconsin–Oshkosh teaching linguistics in the English department. At that point I thought that introducing students to theories of language, language variation, and deep and surface structures was the ultimate conduit to different ways of thinking and behaving. But yet another move reminded me of the need for English proficiency for non-native speakers seeking degrees at US universities. My husband was hired by Mississippi State University (MSU) to help design and implement a master's degree in public administration. He taught in the political science department, and I taught English as a second language (ESL) in the English department.

Teaching ESL for an established program was fine for a while, but I dreamed of creating my own program somewhere. The opportunity presented itself at the end of my fifth year at MSU. Wood Junior College, a two-year private institution nearby, needed a program, and I was ready to create it. For the next eight years I devoted my energies to raising a daughter and a son; designing and establishing an ESL program at Wood; taking courses toward my doctorate in educational leadership at MSU; familiarizing myself with the US system of elementary education while serving as PTA copresident; and learning about secondary education as an invited faculty participant in a National Endowment for the Humanities grant to enhance the linguistic and cultural preparation of Mississippi high school teachers of Spanish.

When my husband and I moved to Texas, those experiences served as the solid foundation for my next job as lecturer in linguistics in the Department of Language and Literature and Coordinator of Bilingual and ESL Teacher Education Programs in the Department of Curriculum and Instruction at Texas Woman's University (TWU). I administered three Title VII grants that enabled teachers in the Dallas–Fort Worth Metroplex schools to earn a master's degree or an endorsement (a statement appearing on a license that identifies the specific subjects or grade levels that the license holder is authorized to teach) in either ESL or bilingual education. Rather than teaching ESL, I was completely immersed in the preparation of ESL teachers. On campus I taught the linguistics courses needed for their endorsements or graduate degrees; around the Metroplex I visited the schools where our TWU students worked; in Washington, D.C., I read grant proposals for the US Department of Education Office of Bilingual Education and Minority Language Affairs. What an opportunity to learn about and empathize with the challenges of my fellow Latinas in the US—teachers and students! After all, I thought of myself as a Latina too, though my new friends would lovingly point out to me that I was not a Latina. I was a Brazilian.

In the late 1980s my husband's career took us to Omaha, Nebraska. After holding a couple of part-time positions—teaching ESL at the University of Nebraska–Omaha and Spanish at Creighton University—I was hired by Nebraska Wesleyan University (NWU) in 1990 as assistant provost for Academic Advising and International Programs. Although the title did not reflect it, this was indeed an SIO position—my first.

SIO: TAKE 1

A few months after my arrival on the Nebraska Wesleyan campus, I experienced my first change in command. On the passing of the provost who hired me, an interim was appointed until a new vice president for Academic Affairs could be hired. With the adoption of the academic vice president structure, my title changed to assistant vice president for Academic Affairs and later assistant vice president for International Education, to better reflect my SIO position.

President John Wesley White was very supportive of international education, and so was Janet Rasmussen, the new VP for Academic Affairs. In 1992, President White established an International Advisory Council and asked me to chair it. The remarkable feature of this council was that both vice presidents—for Academic Affairs and Student Affairs—along with key faculty and students, attended the meetings. The presence of those two vice presidents was critical to the implementation of NWU's Vision 2000, a strategic plan that called for a greater global understanding for its students.

The Vision 2000 plan and the encouragement of the university leadership fueled the writing of a Title VI grant, "Reaching Toward Global Citizenship for Rural Students." Funded in 1994, the grant helped Nebraska Wesleyan enhance its foreign language teaching and infuse its curriculum with global perspectives in coordination with study abroad. As the assistant project director for the grant, I had the opportunity to work very closely with Vice President Rasmussen, the project director, and the faculty. The grant initiated a flurry of international initiatives, culminating with the revision of the curriculum, including the addition of courses that would introduce all students—especially those who could not study abroad—to another culture. One of the original courses approved by the faculty was Brazil!, a three-credit-hour semester course I designed and taught.

My work on institutional initiatives for greater internationalization made me realize that it was time for me to take the last step toward the completion of my doctoral degree at Mississippi State. I then to chose a dissertation topic that would help me better understand the concept of internationalization and its multiple facets and, at the same time, help me in the delivery of my responsibilities as NWU's SIO. For my 1994 dissertation, "Development of an Internationalization Index for US Liberal Arts Colleges," I identified eleven indicators of internationalization commonly cited in the literature and obtained existing data for each of the indicators for each of the 101 Liberal Arts Colleges I (according to the Carnegie Classification of Institutions of Higher Education at the time), a group that included Nebraska Wesleyan University. On the basis of the existing data, I created an internationalization index for the institutions so classified, ranking them from the most to the least internationalized.

Both my own research and the advice of experience colleagues were critical resources for me in my first SIO position at NWU. Soon after I accepted the job, I was encouraged by Thomas Hoemeke, the SIO at North Texas University, to join the Association of International Education Administrators (AIEA) to network with colleagues grappling with issues inherent to the SIO position. Besides attending and participating in sessions at AIEA conferences, I also continued to attend the NAFSA: Association of International Educators national and regional conferences, presenting a paper or conducting a workshop almost every year from 1991 to 2005.

Study abroad at NWU continued to expand in my seven years on campus. In addition to encouraging exchanges through the International Student Exchange Program (ISEP), I worked with the NMU faculty, especially the chairs of the Modern Language and the Global Studies departments, to create additional opportunities for students to earn credit while studying in other countries. For example, the Modern Languages chair and I collaborated on establishing a program at the Instituto Tecnológico y de Estudios Superiores de Monterrey (ITESM), Campus Queretaro, for NWU's Spanish majors. President White and I then traveled to Mexico to sign an agreement with ITESM.

I also partnered with peer institutions to expand study abroad opportunities for NWU students, helping to organize a small consortium of five liberal arts colleges for exchanges with Brazil, Indonesia, and Turkey. On behalf of the consortium, Beloit College successfully submitted an institutional grant proposal to the National Security Education Program (NSEP) in support of the initiative. To launch the program on our campus, NWU hosted a seminar on one of the grant's target countries; Warm Up to Brazil was a perfect name for a seminar offered on a couple of February days in Nebraska. And the seminar lived up to its title, attracting a large audience, including about one-fourth of the NWU faculty.

The presence of international students on campus was also enhanced, especially through the growing number of exchange students. A new short-term, special program added further to the number of non-degree-seeking students on campus. The chairs of the nursing school and the psychology department and I planned and organized a program for students from a Japanese college of nursing. The first group of thirty students came to Lincoln in the summer of 1997 to participate in a two-week program focusing on English skills, American culture, and the nursing profession in the US.

Community outreach was also part of my portfolio. Each year from 1991 to 1996, I led the Nebraska LEAD Program of the Nebraska Agricultural Leadership Council held on the Nebraska Wesleyan campus. Designed to develop the state's agricultural leaders for the future, the program included an international trip and an intensive predeparture orientation. Vice President Rasmussen left NWU in 1996; a few months later President White announced his retirement. Around that time I learned that Agnes Scott College, a liberal arts college in Atlanta, was advertising for a newly created position of director of International Education. With an enrollment of a little over seven hundred, Agnes Scott was among the top ten US colleges and universities in per-student endowment. One of the liberal colleges I studied for my dissertation, Agnes Scott intrigued me because it ranked close to the top first quarter of all schools in the internationalization index I developed. The position appeared to be very challenging, offering the opportunity for its first director to shape the international agenda for the college in collaboration with the Global Awareness Committee. I was thrilled when I learned I had been selected for the position.

SIO: TAKE 2

If office size were a measure, I would say I was making progress in my career. I now had a full-time secretary! I had the challenge of organizing the office inside and out, from structuring the college's international programs to selecting most of the furniture and the office décor, with the help of an interior designer. My goal was to create a "home" that would be welcoming for everyone, especially international students and students interested in going abroad. Before the home was completed, however, I was already meeting with students, faculty, and administrators, eager to become acquainted with existing international opportunities and beginning to plan what additional programs could enrich Agnes Scott's global education.

Not long after I arrived on campus, the VP for Academic Affairs who hired me left the college, and I began reporting to an interim until the new VP was appointed. It was helpful to have the support of the Global Awareness Committee to continue the conversation on international initiatives.

Agnes Scott had two very popular faculty-led international programs, Global Awareness and Global Connections. Combining travel abroad and on-campus courses, those programs attracted a great number of students, in part because of the college's travel subsidies for participants. Each year, three or four faculty-led programs were organized, though mostly to traditional destinations. In terms of independent study abroad experiences, however, students had a paucity of opportunities. Their choices were limited to two universities, one in France and the other in Germany.

To open up the world to Agnes Scott students, I had the college join the International Student Exchange Program (ISEP). With 110 member institutions in thirty-five countries at the time, ISEP offered an immediate diversity of destinations for Agnes Scott students and brought international students to the college. Equally important, the increase in students going abroad did not create a negative impact on the college's revenues. Thanks to the reciprocal nature of the exchanges through ISEP, all tuition, fees, and room and board outgoing students paid Agnes Scott stayed on campus.

Besides ISEP, other programs were added to the roster of academic experiences abroad, including affiliations with universities in Northern Ireland, China, Jordan, and Korea. President Mary Brown Bullock was particularly enthusiastic about the linkages with China. In 1999, two faculty members and I traveled to Beijing, Shanghai, Xi'an, and Hong Kong to explore the establishment of a Global Awareness program in China. The connection with the Middle East, especially Jordan, was made when Her Royal Highness Princess Wijdan Ali, then the president of the Royal Society of Fine Arts and vice president and dean of Research and Studies at the Jordan Institute of Diplomacy, was invited by President Bullock to officially open Agnes Scott's new Office of International Programs. HRH Princess Wijdan Ali stayed an additional two weeks on campus to lead a faculty seminar entitled Images of Islam, an attempt to close the cultural gap between Islam and the West.

Launching new initiatives is important, but so is supporting existing ones. During my three years at Agnes Scott, I worked with the Institute of International Education to bring Foreign Language Teaching Assistants to campus. Each year the college hosted three FLTAs—for French, German, and Spanish—who assisted the instructors by being "a native speaker presence" in the classroom, hosting a "language table" at lunch, or informally meeting with students. At the same time, the program helped the international student teachers refine their foreign language teaching skills, enhance their English proficiency, and learn US culture.

In 2000 I learned that the SIO position at Creighton University was open. After commuting between Omaha and Atlanta for three years, my extraordinarily supportive husband and I thought it was time to have only *one* roof over our heads. After all, Agnes Scott's Office of International Education had been established and organized, the connections abroad it administered had greatly expanded, and the college was making significant strides toward internationalization. I applied for the position at Creighton and was accepted.

SIO: TAKE 3

At Creighton, yet again, the vice president for Academic Affairs who hired me and to whom I reported left the position within my first year at the university. During the fourteen years I served Creighton as its SIO, on average

I reported to a different Academic Affairs officer every 2.8 years. Although each had different notions regarding international programs and activities, they all shared one expectation: as a revenue-generating unit, my office, the Office of International Programs (OIP), had to meet its assigned target.

Neither at Nebraska Wesleyan nor at Agnes Scott was my office responsible for producing revenues for the university through a program or through the recruitment and admission of degree-seeking international students. At both institutions recruitment and admissions were housed in the Office of Admissions, while I handled the necessary documents for the students' entry into the US and coordinated programs designed to support them and facilitate their integration in the community. At Creighton it was different. International recruitment and admission were housed in the OIP, along with international student advising and support, study abroad, the Intensive English Language Institute (IELI), and university linkages.

I welcomed the recruitment of international students for the university now that I was the head of a multiperson office. Counting the IELI director and three full-time instructors, the OIP had six full-time professional staff members, two full-time clerical employees, and one part-time intern. In spite of what seemed to be adequate staffing, the OIP did not have a full-time international recruiter. As a result, my travel schedule took me away from campus too often during my first eight years at Creighton, making it challenging for me to participate in university committees and to make important campus connections. A couple of years after my arrival on campus, I transferred the responsibility for the admission of international (non-IELI) students to the Admissions Office; then in 2008, the academic vice president moved international (non-IELI) recruitment there as well.

With the transfer of recruitment to the Admissions Office, the IELI director position was eliminated and its responsibilities were added to my SIO portfolio. The IELI's low enrollment greatly contributed to that decision. The events of September 11, 2001, had decimated the small enrollment of twenty-two students per academic term. In the summer of 2005, the program had reached an all-time low of only two students. By 2007–2008 IELI was still struggling with fewer than eight students per term and I was unable to find a suitable director willing to rebuild the program. So I had no choice but to accept the direct administration of the IELI instead of overseeing it.

The years 2008–2014 saw the IELI enrollment more than double its pre-9/11 totals. A variety of initiatives contributed to the record enrollment of more than fifty students per term (and the related increase in revenue for the University): the four full-time instructors I hired and their revamping of the curriculum; well-equipped classrooms and a Computer Assisted Language Learning (CALL) laboratory; and agreements with embassies as well as connections with schools and universities in other countries. With the highest-ever number of students, the IELI was in 2013–2014 poised to reinstate the position of IELI director and continue working on its self-study for the Commission on English Language Program Accreditation.

In addition to enrolling IELI students who attend one or more of its five terms per year, Creighton welcomes special groups that come for one term or less. The most rewarding of the connections I helped create was the one with a Jesuit high school in São Paulo, Brazil. The first group of thirty-six Colégio São Luís students came to campus for ten days in late spring 2013 to immerse themselves in the US culture—past, present, and future—and the culture of the Midwest in particular. Besides following a curriculum that focused on colloquial English and its cultural context, the group participated in field trips and activities on campus and in the community, visiting places of natural, cultural, recreational, and historical interest. The program has become an annual event; in fact, Colégio São Luís has made the program at Creighton a part of its high school curriculum.

Creighton's 1999–2000 *Bulletin* (now *Catalog*), published the year before I came to campus, listed "Study Abroad" under "Special Programs" of the College of Arts and Sciences. The section included two paragraphs describing what was then called Semestre Dominicano, a university-sponsored semester in the Dominican Republic focusing on academic courses and community service or business internship, and four paragraphs about other study abroad opportunities. Students at that time could participate in any program they wanted as long as the credits to be transferred were approved by the academic dean's office, the adviser, and the Office of International Programs. There were only five "affiliate" programs then (four in Europe and one in Japan) in which students' scholarships and grants had portability. Overall, European countries were the most popular destination for Creighton students. A part-time intern (a past study abroad participant) in OIP introduced students to available programs and helped them with their application process.

To stimulate study abroad interest and participation, I asked for a new full-time position of study abroad adviser. I hired the first adviser (later retitled "coordinator") in 2001–2002, and in 2003 I carved out a small resource area where students could browse and select programs. Study abroad options for Creighton students increased and became much more varied. With the introduction of ISEP, for example, the realm of possibilities abroad expanded rapidly. Most importantly, I strove to add opportunities for study in nontraditional destinations. Today, Creighton students can study almost anywhere, including the Arab world. In 2008 Creighton became one of the twenty charter members of the AMIDEAST Education Abroad Programs Academic Consortium. Not counting faculty-led programs (they vary in number and destination each year), the OIP, as of June 2014, administered opportunities for Creighton students to earn credits at 168 universities in more than sixty countries.

Many of the new opportunities abroad for Creighton students, and opportunities for international students at Creighton, were the result of connections I made abroad or in the United States through travel, conference attendance, or service to professional organizations. My frequent visits to foreign embassies in Washington, D.C., and to ministries of higher education strengthened ties with Creighton and made our agreements meaningful. My leadership and membership in professional associations or organizations, publications, and presentations also facilitated the promotion of the university and created points of contact. While at Creighton, for example, I was president of AIEA in 2003–2004 and a member of the TOEFL Board in 2006–2010.

With the Office of International Programs in excellent shape—ample study abroad choices, as well as policies and procedures in place to regulate them; software to facilitate study abroad advising, communication, and tracking; a continuous increase in IELI enrollment (now almost three times the enrollment prior to my hiring), creating healthy revenues and enabling the reinstatement of the position of full-time IELI director; the expansion of the IELI teaching staff (four full-time instructors in June 2014); a state-of-the-art CALL Lab and dedicated IELI classrooms; various signed agreements for collaboration, including those with Jesuit institutions in Korea and Japan for student exchanges and with US Jesuit universities for study abroad participation; and Creighton's inclusion in the list of approved schools for Qatari and Saudi students to enroll with their governmental scholarships—it was time to retire. My last day as an SIO was June 30, 2014.

THE SIO POSITION

On the perfect campus, internationalization is defined, and its attributes, goals, and objectives are incorporated into the strategic plan with ample input from the SIO. The plan is supported by fiscal and human resources and followed by pronouncements from an upper administration known for its longevity and the high priority it attaches to internationalization. The SIO and her staff then implement the plan with the enthusiastic support of the entire faculty and with the cooperation of administrators and staff of other units.

However, SIOs—imperfect creatures—work on imperfect campuses. The advancement of the internationalization agenda at a particular institution will depend on many factors, some under the SIO's control (e.g., the ability to learn her campus culture, the progress already made, and the key faculty) and some that are not. The challenge for SIOs comes from those factors they cannot control, such as changes in command and the very nature of the position.

As a middle manager, the SIO position is not well understood. Not only is the position of SIO still new on campuses, but, surprisingly, so is the research on middle management and its performance in strategic change initiatives. The function of a middle manager is typically described in the literature on management as "doing/executing/implementing a strategy created by the top management," whereas an SIO job announcement may read, "Will provide campuswide strategic leadership of all programs designed to promote internationalization." This disconnect may be frustrating for both the SIO and for the upper management. It might be a function of the size of the institution; perhaps at smaller institutions such disconnects do not exist, or, if they do, their impact may be minimal. At Nebraska Wesleyan—and even at Agnes

Scott, where I had the title of "director"—for example, I had greater access to the upper management, having had substantial discussions with the president or the vice president on a variety of international initiatives.

The results of a longitudinal study on the SIO roles and responsibilities that a group of colleagues and I conducted clearly showed that an increasing number of institutions of higher learning in the United States are assigning position titles to SIOs that suggest a closer association with the university's upper administration. The "vice president" title, for example, is steadily growing in preference. (Is this shift caused by the fact that "director" implies a primarily managerial or operational focus?) The study also revealed some changes in reporting lines. Although the overwhelming majority of SIOs report to a vice president, this reporting line is slightly decreasing in favor of an increasing (albeit slowly) trend toward reporting to the president of the institution.

Regardless of the specific title, the SIO's position should be sufficiently elevated to signal the importance of international education, its alignment with the university's academic programs, and its role in helping students develop global competence. The SIO should have a seat at the table in major policy and strategic plan discussions, because international initiatives do affect the entire university, including its finances. Moreover, the SIO should have high enough standing to promote internationalization to all campus constituencies. The SIO may be a manager, but, most importantly, the SIO should be a leader.

Faculty are key SIO's allies, supporting study abroad, teaching and advising international students, incorporating global perspectives in the curriculum, and participating in faculty exchange programs. Conversely, the SIO supports faculty international initiatives. Sometimes, however, this relationship becomes fragile either because of specific situations (e.g., when the announcement of travel warnings or visa restrictions affect faculty plans) or as part of the traditional tension between faculty and administrators. On many campuses the faculty have become resentful of the growth in the administrative ranks. Benjamin Ginsberg recently pointed out that during the period between 1975 and 2005, the number of full-time faculty increased 51 percent while the number of administrators grew 85 percent and the number of "other professionals" rose an incredible 240 percent nationally. It is not surprising, then, that this uneven growth may create a tension between the faculty and the administration. On some campuses, this tension may be directed toward the SIO as well, especially among those who consider themselves experts in the international field by virtue of their study or research conducted abroad. In most cases, however, the faculty international expertise is discipline based and not as comprehensive as the SIO's.

FINAL WRAP

The SIO needs an international advisory council. Where the SIO position is not as elevated as it should be to promote internationalization, and where the SIO-faculty relations need to be clarified and strengthened, the support of an international advisory committee is vital. At Nebraska Wesleyan, for example, the International Advisory Council was composed of key faculty, students, and the vice presidents for Academic and Student Affairs; at Agnes Scott a faculty committee served as an invaluable sounding board for issues related to the international dimension of the curriculum and its alignment with study abroad. Given that most study abroad and international student affairs are under the SIO rather than under academic departments or schools that directly support the academic mission, it is important to establish processes that align both groups. The creation of an advisory group with a well-defined charge and the endorsement of the university's upper administration would bring together international programs and the institution's academic mission. Chaired by the SIO, it would include deans (or their designees), relevant administrators (e.g., admissions, the registrar), and students (at least one international student and one study abroad returnee). It would design and implement initiatives, develop strategic plans, review or create university policies related to international education, and, as the name indicates, advise the SIO on academic matters beyond her scope. Therefore, it behooves the SIO to suggest the formation of an international advisory committee shortly after coming to campus—and hopefully before there is a change in command.

The SIO needs to have a presence on campus. Being on campus during the first couple of years, or at least avoiding long absences, allows the SIO to learn the institutional culture and forge relationships with the faculty and other administrators. The leadership and management functions of the SIO can be seriously impaired if the SIO is also responsible for recruiting international students. Those two full-time positions cannot be effectively combined into one. Prospective SIOs should carefully study the responsibilities associated with the position before accepting it.

The SIO needs to interpret internationalization for the upper administration. The SIO must be prepared to explain to every new vice president or president that takes office the importance of the international unit they lead and its internal and external connections, contributions to the university, accomplishments, needs, and, last but not least, how its mission flows from the university's mission. Nobody else can do this better than the SIO. Although it is not in their job description, SIOs must educate the campus on the need for internationalization.

The SIO needs to explain the complexity of internationalization. It is not uncommon for people on campus to think of international students or study abroad as the only components of international education. How can the complexity of the internationalization phenomenon be disseminated? At the universities I served, I took advantage of the university catalog revision process to create a separate section titled "International Education," which described as many of the institution's global initiatives as possible. This was a small attempt to draw attention to the comprehensiveness of that institution's internationalization and how it connected to the institutional mission. I also tried to use the same strategy on the International Education/Programs website, to bring all the initiatives together, prefaced by a statement signaling the importance of international education for the institution and its students.

The SIO needs to adapt to changes in command. I may hold the record for having had the most bosses in twenty-four years as a SIO. And depending on the boss du jour, my priority could shift among several possible goals, such as assisting the internationalization of the curriculum, developing study abroad programs, caring for international students, supporting foreign languages, ensuring that faculty-led programs had a sufficient number of participants, or meeting my revenue target. I had to be flexible and versatile. In retrospect, the changes in priorities forced me to focus on distinct aspects of internationalization, and I am glad I had the preparation and the resources to meet the challenge. The frustrating side of the revolving door, however, was that there was never enough time (or interest) to discuss a comprehensive plan for internationalization.

As a holder of a protean position, I had to be careful not to succumb to constantly changing directions to the detriment of other initiatives under my purview. To avoid that, I always drew on my research on internationalization—on my doctoral dissertation, revisiting its definition, the literature on the topic, the index I developed, and the most significant components in the prediction of high internationalization. More than helping me attain the doctoral status important for the SIO position, my research served as my sense of direction as I changed to adapt to new and challenging situations. It was truly my compass.

Nine Pretty Hard Lessons from Twenty-five Years as a Senior International Officer

Uliana Gabara

THE PURPOSE of this book is for us longtime SIOs to share lessons drawn from analyses of data and reflections on our extensive experience. Yet memory interferes. Even when propped up by extensive data, it is famously unreliable, affected by all manner of variables, from gaps in documentation to self-image and self-interest. The hope is that awareness of memory's flaws may be a correlative, possibly even a tool, for controlling its vagaries. To what extent today's technological infrastructure for professional work and memory can trump its unreliability is an interesting but not well-explored question. After all, much of the time there is a pattern to our remembering and forgetting. Sometimes we recognize this, but sometimes we don't.

Having dutifully offered this caveat lector, I propose a few lessons in international education from the uncommon perspective of an SIO with twenty-six years' experience at a single institution: a medium-size, private university with Schools of Arts and Sciences, Business, Leadership Studies, Law, and Professional and Continuing Studies. But while my work has been at one university, I have been actively involved in state, national, and international conversations, often as an officer of organizations bringing together senior international officers. My goal here is to approach these lessons analytically and to show how they can be reinterpreted, generalized, and made applicable to various kinds of institutions. My hope is that they will be useful to colleagues considering embarking on an SIO career and to those who are already in the midst of the challenges such work inevitably presents.

A couple of caveats: SIO jobs, and the processes of internationalization, are notoriously varied, determined in equal measure by institutional histories and the vagaries of a historical moment. One of defining differences is between an SIO whose job is clearly administrative and one whose role is both academic and administrative. I was hired for a position that included the creation and coordination of a new interdisciplinary International Studies; major internationalization of the curriculum, and with that faculty development; the creation of study abroad programs; increasing the number and support for international students and scholars; and, very importantly, the creation of programs leading to cultural change across the campus. Such a broad definition of the position clearly called for, and in fact required, a comprehensive approach to internationalization and determined the following twenty-six years of my work.

LESSON 1: KNOW THYSELF

My career as senior international officer began in 1987 when I was hired to create an Office of International Education at the University of Richmond and to be its founding director. The office included a full-time secretary and me part-time while I continued to teach Russian language and literature and, later, International Studies. A returned study abroad student completed the staff. The charge was huge, encompassing virtually every aspect of internationalization.

With a PhD in Russian and Polish languages and literatures from the University of Virginia and an MA in English philology from the University of Warsaw, I felt woefully unprepared for the job. Only years later did I discover that I was in good company. As other chapters in this book demonstrate, nearly all senior international officers at the time had training in an academic field, usually in some way international but not in international education or any other aspect of education. It is only recently that a few PhDs in international education have appeared in the field. Whether this forecasts a change in the direction of international education is an open and interesting question. But I found that the extent to which I was able to pursue a vision of comprehensive internationalization depended largely on faculty support and participation in the project. This, in turn, depended on being accepted not just as an administrator but also as a colleague. My academic background in literatures and cultures, my knowledge of languages, my undergraduate education at a liberal arts college, my life experience in crossing a number of cultural and linguistic boundaries—all combined to give me the credentials necessary, even if not always sufficient, for being accepted as a colleague.

So part of the lesson here is that a SIO should identify and rely on what in her education and past experience will contribute to an understanding of international education and to creating a good working relationship with faculty as equals and partners.

Another reason for my concern about being unprepared for the position of director of international education was my lack of experience as an administrator. And yet, when confronted with the task of internationalizing the campus, I soon concluded that in order to internationalize the curriculum and to work toward a transformation of the institutional culture, it was necessary to begin with the faculty. This could be accomplished by offering its members fully funded opportunities to learn about and experience cultures and countries distant and different from both their academic specializations and their lives. With the support of the president and the provost, the University of Richmond Faculty Seminar Abroad was created. It has continued for twenty-six years, taking place initially annually and then biannually since 2002. Its impact on the internationalization of teaching and research, on faculty involvement in study abroad and international student support, on hiring new faculty with international interests and experience, and more has been documented through a variety of assessment tools.

Only recently, while working on the monograph *Faculty Seminar Abroad: Cornerstone of Comprehensive Internationalization at the University of Richmond*, did I realize that the idea and conceptual structure of the Seminar had its antecedents in a summer course for teachers that I had created at the University of Virginia, "Russia—Physical and Fictional," which began on campus and then continued in the Soviet Union, making it possible for participants to study both the texts and the culture that generated them. This was the "administrative experience" I brought to my new position. On a small scale, this project brought together key elements of my future work as an SIO: an understanding of the need for a more international approach to teaching, a vision for change; an identification of the change agents, their interests, options, and financial limitations; the necessary fund-raising (I secured a grant from the Virginia Foundation for the Humanities). Furthermore, the project had to be done partly within the context of the constraints imposed by the Soviet Union, including the tools for evaluation and assessment of outcomes.

Thus, another part of this lesson is about the importance of understanding how previous training and experience, when carefully examined, can become valuable assets for a new SIO. Additional introspective questions that can be useful in the process of preparing for this work are: Given a choice, what kind of institution do you prefer to be involved in, know, and/or believe in? Does the Carnegie classification matter? Do you prefer to be involved in a sustained, multiyear effort to transform institutional culture, or is your preferred work horizon three to five years, during which you want to move fast and furious, creating new agendas and beginning projects but not necessarily wanting to see them to completion?

LESSON 2: KNOW YOUR INSTITUTION'S HISTORY AND PRESENT

The University of Richmond in the mid-1980s was a small, regional, Baptist-affiliated institution with 3,500 students, a handful of internationals, and a faculty of 205, many of whom were alumni. An ad hoc committee on international studies, composed of three historians, two political scientists, two literary scholars, and an economist, produced in 1986 a report entitled "Enhancing 'International Competence' at the University of Richmond." After delving into the history of American isolationism and the contemporary national and local contexts in higher education, the report pointed to changes in the increasingly globalized world and to the need to offer students an education appropriate for the changed and still-changing times. Its original focus was on the creation of an interdisciplinary major in International Studies, which would require courses in three disciplines in addition to two bookend interdisciplinary courses, a semester of study abroad, completion of three years of a foreign language, and a focus on one of five regional and topical concentrations. The committee also concluded that International Studies was not the only major that needed more courses with international content, study abroad opportunities integrated with on-campus learning, interaction between domestic and international students in and out of the classroom, and a "heightened campus international awareness" involving speakers and programs, student organizations, faculty and course development, internships, and institutional exchanges. Here, then, was the agenda for comprehensive internationalization of the university to be accomplished by a newly created Office of International Education, which was to be staffed by a part-time director, a full-time secretary, and a returned study abroad student. The only flaw in the committee's recommendations was the massive underestimation of what it would take to implement such a bold program.

Many colleges and universities in the United States formulated similarly bold plans that, unfortunately, were never realized. So what was different about Richmond, which had clearly undergone an academic and cultural transformation in the years since the 1986 report and the creation of the Office of International Education?

First some proof of the transformation at UR in recent years: more than 60 percent of students graduate with at least one study abroad experience, with most (75%) having been imbedded for a semester; 81 percent of graduating seniors responding to the 2013 *Cooperative Institutional Research Program College Senior Survey* (CIRP-CSS) said that the opportunity to study abroad was a factor in their decision to attend UR; internationals now constitute 11 percent of the student population, a third of them are exchange students from partner universities; International Studies has for years been one of top three majors; full internal funding for the Faculty Seminar Abroad program has continued since its inception in 1989; 172 participants in eighteen seminars have studied and gone to thirty-eight countries; 25 percent of current faculty have participated in the Seminar; faculty members now come to UR from all over the world.[1]

I think that the most important factor in Richmond's success is that it was faculty members who, reflecting on the state of the world and on the education of their students, concluded that comprehensive internationalization was an urgent need and then recommended ways for bringing it about. Soon after the creation of the position of an SIO, the Seminar gave faculty opportunities for becoming prepared to internationalize courses and research, to take a leading role in establishing exchange agreements, to promote study abroad and advise students on it, and to mentor domestic and international students on living and working in the global world.

The fact that a faculty committee recommended institution-wide internationalization and the creation of the SIO position has helped define my role. Having started my career at Richmond as both SIO and International Studies coordinator and instructor, I was seen by faculty as both an administrator and a colleague. This is how I have been viewed ever since, and this is what made the Office of International Education truly a part of the academic side of the university—not a given at institutions where study abroad and international student support are seen by faculty as merely administrative, especially when they are located in student development offices.

I recommend that new SIOs: examine the history and the present of their institution to find instruments for creating strong alliances with faculty members who already support the program and that they develop new tools for strengthening and expanding such alliances. Too often it is the same few "believers" among the faculty who participate in the work of internationalization. Too often even those who carry out internationally focused research and present at conferences abroad are not involved in comprehensive internationalization of the institution. A Faculty Seminar Abroad program is an effective tool, and far less costly than it appears at first glance, for building a collaborative intellectual community committed to institutional internationalization.[2]

At a time when there are indications that the winds of change might favor an increasingly administrative role for SIOs, consider ways to establish and strengthen your own academic role and that of your office.

LESSON 3: REASONS TO INTERNATIONALIZE

For those in the field of international education, true believers all, these reasons seem obvious and are discussed at length in a number of publications.[3] But institutional realities and the larger societal landscape demonstrate that every SIO has to be prepared to justify the cost and efforts dedicated to the inclusion of the international component in higher education. So, be prepared to deliver everything from an "elevator speech" to an extensive lecture to the board of trustees on why internationalization is an important part of education in the twenty-first century.

The parameters of the justifications have to include the tangible globalization of nearly all fields of human endeavor—from politics to economics to education and the arts, health and the environment, entertainment, transportation, and tourism—as well as a defense of liberal education not as "knowledge for the knowledge's sake" but as real and effective preparation for the world of work. This is a world in which everyone changes jobs many times, in which job training is a dying commodity, and in which critical thinking and articulate and persuasive writing and speaking are essential for all mid-to-higher-level jobs. This is a time when experiential education, civic engagement, and internships have become high-priority elements of higher education and are included in numerous strategic plans, demonstrating and practicing the linkages between the local and global. After all, what is study abroad if not experiential learning, and what is interaction with international students if not preparation for global civic engagement in a post-isolationist world? And why are internships abroad not as valid as those within the US?

At Richmond, we have made these arguments, with various degrees of success, often and in various venues not only in response to the administration's agenda stemming from its strategic plan, but because they are important elements in new approaches to internationalization. There is inherent value in airing the arguments again and again, because at a certain point, perhaps during a lull in the background buzz, they can suddenly be heard.

LESSON 4: UNDERSTAND THE WHY AND WHERE OF A CENTRALIZED APPROACH TO INTERNATIONALIZATION

From the very beginning of my work as an SIO, I have believed that various aspects of internationalization—curriculum internationalization and faculty development, study abroad, international students and scholars, cultural activities, student organizations, and more—can be moved forward most effectively when treated as elements of a single project, a comprehensive internationalization of the institution. Consequently, our approach was to engage participants in the Faculty Seminar Abroad in developing exchange relationships with universities abroad, in study abroad and international student advising and approval, and in outreach to alumni abroad. We gave returned study abroad and international students a key role in the recruitment and orientations for study abroad and international students and invited faculty, students, and staff to continue to shape and implement the agenda for a comprehensive and integrated internationalization.

But early in my career I was made aware of a very different approach to internationalization. Speaking to a senior colleague and mentor about my conviction that international students can contribute a great deal to the education of Americans in and out of the classroom, and that American students can, in turn, be very effective in helping internationals understand the United States, I was surprised when she asked, "What makes you think that international students want anything more than to complete their professional training and to do so as quickly as possible, without contact with any Americans other than their professors?" With the wisdom of hindsight, I can understand the relevance of this question in the context of large research institutions, where many of the international students are in professional graduate schools. But as higher education has evolved around the world, even some of these students have come to see that they can gain more from an American education than what they learn in courses in business, electrical engineering, or animal husbandry. They understand that in dealing with Americans, when they encounter them while working for multinational corporations or even smaller national organizations, they need to understand how to approach cross-national and cross-cultural contacts. It is not an overstatement to assert that the last twenty years, and especially the last decade, have brought about a greater understanding, both in the US and internationally, of the impact of culture on what one learns, even in courses in engineering, and on what one needs to learn, especially in business courses. Consequently, Chinese, Brazilian, and even Russian students who come to the United States to study business and engineering are now more interested in contacts with Americans than they used to be.

Another change in international students' actual or potential connections with Americans stems from the increase in the numbers of international undergraduates who are much more likely to interact with peers and with host families. This is not to say that integration of international students is no longer one of the greatest challenges in international work. In everything from class participation, group work, and the honor code to social life, sorority and fraternity exclusivity, and even language issues, there is need for greater understanding of issues and continued work. There is also the never-ending effort to convince study abroad students to move out into the local student and general population. Even when Richmond students are embedded in local universities and share housing with local students, their tendency is to fraternize only with other Americans; this is not unlike the tendency of internationals, who opt for the comfort of dealing with compatriots or at least other internationals.

Getting beyond explaining to students how much they can gain as a result of interacting with the Other is clearly an ongoing challenge. Mechanisms for success in convincing them to do the hard work of moving beyond their comfort zone are the subject of numerous articles and presentations at conferences. The point is that having study abroad staff work in concert with those supporting international students and, crucially, with the faculty within a comprehensive approach to internationalization offers the greatest hope for success on this front.

At Richmond we focused on the exchange model, in part because the OIE's broad charge included creating study abroad opportunities and increasing the number of international students at a time when attracting undergraduate degree-seeking students seemed nearly impossible. And because the International Studies major and curriculum internationalization were also part of the initial charge, we added faculty development and outreach to alumni abroad to what, by then, was a centralized approach to internationalization. At each step in the evolution of OIE work, we thought of ways we could affect all of our constituencies and the reach of our project of internationalizing the university.

The centralized approach, with its goal of comprehensive internationalization, is never static. You begin by bringing together a few, perhaps originally even only two, elements (e.g., study abroad and international students), and, by conceptualizing the distant horizon, you work toward the time when international education will evolve so as to transform institutional culture and create a truly international university. This approach may be more easily implemented at a small or medium-sized institution, where one can rely on existing or create new connections between departments and schools.

At a very large, decentralized institution, the comprehensive approach may still be possible within individual schools. As such large schools adopt internationalization as a strategic goal, it may be the school dean or associate dean who is also responsible for internationalization. This is one more reason why publications like this one and organizations such as the Association of International Education Administrators (AIEA) should provide help and resources for the significant number of colleagues for whom such work is only a part of their overall responsibility.

LESSON 5: PLAN, STRATEGICALLY AND OTHERWISE

A provost once said to me, "You are opportunistic." My Central European soul crumbled in horror. What—me an opportunist? How did I deserve such an insult? This was more than thirty years after I became an American. I should have known by then that *opportunistic* can be a term of praise in a culture that values the enterprising spirit. But still it hurt. So much for how deep the roots of culture and language can be and how intertwined they are! Now, with a few more years of experience as an SIO, I shamelessly advise all aspiring colleagues to be just that, opportunistic. Yes, it is very important to have a solid, ambitious strategic plan for internationalization. As with all strategic plans, the process of developing one is as important as its final formulation. It is in this process that various groups of people come together, exchange ideas about the past and future, and agree on long-range goals. The final plan should not preclude taking advantage of opportunities, which can appear from all sorts of directions. I am not recommending that you lose sight of what is important or accept funding from dubious sources for unneeded or unwanted projects, but there may well be ways of reinterpreting strategic goals, whether budgetary or conceptual, if they really are strategic and therefore broad and bold.

What happened at Richmond may offer a useful example. For years, the OIE had been moved from one small accidental location to another, never having space for work with faculty committees, programs, or group meetings. For years we talked about how useful it would be to have a center that would enrich the outcomes of our work by bringing it under one roof. It would also serve to demonstrate UR's commitment to internationalization. In 2010 Carole Weinstein, an alumna and board member and longtime supporter, announced that she and her family were prepared to fund an International Center. This was serendipity at it most glorious. So, even though this had not been part of our strategic plan, for the next three years the planning, building, and startup of the International Center became our top priority. After three years of hard work, we had a purpose-designed and -built center where the OIE occupied one-sixth of the space and with seven high-tech classrooms to accommodate online collaborative teaching with faculty at partner universities; offices for visiting international scholars; spaces for ESL, for Cultures and Languages Across the Curriculum, and for seven departments and interdisciplinary international programs, including not just International Studies but also American Studies, (which was focusing on becoming international in scope); the Global Studio for languages and communication; the Spatial Analysis Laboratory; the all-purpose International Commons; two art galleries; a café; and a courtyard, which could house all kinds of events, planned and spontaneous, and socializing involving students, faculty, and staff.

There is also the issue of where internationalization fits within the broader institutional strategy. Accepted wisdom tells us that in order to move forward, international education must be part of this strategy. There is no question that it is important and useful to be so included. In this volume, colleagues with experiences different from mine speak of the advantages of the SIO having a very close relationship with a president, who becomes closely involved in promoting and supporting the international project, travels with the SIO, and pursues his own agenda in this area. But for all of its advantages, internationalization from above has the potential for alienating the faculty if they do not feel sufficiently consulted and involved in decision making. It can also alienate other administrators if their prerogatives are being abrogated. Its roots can be shallow, and the SIO can become a scapegoat in intra-institutional turf wars.

So what happens if—or when—a new president arrives with an agenda that does not include internationalization? Is the initiative doomed for the tenure of the new president? Never having worked under a president who was personally involved in internationalization, my experience has been different from that of many of my colleagues. Consequently, my belief is that *if* international education has established a significant role in the life and culture of the institution, *if* it has clearly demonstrated its contribution to the successful implementation of the academic mission, *if* it can demonstrate positive impact on rankings and on attracting both domestic and international students, and *if* it has managed to attract external resources (such as funding for a center or a chair), then the worst-case scenario on the arrival of a new president is a status quo—no infusion of new resources, no new positions, perhaps even lack of support for no-cost new initiatives, but no interference with the essential work of internationalization such as study abroad, international students, faculty internationalization, and programs. Whether this is reason enough to warn SIOs about becoming too dependent on presidential support, I leave that to the reader's judgment. Unfortunately, my own experience, as well as others', suggests that one should be cautious about making assumptions about long-term support for international education. It's better be prepared to move forward on the strength of past accomplishments, even if more slowly, and to survive a dry spell in institutional support, if need be.

LESSON 6: CONSIDER THE BUDGET

Part 1: On Institutional Funding

The first question SIOs often have about the budget is, of course, what money is available for staffing—How much will it cost and can this cost be justified. The first response from an SIO—or, better yet, from a faculty committee charged with the oversight of an office of international education—should address the academic rationale and the impact of internationalization on the institution's ranking and ability to attract good students. Equally important are responses that point to the pragmatic value of study and internships abroad and to interaction with international students as preparation for entering the global workforce.

Other big budgetary questions are: How do we reconcile statements about the value of study abroad with access to it? And, how do we attract undergraduate international students without offering a great deal of financial aid? The solution we adopted at Richmond addressed these issues together by creating exchanges with universities abroad. Our thinking soon after the creation of the OIE in 1987 focused on semester study abroad. The reasons had to do with academic content, cultural immersion, and the fact that, unlike short-term and summer programs, financing of a semester is part of each family's financial plan, not an add-on. But since financial aid was not portable, it was available only to students who didn't depend on aid, and disadvantaging students on financial aid countered all of the university's pronouncements about its commitment to diversity. We also realized that in the prevailing climate in higher education, international students were not likely to come to the University of Richmond, a largely undergraduate institution, if they had to pay full tuition, and certainly not from Europe, where most of our students wanted to study abroad.

On campus, our goal was to integrate American and international students; we did not want to reproduce the situation common at many universities where incoming students are mostly from Asia while the outgoing ones are headed to Europe. Consequently, very early on the OIE decided to establish exchanges with carefully selected, excellent institutions in Europe but also in Latin America and eventually in Asia and Africa in order to expand our students' interests beyond Europe. Our financial and administrative arrangements reflected these priorities. Richmond students and those from partner institutions were to pay tuition to their home institution, which meant our students could continue to receive full financial aid. Incoming students filled beds vacated by outgoing students and paid for room and board. To avoid the problem created by the greater number of Richmond students going to partner institutions than those institutions' students coming to UR, we agreed with partners that we would pay direct enrollment tuition for additional students. This became quite simple by the mid-to-late nineties when most of our partners had established procedures for accepting visiting students from abroad, but in the first few years we had to help some of them understand and develop appropriate procedures.

As anyone who has dealt with study abroad knows, direct enrollment is not the easiest model for students because it does require significant independence, both academic and social. But most students can benefit from it if persuaded to consider it and prepare well. Our experience demonstrates that, with time and increasing numbers of students on campus who return with very positive reports, most students become eager to enroll directly at a partner university. Still, it is not for everyone. And it is also not the easiest model to administer. Historically, of course, Americans have tended to study abroad in "island" programs directed either by faculty members from an individual institution or by providers such as the Council on International Educational Exchange (CIEE), the School for International Training (SIT), the Institute for the International Education of Students (IES), and others.

Aware of both of these issues, we provided the possibility for some students to study in selected and approved provider-offered programs. It should be stressed that throughout the process of selecting both partner universities and American programs, it was the faculty-led Committee on International Education that reviewed and approved proposals by the OIE. It acted as the judge of academic quality and in so doing kept the number of programs small enough to allow for faculty involvement.

The key to implementing the new structure for study abroad was a policy adopted by the Committee on International Education which required that students participate in a Richmond-approved program or petition for an exception. Exceptions would be granted by a subcommittee on the basis of demonstrated academic need.

As a result of the new policy, all students going abroad during the academic year would pay the same tuition for a semester abroad as they would for one on campus. This made it possible for all students to participate in study abroad, regardless of whether they were on financial aid or not. Predictably, we encountered a certain amount of resistance—almost exclusively from parents and students with no financial aid who saw a semester abroad either as a means for saving money or as a time when they would be free of Richmond's academic standards and yet receive credits toward graduation. In response, we created a document explaining why all students would have to pay Richmond tuition for a semester abroad: while abroad, UR students continued to accrue preapproved credits toward a UR degree; moreover, UR faculty and staff continued working with students on everything from housing and registration for the semester after study abroad to library access, advising, health and safety issues, and more. Resistance essentially disappeared within a few years, and almost no one took up the very real option of taking a leave of absence and reapplying, even though we made it clear that the process would be simple and the chances of readmission and even getting the credits earned abroad almost certain.

In 1991 there were twenty-four degree-seeking international students and four exchange students from two partner institutions; by 1993, as the number of partnerships increased rapidly, exchange students constituted half of the total international population. In recent years, as the number of partnerships reached almost seventy, the number of exchange students grew significantly, and, as a result of increased efforts at recruitment abroad, so did the degree-seeking population. Two other factors played a role in this integrated approach: the new national trend of increasing numbers of undergraduate internationals and the fact that UR had become well known in some countries, especially in China.[4] By 2013 the situation had stabilized, with exchange students constituting 33 percent of the total international population, which has reached 11–12 percent of the total student population.

I offer all of these statistics in order to emphasize the extent to which growth in study abroad, exchanges, and international student populations is connected and how they support each other. Explaining this to the top administration, and also possibly to the trustees, is not easy, but it is necessary if the institution is to benefit from the opportunities such an approach creates. An integrated approach can be the basis of fiscal stability in international education and can impact the university's reputation as an internationalized institution.

Part 2: On How We Moved from a 1.75-Person Office to a Staff of Eleven

"Slowly and cautiously" is the basic principle. Securing funding for new positions is never easy. Institutions resist even the best of proof that a new position is needed in order to keep up with increased demands on the office. At Richmond we relied on expanding our work as far as humanly possible without adding staff. Only after demonstrating how much we were doing did we ask for a half-time position, requesting its change to full time a year or two later. UR's growth in study abroad, international students, and exchange agreements worked in our favor. For example, in 1989 there were fewer than 100 study abroad students; by 2001 there were 380 and by 2013 just under 700. Similarly, the number of international students increased from 31 in 1991 to 165 in 2001 and 399 in 2013. In that time we also went from one partnership agreement in 1991 to 40 in 2001 and 73 in 2013. In 1990 1 staff member was responsible for study abroad and international students; by 2013 the study abroad team consisted of 5, and 2 full-time staff were responsible for international students.

In OIE we stressed that fiscal predictability was the result of the system we had put in place: students going abroad continued to pay Richmond tuition even as they received financial aid; exchange students decreased the impact of room and board fees lost when students went abroad; degree-seeking internationals were attracted to Richmond by the presence of exchange students, while domestic students were attracted by its reputation for study abroad.

Part 3: On External Support

Raising funds is part of every SIO's job, whether it is made explicit in the job description or not. Success in this task has significant real and symbolic implications. It defines how an SIO is viewed by the administration, first and foremost, but also by faculty, especially if faculty members benefit from the new resources.

There are some opportunities for funding projects through Title VI, Fulbright, and other federal programs, as well as through organizations as the Institute of International Education (IIE), the Association of International Educators (NAFSA), the School for International Training (SIT), and IES. At Richmond, Title VI funds made possible the creation of International Studies concentrations in Latin America, Africa, and the Middle East. They also supported self-instructional language training in Swahili and Turkish. The Fulbright program brought us some of the first international visiting scholars, and a number of faculty went abroad on Fulbright grants and became advocates and participants in "internationalization at home," in study abroad and international student advising, and in bringing visiting scholars to campus.

But what about funding by a donor? There is no question that a dedicated fund can be a game changer. Soon after the creation of the Office of International Education, a conversation began between the director and alumna and board member Carole Weinstein. The conversation began with a focus on the ways in which Richmond students should and could be educated and moved on to a range of issues, including how faculty, staff, and students could be involved in creative individual projects with a potential for affecting the university as a whole and what the impact would be of having more international students on campus. Weinstein was excited by the conversation and these prospects. The annual fund she offered became the enabler of various initiatives that could not be realized through the institutional budget. After a number of years, she decided to create the Carole Weinstein Chair in International Education. The dean, who became the holder of the chair, now had a continued, and by that time significant, source of support for new ideas and new initiatives around international education. A distinguishing feature of this funding continued to be its support for creativity by all segments of the university community, including the staff, which is usually not included in institutional funding opportunities and yet is so important in the process of internationalization. The funding for the chair also made possible financial aid for international students beyond what the UR had in its pool for this population.

The final chapter in this story of external support was the funding of the Carole Weinstein International Center, a purpose-designed and -built 57,000-square-foot structure that houses the OIE, seven departments and interdisciplinary programs, faculty in international law, high-tech classrooms, the International Commons, the Global Studio for languages and communications, the Spatial Analysis Laboratory, ESL, Cultures and Languages Across the Curriculum, the Global Music Studio, two art galleries, and a café. As its occupants demonstrate, the goal of the International Center writ large is to reflect existing and facilitate ongoing comprehensive internationalization. So, while international courses and programming take place in campus locations not in the International Center, and not everything that happens at the Center is international, the importance of the Center, real and symbolic, cannot be overestimated. It is a key demonstration of the extent to which internationalization has been inserted into the DNA of the institution; it is a presence resistant to changes of leadership and vagaries of budgets.

LESSON 7: ASSESSMENT—PAST, PRESENT, AND FUTURE

Assessment in international education can mean a number of things. It can be simply the number of students who study abroad and the number of international students attending the institution. Observing that number, and the percentages of both populations over time, since class sizes and the total populations vary, gives us a sense of change and trends. As everyone in the field knows, the most widely used national data is that collected by the Institute of International Education (IIE) and published in its Open Doors report. As reliable as this data is, there are problems inherent in it. For example, institutions are ranked on the basis of raw numbers, not the percentage of students who study abroad, which skews the picture in favor of larger institutions. And since individuals, rather than a sum of attendees in all programs, are counted, the workload of study abroad advisers is underrepresented. Similarly, the raw number of international students is the basis of ranking, which again gives larger institutions an advantage.

Assessment of the quality of study abroad programs and their outcomes is a source of unending discussion and disagreement. How should we measure cross-cultural outcomes, and what about the academic quality of programs? When should we measure these outcomes, and can we measure them reliably at the point of students' return to campus? Many agree that outcomes become clear only years after the students have graduated, at a point when getting responses from them becomes very difficult, if not impossible.

Assessment of issues related to international students receives much less attention, though with the increase in the recruitment and numbers, especially of undergraduates, it seems appropriate to assess learning outcomes, services, the level of satisfaction and integration, and the contributions internationals make to cross-cultural learning on campus.

At Richmond, we have made various attempts at assessment, none more reliable than the numerical data, which demonstrate clearly that more students, and a larger percentage of the total population, have participated in study abroad and that there are more internationals on campus. Significantly, self-assessment offered in CIRP-CSS demonstrates that participants in study abroad believe in its outcomes: in 2013, 94 percent "strongly agreed/agreed somewhat" that study abroad made them more self-confident; 89 percent said they used what they learned abroad in their academic work (an issue we had been working on with the faculty for years); 86 percent saw themselves as more informed about global issues than prior to study abroad; 84 percent said they were more interested in global issues; 75 percent said they felt more comfortable interacting with Americans of different ethnic backgrounds; and 74 percent said study abroad helped them with career/graduate school plans. These numbers have remained steady since 2009. The exception was the percentage of students who said that the opportunity to study abroad was a factor in their decision to attend Richmond; this grew from 64 percent to 69 percent and, in 2013, to 81 percent.[5]

Two lessons can be gleaned from this. First, the international office does not need to collect all data. It should, instead, partner with various units that gather information. At UR, for instance, the Office of Institutional Effectiveness agreed to add questions about study abroad to the senior survey. Second, we need to interrogate such self-assessment to learn more about its reliability. Can students be telling us what they know we want to hear and what we told them while preparing them for study abroad?

Assessment also presents challenges in faculty development. Consider the Faculty Seminar Abroad. Here, too, the question posed by administrators is, "What are the outcomes and how can you demonstrate them?" Yet participants tell us repeatedly that the "outcomes" are many and varied—some that are visible immediately following the return from study abroad, some that become visible only years later. In addition to writing a required report, faculty may revise a part of a course in the first year, add an international module to an existing course, and/or create a new course only when the department decides that it wants to add another course. Some faculty will collaborate with a colleague they met at a partner university on research or on the mentoring of each other's students. All of this may take some time. It is also clear from the survey we conducted in 2013 that faculty participants also see themselves as better study abroad promoters and advisers and as better mentors for international students.

LESSON 8: THE SIO'S WORK OUTSIDE THE CAMPUS

Even for an SIO with a significant staff, there is plenty of work to do on campus—creating new conceptual structures, policies, collaborative agreements abroad, and curriculum internationalization; reaching out to all units, from admissions, alumni, and student development offices to organizations such as study abroad and international students and scholars, to collaborative art exhibits, concerts, and fashion shows, to OIE-run film series. And then there is the work focusing on faculty and staff development and on finding ways for bridging the chasms between schools and departments, between the institution's strategic plan and the plan for internationalization.

Still, it is important for every SIO to become involved at the state, national, and international levels. There are various reasons for such involvement. I remember joining the International Studies Association thinking that it would help me with my work as coordinator of our new interdisciplinary International Studies major. I quickly found out that some of my expectations were not to be met; this was an association of political scientists, with a few economists thrown in for good measure. But somewhere in a corner of the organization was the International Education section, which I joined and before long chaired. The few of us who were trying to figure out what our new jobs meant, and what we could do in this field, turned it into a useful support group. In another effort to learn from experienced colleagues, I attended one of the early AIEA meetings. Here the problem was different. This nascent organization then consisted of chief international officers at large land grant universities, and their concerns were quite different from my own. The fact that there were almost no women in attendance did not help. But the few of us who were there managed to join forces and help redefine the scope and work of the organization. Eventually, after a number of years of progressively greater involvement in the organization, I became its president and continued working toward creating a broad-based organization for senior international educators.

I have been involved in numerous other professional organizations, among them: NAFSA, serving at one time as the Virginia state representative; the Virginia Council for International Education, as its president; the European Association for International Education; SIT, as a member of the Partnership Council; the FORUM on Study Abroad; the Foundation for International Education, as academic board member; and the Greater Richmond World Affairs Council Board.

There are many reasons why such involvement is important. One reason is to learn from the experiences of colleagues and other institutions; another is to compare the extent of international work on various campuses and use this information to persuade your administrators about the current and potential comparative advantages of internationalization. Also useful are the opportunities to network for future job opportunities, if one is looking for mobility. And finally, contribution to the field itself is an important civic duty, an issue many of us have taken seriously over the years.

LESSON 9: THE SIO'S ROLE IN ACADEMIC AFFAIRS

At the beginning of the long process of internationalization at Richmond, in the late 1980s, there were some who were not convinced this was a necessary or a lasting endeavor. In creating the Office of International Education and the position of its director, the university made a commitment to comprehensive internationalization. This was an exceptional move for a medium-size regional institution at the time, as was the inclusion of other cultures and civilizations in its courses. But because it was a process led by dedicated faculty members, in collaboration with some administrators, it has been successful. The culture of the institution has been transformed to the point where study abroad is an expected part of most students' education. Because of the system put in place by the university's policy on study abroad, no student is excluded because he is on financial aid; 11–12 percent of students hold F or J visas and have an impact on what happens in classrooms and in residence halls; many students come from immigrant and minority homes; the faculty includes people from around the world, not just from around the country; and a multitude of courses look at issues from cross-cultural and international perspectives.

But these accomplishments do not mark the end of the road. There are important opportunities and needs in the area of "internationalization at home" for Richmond. This is not a means for diluting study abroad; instead this is a way of offering enrichment and other ways of deepening the Richmond education to make it ever more intercultural and international.

One way of furthering this mission is through language study. Languages are prisms through which people and cultures look at themselves and at others. They define what we see. As the popular idea of the phrase *lost in translation* suggests, we lose something when we have to rely on translation, and yet we gain something when we read, work, and study in a second, local language. SIOs who see their role as academic leaders may want to consider

Cultures and Languages Across the Curriculum (CLAC), a project in which students of a foreign language are able to use their varying degrees of knowledge to supplement their learning in English-medium courses in various academic fields. For example, in a course on the politics of the European Union some students, often those who have returned from study abroad, meet for an extra hour, during which time they read and discuss texts in German, French, or Polish. These supplemental hours are sometimes taught by a faculty member but more often by native speakers, international students, or Americans fluent in the language. The faculty member of record need not be teaching the CLAC hour. The point is the active use, rather than the study, of a foreign language. UR is a member of a small consortium of institutions attempting to make CLAC part of the curriculum. As promising as this project has been, it has not taken flight, so it should remain on the agenda for *future* internationalization.

Another opportunity for the next stage of internationalization is the Collaborative Online International Learning (COIL) project. At Richmond, COIL would build on the significant number of partner institutions abroad for developing joint courses. With the current national and international focus on exchanges and the use of Internet technology, SIOs at many institutions may want to consider adding globally networked learning, virtual exchange, and online intercultural exchange to their campus agenda. Such courses could lead to faculty collaboration in research and to collaborative student projects. This initiative would also strengthen, rather than take the place of, study abroad. COIL courses would better prepare students for the semester abroad and allow those returning to use the knowledge and experience they gained in the rest of their coursework. Both of these projects for the future are based on the comprehensive approach to internationalization, which has long been Richmond's trademark. As everywhere, whether they become realized will depend on the positions taken by the future dean of International Education, the next president, and the new provost. With both, tangible incentives will be necessary in order to encourage faculty participation, and only the administration can offer such rewards.

Internationalization has long been seen by some as part of the future of higher education rather than a part of its present. The result is that when new priorities or needs are declared and something has to be postponed, it is often internationalization that is suspended, delayed, or, in the worst-case scenario, even disassembled. Dealing with this reality should become part of the agenda of national organizations such as AIEA and NAFSA. As the inextricable connection between the United States and the rest of the globe becomes linked with higher education, with what colleges and universities are expected to deliver to students and society as a whole, with job preparedness for alumni and proof of students' postgraduation employment, can an uneven and often only intermittent commitment to internationalization be justified? Since the answer to this question seems to be an obvious and resounding *no,* the question before us is really how to develop the best, most productive, and truly sustainable process of internationalization for each institution.

CHAPTER NINE

Reflection on International Education Leadership Experience at a Small Liberal Arts College

Joseph Tullbane

MY ARRIVAL at St. Norbert College in August 1999, as the newly appointed senior international officer is not where the story of the internationalization of this small, midwestern liberal arts college begins. The story really begins with a description of my unusual pathway into the field of international education and how that background affected the changes introduced at the college over the next fourteen years.

MY PATH

How does a person born in the southernmost tip of Texas qualify to be an international educator? In my case, it began with my father being recognized for excellence in teaching with a national teaching award in 1958. The recognition ultimately resulted in him being recruited by the State Department to teach at a military dependents' high school in Spain. The summer after I finished third grade, we moved to Madrid, and for the next ten years I attended American elementary, middle, and high schools while living in that amazing Spanish capital city. For three months every summer, our family traveled throughout Spain and the rest of Western Europe. Experiencing the different peoples and places of Europe was the best of all worlds for a young man growing up.

Returning to the United States for college in 1967, I was privileged to attend Rice University in Houston, Texas, majoring in architecture. A four-year Army ROTC scholarship paid my way through college, and at the end of five years (having completed both a bachelor's degree and professional degree in architecture) I entered the US Army as a second lieutenant. While in college I met and married my wife, who has been my life partner in living around the world.

My twenty-three-year army career was atypical, to say the least. After six years serving in various armored cavalry, armored, air defense, and staff units, I was selected to enter a regional specialist field studying Soviet (later Russian) and Eastern European political, economic, cultural, and military affairs. My training in the field entailed getting a master's degree in international relations from American University and, later, a doctorate in Russian area studies at Georgetown University. Adding Russian to my almost-native Spanish was a side benefit to these studies. I spent the rest of my military career working in Washington, D.C., Europe, and Eurasia. During this time, I taught at the US Army Russian Institute (a postgraduate intelligence school concerned with learning more about the Russian and Eastern European regions) located in Garmisch-Partenkirchen, Germany; served as a regional analyst and later as manager of analysts at the Pentagon in Washington, D.C.; and as a military attaché to the US embassy in Madrid.

Throughout my military career I continued to travel in Europe, Eurasia, Latin America, and Asia, picking up bits and pieces of languages, customs, and cultural understanding. I believe that the opportunity to live and travel extensively abroad gave me a functional understanding for and deep appreciation of other cultures and societies, as well as an ability to deal successfully with professionals from around the world.

As I matured in the army, I was also exposed to more and more sophisticated management, communication, and leadership techniques, as well as business and fiscal program management of large-scale independent and semi-independent operations. Ultimately, I supervised and managed the army's regional specialist office, which took care of the career management for the 1,900 officers of the program (650 of whom were in training in various locations around the world) and controlled an annual operating budget of around $6 million. The organizational skills I learned in this and other jobs paid enormous dividends in designing and managing the campus internationalization programs at St. Norbert College.

THE COLLEGE'S PATH

St. Norbert is a four-year, religiously affiliated, liberal arts institution with around 2,100 students. It enjoys a good academic reputation within the region. It also has a tradition of internationalism based largely on a shared history with its founding Catholic order (the Norbertine fathers) and has had international full-time, degree-seeking students on campus in small numbers since 1918.

In terms of overall internationalization, the general education program underwent a transition in the early 1970s that added major aspects of internationalization to its core curriculum. Then, in the early 1990s, there was a concerted effort to begin recruiting international full-time degree-seeking students. That number peaked in 1994 at seventy-five (roughly 5 percent of the student body) but by 1999 had fallen to a total of only fifteen. A significant portion of the international student population during this period was Japanese, and the combination of the downturn in the Japanese economy and the lack of national diversification in the international student population at the college contributed heavily to the loss in these student numbers and to an overall downturn in international recruitment funding.

The study abroad program during this same period focused on semester abroad provider-based experiences and sent approximately ten students abroad each semester. Additionally, there was a single active faculty exchange program with the University of the Philippines–Diliman. The president at the time believed strongly in internationalization as a concept and had directed a number of far-reaching changes to accomplish it, including the creation in 1995 of the International Center. With board of trustee support, he settled on a business-oriented, revenue-generating model for the new Center, structured to be largely independent of the college's academic programming. The vision for the new Center sought to leverage the growing business community in the region and was intended to offer advice and college resources to that community as local and regional businesses expanded their global partnerships. In 1996 the separate, independent International Center opened. At least on paper there was a foundation for internationalizing the campus. However, the preexisting study abroad and international student services operations were not housed in the new Center but under the associate dean for Academic Affairs.

The idea of a college–business community partnership seemed very progressive at the time, but the expectation of a resultant strong revenue stream that would pay for the Center's expenses failed to materialize, leaving the institution with a significant deficit where a surplus had been predicted. Further, the faculty never fully bought into the concept behind the new Center, seeing it rightly as a drain on limited institutional resources without a commensurate pay back in terms of net profit or further internationalization of academics. This lack of support by a major campus constituency combined with the less-than-expected operational performance to bring the Center, figuratively, to its knees.

Even though the initial four-year experience had been somewhat negative, there were positive takeaways for St. Norbert. First and foremost, it reinforced an institutional commitment to internationalization as a key element of the college's mission and heritage. Further, it illustrated that there was a commitment of funding and resources by the upper administration to advance this effort. The creation of a centralized International Center was a huge step forward for a college of its size. The Center was an infrastructure with the potential to bring disparate international elements together from various parts of the campus. Last, many of the individual programs internal to the Center, such as community outreach and the English as a Second Language (ESL) Institute, had real potential to affect positively both the college and the local community while at the same time developing as profit streams for the institution.

In 1998–1999, a faculty-led campuswide task force spent an intensive year and a half (meeting weekly) developing and refining a conceptual framework for a new and more academically oriented Center. The fact that the faculty accepted the task of restructuring the International Center was incredibly significant. By doing so, they became the de facto sponsoring force behind the idea of campus internationalization. While extensive in its recommendations, the task force study purposefully left considerable operational flexibility for the new SIO, leaving room for imaginative development of both the Center and the larger issue of campus internationalization. The overall intent of the study was to find a method for expanding and enhancing the college's international aspects.

The final study report further suggested a reorganization of the Center that expanded the basic structure to encompass certain heretofore independent entities, such as study abroad and international student/scholar services. A major change championed by this report was that the director position be elevated to the associate VP/dean level, reporting directly to the academic vice president and dean of the College, and that a doctorate degree be a requirement for anyone holding the position. The report also suggested that faculty status for this director would encourage the collegial process of discussion and understanding between him and the faculty at large. To give the new position still more academic significance, the various international interdivisional majors and minors, including such programs as International Business, International Economics, International Studies, Japanese Studies, Leadership Studies, Peace and Justice Studies, and Philippine Studies, were brought under the new associate dean's purview.

INITIAL CHALLENGES AND OPPORTUNITIES

On my arrival at St. Norbert College, I was presented with some difficult challenges but also some significant opportunities relating to internationalizing a small college somewhat isolated in northeastern Wisconsin. This dichotomy was more than simply a "glass half empty or glass half full" view of a situation; in fact, it represented the complex and wide-ranging elements that constitute campus internationalization on a broad campuswide spectrum. Fiscal and personnel constraints were somewhat unusual because of the tuition-driven nature of the institution, but the opportunities for "out-of-the-box thinking" and "cutting-edge solutions" within those constraining factors was amazing.

During my first weeks on campus, certain demands were laid out for me by both the dean/VP for Academics and the president. Some of these were fairly obvious given the current condition of the International Center and its operations. The first and foremost demand was to bring the Center operation under control fiscally, essentially moving it out of the red and into the black on the balance sheet—by any means within reason. The second challenge was to bring staffing in line with available resources. Third, I was ordered to adopt the task force recommendations (which had already been approved by the board of trustees) to change the Center's orientation and restructure it from primarily business support to a more institutionally integrated and academically oriented operation.

A very positive aspect of these challenges was that the demands for change and reorientation of the Center, and by extrapolation campuswide internationalization, opened up fairly significant opportunities to create something new and far-reaching for the institution. Obviously, the key challenge was to resolve the budgetary issues facing the Center. On the surface this meant cutting personnel and funding. At the same time, reorienting the Center seemed to suggest strongly a positive inclination by the institution toward growing campus internationalization for the future. This idea of building infrastructure for the future seemed to contradict the emphatic budgetary guidance from the upper administration. The fact, though, was that both objectives were important to the institution. The college would have never conducted a national search and hired me as a new SIO if it had been intended to curtail the drive toward campus internationalization. It was essentially left to me as the SIO to define and execute the guidance in such a way as to create a successful operation.

Accepting the president's challenges, and in consultation with the Center's professional staff as well as key faculty supporters of the concept, I adopted some further goals that fleshed out the spirit of those seemingly contradictory directives.

- Develop the trust, support, and ownership of the internationalization effort by the institution's faculty, staff, students, administration, and board of trustees.
- Create a growth model for internationalization of the campus and develop the internal infrastructure within the Center that would contribute to developing said institutional model successfully.
- Review each component within the Center for viability and either disestablish or reorganize, redesign, and augment as necessary.

- Integrate the newly added academic support components into the Center, building a support base within the faculty as well as a synergistic relationship between each of the separate Center elements as a method of increasing resources without immediately expanding staffing.
- Explore and develop methods of improving the Center's economic self-sufficiency and follow these efforts up rapidly with the creation of institutional revenue streams within the Center.
- Extend the Center's influence throughout the institution and, through outreach efforts, expand the influence beyond campus into the local community. (This goal was a bit more complicated than simply offering lectures to the community and entailed engaging on an ongoing basis the needs and interests of the community at large.)

After detailed individual discussions with each of the Center staff members and a number of outside observers, I realized that certain internal changes had to be implemented to rebuild personnel confidence. The past few years of constantly being under fire from various constituencies on campus had left many of these professionals unsure of themselves and hesitant to make critical decisions to implement needed changes at the lowest level possible. In essence, I was faced with an enormous job, and I found that it was inefficient at best to attempt to direct personally every phase of its varied operations. I needed to be able to rely on my directors to resolve and implement solutions within their own defined operational areas, and that demanded rebuilding their confidence and the internal transparency of the organization's decision-making structure.

The process of instilling confidence in the Center leadership and developing a positive dynamic relationship with and among my directors became one of the foundational pillars on which the reorganized and rebranded center stood. To plug staffing gaps that had become apparent during the initial organizational review and to also build the new infrastructure needed to support a growth model for campus internationalization, it was necessary to recruit and hire imaginative, innovative new employees, individuals with the potential to advance quickly within the system but who were also willing to initially perform as chief cook and bottle washer in our inherently resource-constrained environment. When hiring entry-level staff, I also looked for individuals who had the capacity to efficiently run an office/department once developed.

Ultimately, the Center needed to be viewed as a successful, mainstream element of both the institution and the community, but always within the conceptual context of internationalization being a campuswide mission. My goal, therefore, was to ensure that eventually, when campus internationalization was mentioned by a visitor, the natural response would be that "we all do internationalization," not "oh, internationalization—you need to visit the International Center."

A NEW CENTER FOR A NEW ERA:
THE HYBRID INTERNATIONAL CENTER

The Center was largely reinvented in the period after 1999. While endeavoring to retain the best elements of the old Center (mainly community outreach), the new Center's infrastructure was expanding to meet the needs of an increasing number of full-time degree-seeking international students and a robust semester abroad program; improving high-visibility community outreach programming; and developing a viable self-sustaining model for the internationalization efforts on campus. Before we could implement any real change, I had to reengage the faculty at large.

The Faculty-Center Relationship

Traditionally at St. Norbert, a small number of dedicated faculty members had overseen a few specific individual international programs. They were connected in an informal, loosely configured collegial relationship. These individuals often were highly sensitive about the independence of their individual programs. Over time, as the college expanded, fewer of these dedicated individuals had the time available to commit to running increasingly complicated programming. Further, even those who did contribute their increasingly scarce time to these programs began losing touch with the detailed, day-to-day issues. The weakening of the critical link between faculty and international programming (small to begin with), as well as the faculty's complete separation from the Center, contributed greatly to their general discontent with the situation.

At the same time, expansion of campus internationalization and demands for additional related programming strained the capacity of the Center's professional staff. Coincidentally, increasing professionalization of the international education (IE) field strongly argued that the day-to-day international operations should be placed in the hands of the full-time IE professionals, whose sole job was to efficiently and effectively run international programs. This solution was far more effective than using faculty as part-time program managers, especially given their increasingly constrained availability.

The faculty role in campus internationalization was still paramount to its success. With direct faculty participation increasingly unlikely, the solution had to focus on some form of supervisory involvement. The first step in this process was to consolidate three separate existing informal faculty and community committees into a single formal standing committee within the faculty governance structure. With this move, I both institutionalized the oversight structure and brought a more precise focus to the involvement of the faculty in the campus internationalization process. At the same time, I encouraged the direct participation of interested campus staff members in the individual international programs sponsored by the Center. This change also gave more precise focus to community interests.

The elected faculty standing committee was, and still is, tasked with reviewing study abroad sites at least once every three years and with adding new sites and eliminating old sites as recommended by the professional staff. Beyond that, the committee was briefed regularly on the operations of each of the offices of the Center and had both the right and responsibility to comment on current operations and suggest new ideas. Further, the committee was expected to serve as an informal conduit to the rest of the faculty body, keeping it informed of the evolution within the Center specifically and of the campus internationalization efforts in general.

Essentially, while faculty participation in the field had been expanded, its nature changed from being direct involved in specific programs to assuming a broader overall responsibility for academic supervision of the entire internationalization effort at St. Norbert College. This new faculty relationship did not restrict individual programmatic involvement by a faculty member, but it simply no longer made it the focal point of the campus internationalization efforts. This, in turn, allowed me to hire proven professionals to meet and anticipate the requirements for a growing internationalized college.

Development of the Center's Infrastructure

Once the concept of a professionally staffed center was established and generally accepted by both the faculty and administration, measures to better integrate the disparate elements under my supervision as SIO, to redevelop the center as a more fiscally self-sufficient entity, and to embrace an across-the-board commitment to flexibility and adaptability had to be explored and implemented. I addressed these three very disparate requirements by designing a type of hybrid organization for the new Center. The organization combined academic support, community outreach, and revenue generation under a single umbrella.

There are a few aspects of the Center that make it somewhat unique for a small liberal arts college. First, its operations encompass all campus internationalization efforts at St. Norbert College, both curricular and cocurricular. This is rare, though not unheard of, at small liberal arts institutions. Second, the reliance on a professional IE staff for all aspects of Center operations is more normal at larger public or private institutions. Third, the inclusion of vibrant local community outreach as an integral part of the Center is seldom found at institutions of this size. Some examples of these outreach programs are afterschool foreign language training for elementary school students, national speaker programs for the community on current international issues, an annual international simulation role-playing exercise for local high schools, and for-profit translation and interpretation services for local and regional businesses.

Implemented in 2000, the new hybrid organization responded to the needs of both the local community and the college. During its first five years, it was recognized nationally as a relatively new, aggressive growth model dealing with internationalizing a small campus. While tailored to St. Norbert's needs, it proved to be generally replicable at other similar institutions. The organizational structure, at least at the conceptual level, has been copied by many other small liberal art colleges as they seek to internationalize their campuses on limited budgets.

Because its structure is constantly evolving based on the needs of the college and the local community, the Center tends to be extremely diverse in its offerings. This broad-ranging and inherently diverse approach to campus internationalization demanded that many of the Center's offices be regularly redesigned and reorganized. It also required that directors of these divisions and offices be leaders in their own right. Beyond their more traditional role as managers in their respective areas of expertise, they had to be creative, imaginative, out-of-the-box thinkers.

With its reorganization and revitalization, the Center evolved into a major revenue stream for the institution, with its ESL Institute programs, translation and interpretation services for businesses, and a number of for-profit programs, such as the evening adult language and cultural awareness classes. Three unplanned consequences of the success in creating a new revenue stream were that the rest of the campus constituencies appeared less threatened by a generally self-sufficient, integrated set of operations; it moved the overall campus internationalization effort from a position on the periphery of campus activities to one at the center of the institution; and the Center operations were increasingly protected from major personnel and funding cuts affecting many of the other campus departments in the economically constrained environment.

At the same time, however, there were some negative aspects to this financial success. Any time that revenue streams become significant elements of an equation, there is a real possibility that demand for said revenue will become a driving force in and of itself. Such revenue becomes an expectation and is often spent in anticipation of it being produced, and sometimes with complete disregard to the financial realities of the economy that might constrain its availability. This danger is especially serious in a smaller tuition-driven college. Ultimately, this might lead to non-revenue-producing (but essential) aspects of the operation being threatened with downsizing or elimination.

The real issue, as it related to the Center, was that its operations were so interrelated and mutually supporting that any downsizing or termination of non-revenue-producing elements would almost certainly negatively impact the overall revenue streams of the Center itself. Maintaining the complex interlinked personnel and organizational aspects of such an operation, defending its very flexible and adaptive nature, and at the same time managing institutional revenue expectations within reasonable bounds all contributed to a major balancing act for the Center managers, but especially for me as its SIO.

The Completed Organization

In its completed form, the Center consisted of three basic activities: revenue-producing operations, academic support operations, and community outreach operations. The actual component elements of the Center were: the ESL Institute, representing a major revenue stream but also academic support as a feeder to admissions; the International Student and Scholar Services Office, representing academic support; the Study Abroad Office, representing academic support and a major recruiting tool for the college; the Language Services and Community Outreach Department, representing both institutional revenue stream and community outreach; and the Office of International Programming, representing both academic and student affairs support. Other offices such as Export Management, International Contracts, and, most recently, International Student Marketing and Recruitment have come and gone as the Center has evolved based changing college needs. Even within each of these areas, programming is extremely diverse and continually evolving, reflecting the dynamic nature of the Center.

ACCOMPLISHMENTS AND SUCCESSES

Internal Successes

In terms of measurable advances and improvements since the redefinition, restructuring, and rebranding of the Center approximately fourteen years ago, there have been a number of recognized successes.

Financial stability and growth. Within two years of the initial reorganization of the Center, one of the primary concerns of the institution's senior administration had been addressed. The Center had turned its bottom line from the red to the black and had asserted itself as a source of a growing revenue stream for the institution. Since then, the Center has developed a number of small revenue-producing operations that together offer additional help to the college not only in fiscal terms but also in terms of local outreach and expanded internationalization.

Semester-long study abroad. In order to maximize the efficiency of the Center's small staff and at the same time ensure that our students experienced a more full and meaningful experience abroad, I reorganized study abroad in the spring of 2001 to exclusively emphasize semester abroad programs. To ensure greater control over the academic and administrative quality of these programs, as well as maintain better cost control, we developed and negotiated direct enrollment and exchange agreements with selected partner institutions around the world. This change increased study abroad's popularity with students, allowing them to use institutional aid and thereby reduce their individual costs. Independent summer programs and individual faculty-led short-term programs were still encouraged, but they were not supported by the limited available study abroad resources.

Revamping the study abroad program resulted in 7.5-times greater participation between the 1998–1999 and 2012–2013 school years. By 2012, Admissions credited study abroad with having a major impact on domestic student recruiting for the college. Further, roughly 33 percent of the graduating class of 2013 had studied abroad on a semester or longer program, another 3 percent on a summer program, and still another 12 percent on a short-term faculty-led program.

The ESL Institute. The ESL Institute has gradually expanded its enrollment since 1999 and is one of a comparatively few college-prep operations nationally to successfully negotiate the negative immigration aftermath of the 9/11 attacks. During this period, the ESL Institute strengthened its niche market status as a successful small-class, tailored, high-support, intensive college-preparatory program. By 2013, the ESL Institute was developing an integrated program of preentry bridging courses in mathematics, US history and politics, and Western philosophies and religions, emphasizing academic areas traditionally weakest for international students matriculating to colleges and universities from their home nations. This add-on curricular bridge was intended to round-out the preparation of students hoping to succeed in college. I believe that this integrated bridging program, if fully implemented, will set the Institute apart from its peers both regionally and nationally. Regardless, the ESL Institute operates as a significant college revenue stream, but it also produces an annual cohort of qualified international full-time degree-seeking recruits for the college.

Language services and community outreach. The Center has also expanded its various community outreach programs significantly since its inception. In

2013 it continued to offer local schoolchildren (second through sixth graders) the opportunity to study foreign languages and cultures as an afterschool activity; approximately four hundred elementary school children participated at a number of local private and public elementary schools. It offered adults evening non-credit-conversation courses in roughly fifteen languages each semester. The Center also offered a variety of workshops on foreign cultures and basic language communication/interaction to local law enforcement departments, K–12 educators, and the general public. It also offers for-profit translation and interpretation services to local business, having grown from eight to roughly fifty-nine languages in fourteen years. Finally, it rolled out ethnic cooking classes for the local community, some taught in English and some in the native language.

The International Student and Scholar Services Office. This office has expanded its services to now take care of *all* of the college's immigration needs, including both student and scholar visas as well as work permits for permanent international staff and faculty members.

International Student Recruitment and Marketing. In 2010 this office was moved from the Center to the Office of Admissions, with disastrous results for international recruiting at the college. That noted, while this operation was under the purview of the Center, international student recruitment had roughly doubled in size in less than four years (2007–2010) while the academic quality of incoming students improved significantly. The synergies inherent in locating international student recruitment within the Center were becoming apparent while at the same time keeping costs of recruitment within reasonable bounds.

The Office of International Programming. Established in 2011, International Programming is dedicated to creating links between the campus community and our international students. The idea behind it was to better integrate our international students into the fabric of campus life and local community. It sought to introduce them to the United States but at the same time work with other offices across campus, from Campus Ministry to Athletics, to build a better understanding of the amazing home cultures and ways of life that the international students bring to our community.

External Successes

Nationally, St. Norbert College has gained visibility and recognition in the field of campus internationalization. In 2004 it was recognized by the Association of International Educators (NAFSA) as one of five awardees (with Duke, SUNY-Binghamton, UNC–Chapel Hill, and Bellevue Community College) of the inaugural Paul Simon Award for campus internationalization. In 2005 it was recognized by the American Council on Education (ACE) as one of eight institutions of higher learning nationwide with best practices in the field of international education. In 2008–2009 St. Norbert was the first college or university in the United States to be recognized by the Forum for Education Abroad for meeting new national standards in best practices for study abroad operations, having completed that organization's Quality Improvement Program (QUIP).

Success as a Problem?

Within four years (1999–2003), the overall program had begun to gain national recognition for its improving quality, while internally it was making visible changes to the face of the campus community. Because of its perceived early success, a common misperception seemed to grow within the senior administration that campus internationalization had been largely completed, that they could declare it a success (or successful enough) and move on to other projects. They failed to understand that campus internationalization is a process, not a project, and that the early successes, while welcome proof of an improving campuswide effort, are really milestones for an ongoing and iterative change process. This misunderstanding of internationalization as a process allowed them to justify a shift in strategic emphasis (with obvious funding and personnel implications) to other worthy causes that were favored by the upper administration.

At times, my directors and I were forced to expend considerable energy and effort defending and justifying the continuation of specific programs, rather than using our time more fruitfully expanding campus internationalization. Our flexibility and adaptability—the hallmarks of our overall operation and what gave it a significant vitality—were increasingly constrained. We were expected to do more with less and less.

International Recruitment and Where to Locate It

At many colleges and universities, the question of where to locate international student recruitment and marketing is an ongoing discussion. The discussion is whether this effort should be located with the professionals who understand the needs and demands of prospective international students or with the professional recruiters within Admissions. Key to this discussion is whether or not there is a substantial difference in domestic and international recruitment and marketing. At St. Norbert an early decision to locate this recruitment and marketing effort in the Center was based on a general recognition that international recruitment and marketing are significantly different from domestic recruitment and marketing. The idea was to take advantage of the international knowledge available and the potential synergies within the Center (for example, the utilization of the ESL Institute and study abroad site visits) to rapidly and aggressively increase the number and academic quality of full-time, degree-seeking, international students.

As international student recruitment became more and more successful, an impression at the vice presidential level grew around the idea that the operation was fully developed and that therefore it could and should be shifted away from the Center. In the case of St. Norbert, this was a serious misstep, although one mainly of timing. Our original plan already called for international recruitment to be moved from the Center to the Office of Admissions, but only after it was fully developed as a successfully functioning, independent operation. In this case, however, the operation was moved from the Center before it was completely staffed and funded. The agreement between the VPs of Academics and Enrollment Management to move the operation in 2010 was seen by them as simply an early execution of the original plan. The problem was that the visible successes in recruitment still largely relied on the internal synergies derived from the operation's structural integration into the Center.

The original plan for the international recruiting and marketing effort at the college called for the establishment of a three-person office (a director/recruiter, one recruiter, and one recruiter/office manager) over a five-year period (which included a settling-in period) before any move would be attempted. Projected increases in personnel and operational funding of these changes were to be covered by a small part of the increased revenue brought in by the expanding number of international students. To bridge the initial gap in lack of dedicated personnel and funding, other subunits of the Center contributed in-kind support to the recruitment effort. For example, the ESL Institute director committed roughly 25 percent of his time to this effort, the Study Abroad Office committed about 20 percent of its time to it, and I committed 15–20 percent of my own time to direct recruiting. So short-term success was actually working against long-term progress, namely adequate staffing of the recruitment effort.

The negative effects of the decision to move the operation were felt almost immediately. In the first year after the move international recruitment fell by more than half (from 45 to 20 new students). The second year results dropped by half again (to 10 new students), and the school was now graduating more students than it recruited. Finally, in the third year numbers fell to under 5. This was a disaster by any measure. In just three years the overall international student degree-seeking population had dropped from 7 percent of the student body to under 2 percent. Finally, in the fourth year, 2014, the operation was returned to the Center, and the numbers and the overall recruitment process (contacts, agents, etc.) are being rebuilt, essentially from scratch.

Maintaining Momentum and Leadership

Maintaining staffing and replacing top-flight directors and key players was an ongoing issue for the Center. An aggressive growth path demanded that the Center have a staff composed of bright, forward-thinking, self-initiating individuals willing to take risks to succeed but who also can understand the constraints of a small organization and have egos that allow them to function with little or no staffing support. Identifying and recruiting such individuals to a small college with limited resources is always a challenge. Retaining them is even more so at a small college where there is, by its nature, little opportunity for internal advancement.

I provided professional development for the staff so that they could move on as they outgrew their current duties; we were literally training them to progress from their current work to better jobs at other institutions. On the surface, this seemed a bit perverse, but in fact it resulted in better-trained and happier personnel, because they understood that I would be their advocate for promotions, internally if possible but elsewhere if there were no positions open at the college.

PROGRESS AND ACHIEVEMENTS

From August 1999 to August 2013, my team and I took a small, isolated, midwestern liberal arts college further along the road to campus internationalization than many of my faculty and administrator colleagues thought possible. Much of what we established internationally has been institutionalized within the curricular and cocurricular segments of the college and will withstand the vicissitudes of subsequent shifts in the visions of future presidents.

However, at the end of this period, St. Norbert had a new president and dean of the college whose visions no longer shared the views of the president and dean who had welcomed me in 1999. The new leadership wanted St. Norbert to compete for national prominence and downgraded the internationalization goals of the past. I found myself and my directors fighting to just maintain what had been achieved. The growth of internationalization was no longer possible as it had been in the past. I realized that my vision was no longer in step with that of the upper administrative leadership.

With mixed feelings, I decided to retire from St. Norbert in 2013. I felt that I had taken campus internationalization as far as it could go at that time. I knew that I had left some things unfinished and that my vision had not been fully realized. Nonetheless, I could see the progress made over the last fourteen years and the very real possibilities for the college in the future. I will always be proud of what my team and I were able to achieve for St. Norbert College.

CHAPTER TEN

SIO—the Hardest Job You'll Ever Love

Riall W. Nolan

> If you expect to see the final results of your work, you simply
> have not asked a big enough question.
>
> —*I. F Stone*

I HAVE ALWAYS considered myself to be an average sort of person, and so I was gratified to read a few years ago that the "average American" will hold twelve different jobs over his or her lifetime and move through three different careers. This describes me almost perfectly. I began my professional life over forty years ago as a development anthropologist, moved decades later from that to a second career in international education administration, and am now on my third reincarnation as a full-time university professor.

This is my account of the twenty years I spent as an SIO in four different universities. What ties this rather patchy career together is my overriding curiosity about how we learn cross-culturally and what we do with what we learn.

HOW I GOT INTO IT

My international career began in a rather haphazard way. In 1965, the spring of my senior year at Colgate University, I had a fateful conversation with my adviser. Shortly thereafter I was a Peace Corps volunteer in a very remote Senegalese village, living in a grass hut and listening for the lions at night. I developed a taste for highly spiced food, learned to speak several languages not taught at Colgate, and developed a keen interest in the people living around me.

I also became fascinated with the behavior of the other foreigners who occasionally visited our remote town on one development "mission" or other. Many of these were highly trained specialists in economics, agriculture, or engineering, but few of them seemed able to actually make things work in the local culture. In time, as my own interest in development work grew, I began to search for better ways to uncover and use local cultural knowledge in projects and programs. Anthropology seemed to offer both a perspective and a methodology for understanding other societies, and so, when I finished my Peace Corps stint, I headed for the UK and a doctoral program in social anthropology.

Degree in hand, I then spent the next fifteen years doing development work in a variety of places around the world—Papua New Guinea, West and North Africa, and Sri Lanka. As I learned to design and manage development projects, I also became curious about the development agencies themselves. How did these organizations, so influential in the lives of poor people, actually think about what they were doing? How did they learn as organizations about different cultural environments, and how did that understanding find its way into their plans and projects?

Over time, I progressed from being a development field person to being a development agency bureaucrat. Instead of living in a thatched hut and walking miles every day, I now sat behind a computer and directed the work of others. I spent most of my time writing reports and sitting in meetings discussing policy. And while the work still seemed important, it also seemed a long way from the grass roots where I had begun. And so in the mid-1980s my wife and I eventually made the decision to leave development work, move back to the United States, and start again—in a university.

I settled into my new role as an assistant professor of anthropology. I found most of my students to be delightful, very interested in understanding societies far removed from their own, and anxious to make a contribution of some sort to the world of tomorrow. I felt that I was helping to open their eyes to the world around them and, in some small way, building their capacities for engagement with that world.

By the end of my first year of teaching, however, I had to face the hard truth that it would never be possible for me to give most of my students the opportunity to discover the world beyond the shoreline in any but a superficial and remote sense. If I tried hard, I might be able to help two or three of them every year to get overseas and to experience the kind of growth in understanding that I myself had benefited from in the Peace Corps. And although I enjoyed the teaching, I was less interested in, and less impressed with, other aspects of my new academic career. In particular, I found departmental politics odd, occasionally vicious, and, overall, somewhat boring.

I realized, just as I had in development work, that someone who wants to make a long-term difference needs to be involved in setting policy. It was at that point that I decided to join the dark side—to get involved with academic administration. Although I hoped that I would be able to retain some connection to the teaching that I loved, I was mainly interested in helping to promote international education within an entire institution.

Three years later I got the chance to direct one of the US's few multilingual international training institutes for development professionals, located within the Graduate School for Public and International Affairs at the University of Pittsburgh. No longer dealing with US students, I was now responsible for designing and offering training to experienced public-sector officials from Africa, Asia, Eastern Europe, and the Middle East. Our program offered instruction in French, Arabic, Indonesian, and Russian. Here, the challenge was to design and manage cultural transitions for skilled professionals coming to the United States, many of them for the first time, and to build their skills in development management.

This, my first job as an actual SIO, was very different from my previous experience as an anthropology professor. What mattered here was not individual accomplishment—the publication of academic papers or the getting of grants—but, rather, the creation and support of a team of people whose collective efforts would touch a great many others. My work, in other words, succeeded to the extent that it facilitated and enhanced the progress of others.

I spent six years in this job, directing the work of a multilingual and multidisciplinary group of teachers and trainers.

At the end of that time I accepted a position at Golden Gate University in San Francisco, partly to be closer to my family but primarily because it offered me an opportunity to become their first-ever dean of International Programs. Here I had the chance to engage in high-level strategic planning and to design new international master's programs. But in other ways the opportunity proved a disappointment. Although I was more or less where I wanted to be, there just didn't seem to be enough to work with, and so three years later I moved again, to the University of Cincinnati—again, as its first SIO.

Cincinnati provided me with more responsibility, more resources, and more opportunities. I also had a new job title, associate provost in charge of the Institute for Global Studies and Affairs. I stayed in that job for six years, and I left mainly because I felt that I had done all I could do. The institute had moved the university forward on a number of fronts, but we had also reached a plateau, and moving forward would probably require some fresh thinking and a new leader.

So when an opportunity came up to be the SIO at Purdue, I applied and was eventually selected, becoming first dean and then (déjà vu) associate provost for International Programs. At Purdue I managed a staff of about forty-five and a budget of over $3 million. After six years there, I reached the mandatory retirement age for senior administrators and "retreated" to my tenured faculty position in anthropology, which is where I am today.

SENIOR INTERNATIONAL OFFICER—
THE HARDEST JOB YOU'LL EVER LOVE

As an SIO, I used many of the same skills and perspectives that I had learned first as a Peace Corps volunteer and then as a development anthropologist: get the lay of the land, develop contacts, and figure out what's worth talking about.

I usually had to do these things pretty quickly. "Drinking from a fire hose" and "building the canoe while shooting the rapids" were both phrases I remember from these early days. Eventually, of course, things settled down a bit, and I began to meet people and get down to work.

And as one gets to know one's constituents, aspects of institutional character appear. Although each person in an institution is a unique individual, the parts do indeed work to create a coherent whole—what anthropologists call an "organizational culture." The institution will have its own way of raising issues and resolving them. The institution will be broadly driven by a relatively small number of important concerns, ranging from budgeting to academic quality, to diversity, rankings, or anything in between. The institution has a history and has learned important lessons from its history while at the same time developing skill at doing certain things. And finally, of course, the institution has aspirations.

In each of my four institutions, uncovering these aspects of institutional culture was an essential step for me in understanding how to move toward the strategic conversations about internationalizing that are such an important part of an SIO's work. My developing understanding of the institution's culture gave me things to talk about—and often steered me away from certain things—as I began to engage with my new colleagues.

In each of my four universities, almost everyone around me was a stakeholder in one sense or another, because all of them had interests of one sort or another in what was happening. If you are stepping into a mature internationalization effort, as I was at Purdue, then people are naturally going to be interested in whether or not you're planning to make changes. If you are the inaugural SIO at an institution, as I was at both Golden Gate and Cincinnati, there's even more scrutiny.

Stakeholders in a university come in all shapes and sizes, and it takes a fair amount of time to get to know them all. Stakeholders can help you in many ways, but they also have needs, hopes, and fears that have to be dealt with. Understanding these as fully as possible before embarking on complex endeavors is almost always a good idea. On each campus where I worked, I needed to find and work with opinion leaders—individuals, whatever their position, whose ideas and attitudes "count" for others. And from among that group, I needed to find champions, people who would advocate for internationalization at crucial times.

SIOs aren't technicians; they don't come with ready-made answers for things. Or, even if they do, they need to adapt these answers to the local context in which they are working. SIOs, in other words, combine technique with artistry. Donald Shön, in his work on reflective practice, describes the work of certain professionals as a process of talking to the environment about what is needed and what is possible. The environment, says Shön, talks back, and from this ongoing dialogue original and creative solutions emerge.[1] It is through the process of engagement and collaboration that the shape of a solution arises.

Nowhere is this truer than with SIOs inside the university. But the engagement and dialogue is with multiple constituencies at the same time at a variety of levels.

If, as some believe, nothing significant happens on a university campus without the blessing of the faculty, it is equally true that nothing important will happen without the understanding, consent, and support of the three or four individuals who actually run the place. These are usually the people an SIO works for, in one way or another: the provost, the president, and, in some cases, the chief financial officer and/or the chair of the board of trustees.

There is no one right way to develop and broker what I call the "strategic conversation," but the way that seemed to work for me was to get a clear, if somewhat general, sense of who the faculty were and what they might respond to, and then to begin to talk about broad strategic directions with the provost and president. This is much easier to explain than to actually do, of course. There will be pressure on the new SIO to get things done quickly and, in most cases, before an entirely clear picture has emerged of institutional strengths and weaknesses.

In other cases, of course, the faculty and the administration may be at odds with one another. Ideas that appear to come from the top, in such situations, are likely to be rejected out of hand, and I did indeed have several such experiences at two of my institutions. At Golden Gate, the president became an increasingly embattled figure, bringing much constructive change to a halt. At Cincinnati, the faculty and the president had settled into an attitude of mutual disregard, an atmosphere which, while not actively hostile, certainly impeded discussion. At both institutions, key internationalization issues were eventually decided and resolved to everyone's satisfaction, but not before a great deal of time and energy had been expended.

The strategic conversation, in other words, is a delicate and time-consuming process, but it is absolutely essential to putting in place a clear framework to guide future activities. Without some sort of a strategy, any international collaboration looks as good as any other, any study abroad destination will do, any grant opportunity is a good one, and any request for funding support is worthy.

ONCE YOU START TALKING, WHAT DO YOU TALK ABOUT?

A reflective conversation takes time and proceeds slowly. It takes place among and between multiple stakeholders and has to include those to whom you report. These are the people—the president, provost, dean of faculty, and trustees—who control resources and who have the power, should they so choose, to make major policy changes and nudge the institution in a new direction.

As I worked my way through a succession of SIO jobs in several large universities, I became acutely aware of how unprepared these institutions were for the challenges and opportunities presented by today's interconnected world. The mechanics of designing and carrying out a high-quality study abroad program, a joint international research endeavor, or an international student recruitment campaign, while complex in some ways, are not hard to describe. And although there are several different ways to do each of these things, there is not infinite variation.

The problem, as I came to realize, wasn't in the techniques but in identifying and nurturing the *motivation* for international engagement in the first place. Presidents, provosts, deans, and trustees have a lot on their minds, and international work may not be a particularly high priority at the start of the conversation.

And so the need for a series of reflective, strategic conversations. These are very much of an emergent dialogue; one talks to the stakeholders, the stakeholders talk back. Each conversation adds a bit of meaning; each party to the dialogue learns new things. Eventually, original and creative ideas emerge from the conversation.

At several of the institutions I worked at (Purdue and Pitt, for example) internationalization had been going on for some time. At others, however, people were starting more or less from scratch. It's not that no international activity had occurred, but no attempt had been made to think about what had happened and what might happen on an institutional scale. In both cases, the shape of the strategic conversations turned out to be very much the same. Where do we want this institution to be in five years? What do we need to do in order to get there? How will those tasks be identified and assigned, and how will they be supported?

In the end, an internationalization strategy needs to incorporate thinking about the basic elements, or building blocks, of change: clear objectives, financial support, policy support, and enhanced human capacity. At each institution I focused on helping stakeholders (and particularly organization leaders) define clearly what they wanted to achieve. Sometimes, this was the maintenance of a successful program, or its expansion. Often, however, it was a new direction. In either case, it was necessary to outline not only the objectives and the means for achieving them but a rationale for action that could capture the attention and support of other stakeholders later on.

Leaders think mainly about where to go, but, in my experience, they often do not think very much about how to get there. And so my job much of the time was to explore alternative pathways to a destination, outline what would be necessary, and recommend specific courses of action. Usually, "getting there" involved four main things: making sure *resources* would be in place; building *capacity* in people in order to enable them to succeed; making sure that *policies* were also in place to support things; and establishing or reinforcing the relevant international *connections*.

Resources

Resources were, at most of my institutions, issues of money. So a large part of my work involved finding money (and, on occasion, time) for the various activities that promoted internationalization. At Pitt, no money whatsoever came from the university's budget; my entire operation, from staff salaries to overseas trips, had to be funded through outside sources, mainly in the form of grants and contracts. At the other three institutions, core financial support from the central budget was available but had to be supplemented in various ways in order to extend present activities and engage in new ones. Finding the money and securing it for internationalization purposes is often a hard job, and other stakeholders on campus can be resentful of this. Finally, at each university I attempted (with varying degrees of success) to involve the institution's fund-raising arm in international activity.

Building Capacity

Building faculty and administrative capacity for international activity was a major part of my job at each institution. Training the vice president's office at Golden Gate on how to communicate effectively with overseas partners consumed quite a bit of time. Putting in place transfer arrangements for overseas credit became a major operation at the University of Cincinnati, as did setting up a process for tuition swaps. And at Purdue our office worked for several months with others across campus to craft a comprehensive risk and safety policy for overseas programs.

At Purdue we also set up and ran a highly successful series of faculty tours to selected strategic locations overseas to permit our people to see the region, to meet their colleagues there, and to discuss possible collaborations. Over time, these learning tours involved a significant number of our faculty and staff and contributed greatly not only to support for internationalization but to the skills needed to make it work. Finally, at both Purdue and Cincinnati I led teams responsible for increasing our number of Fulbright scholars, an effort that involved not only working closely with student applicants but also training the faculty in how best to support students who wanted to apply.

Policy Support

Internationalization is a complex, multifaceted undertaking, and it must be supported by policies that encourage—or at least do not discourage—internationalization activities. Probably the most important aspect of my work as an SIO involved looking at policy. To policies on credit transfers, tuition swaps, and risk and safety procedures could be added policies at both Cincinnati and Purdue on study abroad scholarships and institutional collaboration agreements. All of these consumed a great deal of my teams' time and energy. These efforts were enormously worthwhile, in that the results were highly positive in all cases, the changes made were permanent, and the process of discussion and decision taught all of us within the institution a great deal.

International Connections and Agreements

What linkages, partnerships, or collaborations should a university seek to form, and why? At all of my universities, there were dozens (in some cases hundreds) of signed "agreements" of various kinds, few of which had any active life at all. Why had they been signed? In some cases, presidents had signed them following a visit overseas. In other cases, faculty had signed them during the course of an international conference or site visit—or perhaps after a particularly convivial dinner together.

One of my first jobs at each institution was to wade through these agreements and carry out a form of triage. Some agreements were worthwhile, some were mainly symbolic, and a few were actually detrimental or risky. Others, while essentially harmless, could not be rescinded without giving offense. Many such agreements were owned by particular faculty members or departments, who clamored for additional funding to keep things going.

The strategic conversations centered on both the why of agreements and the how. Which agreements were worth having, and what purposes should they serve? How should new agreements be drawn up, and by whom? At any university of any size, these are complex questions requiring discussion among and between a range of stakeholders. As I gained experience, I began to see ways to broker these conversations more effectively. At Purdue I had gained sufficient wisdom and insight to understand that agreements could be made for several different broad purposes and that policies should be in place to facilitate each type. Agreements involving a single faculty member, or a small group of faculty, could be drawn up quickly and with minimal review or oversight. Agreements involving an entire department, however, were commitments of a different sort. They obviously involved more than one person—faculty, students, and staff—and they contained multiyear obligations of various sorts, not the least of which was financial. These agreements, therefore, needed more structure, more discussion, and more review. Finally, there were those strategic agreements involving the top leadership of the institution, generally establishing some form of long-term structural tie with an overseas entity (usually a university, but not always). These involved the entire university, were designed to be very long-term in nature, and often required a considerable shifting of resources and important legal commitments.

It is this last category of agreement that has proved to be most problematic. There is no doubt in the minds of most SIOs that the successful universities of the future will be those that have forged strong and meaningful structural connections with institutions overseas. Through these connections will flow students, faculty, research, and funding. But imagining, planning, and setting up such linkages is incredibly difficult and demands, ironically, the very degree of international understanding that internationalization is supposed to bring about as a prior condition for success.

In the past two decades, we have seen some of our most prestigious institutions fail in their attempts to establish branch campuses overseas. Purdue was invited several times to set up a campus overseas, and once came very close to doing so. It is perhaps fortunate that we did not, for it became clear as negotiations proceeded that many in our institution knew far less than they should have about how to envision, construct, and carry through international partnerships.

INSTITUTIONAL CULTURE AND THE ART OF THE POSSIBLE

At each of the institutions where I worked, I engaged in reflective conversations with faculty and administrative leaders about strategic directions. The results of these discussions turned out to be, though uniformly positive as a whole, quite different from one another in terms of focus and content. Institutional context makes all the difference in terms of closing some doors while opening others.

Golden Gate University, for example, had adopted a responsibility-centered management budget model, requiring each unit to be "a tub on its own bottom." Whatever advantages this system might have theoretically had, its direct effect was to encourage competition between internal units, thus making collaboration and long-term strategic planning extraordinarily difficult. At Pitt we ran a totally soft-money operation, but without the intramural competition, which made the job much easier. Our strategic planning at both institutions, such as it was, centered largely on where we could go to get the next grant or contract.

At Golden Gate and Cincinnati, a significant lack of trust existed between the faculty and the upper administration, which meant that considerable time had to be spent creating workable relationships with members of the faculty who viewed international programs as something emanating from "one of them." This directed resources and energy away from more positive and worthwhile activities.

Finally, I learned that academic quality and high institutional rankings were not necessarily a guarantee of receptivity to internationalization. In fact, high rankings may work the other way. At Purdue, it proved very difficult to get the faculty in one department interested in semester-long exchanges with top overseas universities. "We're ranked number six in the nation," they explained. "Nobody teaches our subject as well as we do. Why would we need to send our students overseas?"

Such hubris can also generate large areas of ignorance. At this same institution, my associate dean and I once attended a faculty meeting where a prospective candidate for the job of school head was giving his campus interview presentation. There were several hundred faculty in the room when the candidate opened his talk with a question: "How many of you know what the Bologna Process is?" After a long moment, two hands went up. My associate dean turned to me and whispered, "We're doomed."

Another aspect of institutional culture that affected my work is probably familiar to every SIO: high turnover among upper faculty and administration. As Edgar Schein reminds us, institutional culture starts at the top, and when the institution's president leaves, the results are generally felt throughout the system.[2] In some cases, a leader's departures are messy. But all departures are disrupting to one degree or another. I experienced turnover at the top in every single one of my institutions, and never did it have a positive effect on what we were attempting to do.

None of these things is particularly surprising to people with experience in higher education, but all of it goes to underline the basic point: institutional culture matters in internationalization, and institutional culture, to an extent that perhaps not everyone appreciates, emanates from specific individuals.

Despite all of these difficulties and obstacles, I am happy to say that significant success was achieved on each of the campuses. In each of my four jobs as SIO, my team and I, together with the support of faculty and upper administration, were able to significantly improve the policy structures that supported international activities, things like budgeting, allocation of grants and support, risk management, international linkages, and program design and implementation. These were significant to me because they were long-term and institution-wide and relatively unaffected by changes of leadership.

At two campuses I led strategic planning efforts to help set the course for future activities. In the process of strategic planning, the capacities of all of the stakeholders, including the SIO, tend to increase as the all-important reflective conversations proceed. At both Pitt and Purdue I was successful in obtaining major new funding for important activities to support new initiatives. At all of the institutions, building faculty capacity was a major emphasis of mine; designing and putting in place programs to support faculty financially, to train faculty, and to bring faculty overseas were major parts of my job. Here again, the results of such efforts tend to be long-term and relatively safe from changes of leadership or emphasis.

The programs I am most proud of, however, are the international linkage programs that my teams and I designed and set up at Pitt and Purdue. At Purdue we led a three-year effort to connect our institution with institutions in India and China and to focus on research partnerships, student mobility, and alumni development. At Pitt our group spearheaded a five-year program to build faculty capacity in nine selected universities in Russia and the former Soviet Union. This program had multiple facets, including training, support for joint research and opportunities for scholars from Russia and Eastern Europe to come to the United States as visiting professors to work with their counterparts. The program encompassed nine overseas universities and fifteen US institutions. Both the Pitt and the Purdue programs created an "invisible college" of faculty participants, and both provided training, experience, and funding that would enable work to continue for years into the future.

WHAT I'VE LEARNED

As I said at the outset, my years in development work taught me several things that helped me later as an SIO. One of the most important of these was the need to treat the local culture as an asset and opportunity and not as an obstacle. In development work, projects and plans at odds with the local culture are unlikely to work, and so it becomes very important to acknowledge and understand those around you before attempting to nudge them in any particular direction. So, too, at universities. Each institution has its own way of doing things, and although this can and does change through time, it's best to start by riding the horse in the direction it's already going.

University cultures are not monolithic, however; they contain distinct subgroups with particular interests, hopes, and fears. And so understanding differences within an organization is also a very necessary part of fitting plans to place and people. In this process, interactive, highly participatory approaches to planning and implementation work best in almost all circumstances.

At the same time, I learned to never underestimate the weight or significance of past experience. Institutions, and the individuals who comprise them, bring previous experience into the present, and this experience helps shape their perceptions of possibility, constraint, threat, and safety. Local beliefs and attitudes do not arise from nowhere; they are the product of years of past history, a great deal of which finds its way into the present. Faulkner could have been speaking of universities when he wrote, "The past is never dead. It's not even past."

An SIO's work should be sustainable. If change has been successful, if improvement has occurred, if outcomes are satisfactory, then it is critical that these gains be maintained. Institutionalization, not innovation, is the true hallmark of change. SIOs, like college presidents, will come and go, but the best of what they do ought to stay behind to form a foundation for others, in their turn, to build on.

What I have learned after twenty-odd years as an SIO can be easily summed up briefly: internationalization takes many different forms, but it is based on the development of strong and durable relationships between people. Without good relationships, little of consequence is likely to happen. SIOs must therefore be both willing and able to connect with faculty, with students, with partners overseas, and with top management in order to initiate and develop those reflective conversations that will result in long-lasting and useful outcomes.

Institutions have specific characters and histories, and these will help frame and determine what is possible. In this sense, all possibilities are local ones. Institutions have individuals within them who can make a real difference at the right time and place. So much of the success of an SIO's work is bound up in the nexus between agency and contingency. Fortune's hand looms very large in SIO work.

I have had an enormously satisfying career as an SIO. It has been at times discouraging and frustrating, but it has never been boring. As an SIO I never stopped learning never stopped trying to develop the skill and artistry essential to success. Along the way I have been privileged to meet and work with a variety of very fine and gifted individuals, both here and overseas. The work of changing our institutions is long and hard, but it is surely worthwhile, as we prepare ourselves for the challenges and opportunities ahead. I am happy to have had a small role in that endeavor.

CHAPTER ELEVEN

A Contemporary Odyssey to Senior International Leadership

William Lacy

FOR US UNIVERSITIES, the emphasis on internationalization is a relatively recent phenomenon. Just twenty-five years ago, international education via study abroad was a limited program, providing a small number of middle- and upper-class humanities and social science undergraduates an opportunity to study in Western Europe. For the large majority of institutions, international students were a very small percentage of their student body, particularly among undergraduates. The international faculty was equally small, and campuswide leadership in the form of senior international officers was generally nonexistent. In addition, the application of new knowledge internationally was primarily focused on agricultural development. Finally, the strategic plans and goals of most US institutions rarely included an international agenda, or a senior international officer.

As a consequence, unlike other academic and campus administrative positions, few role models or clear career trajectories for such positions existed. Some of my fellow SIOs have referred to the journey to leadership for campus internationalization as an odyssey. That particularly characterizes my personal journey, which began with a military tour in the demilitarized zone in Korea and eventually included professorships in the Departments of Sociology, Rural Sociology and Agricultural Economics, Development Sociology, and Human Ecology at four research universities (the University of

Kentucky, Pennsylvania State University, Cornell University, and the University of California, Davis) and five distinct administrative positions at Colgate University, the University of Kentucky, Penn State, Cornell, and UC Davis.

Like Ulysses, my thirty-year odyssey began in Ithaca in the early 1960s, as an undergraduate at Cornell University, and temporarily ended in Ithaca in the early 1990s, as a Cornell administrator. When I considered moving to UC Davis in the late 1990s to assume the newly created vice provost position in University Outreach and International Program, my wife, Laura, reminded me that odysseys are supposed to end in Ithaca. Not to be deterred, I countered that Ulysses then left Ithaca on a second adventure. She smiled sweetly and replied that, once again, Penelope did not join him. Despite her serious reservations and strong connections to Cornell (four generations of Cornellians in her family), Laura did, however, agree to move to Davis with me in 1999, and she assumed a research leadership position in the newly created MIND (Medical Investigation of Neurodevelopmental Disorders) Institute.

THE LEARNING YEARS

My initial awareness of a world beyond a few states in the Northeast and Virginia began modestly at Cornell as an undergraduate. I met international students in my residence hall, enjoyed fraternity brothers from Europe and Asia, served as big brother for a Hong Kong undergraduate student, and met and dated a lovely Chinese American student. However, my undergraduate degree in industrial and labor relations and pre-law involved no language or area studies courses and no study abroad.

My first significant international experience was atypical, compared to that of my SIO colleagues. In the mid-1960s, having completed my undergraduate degree at Cornell and a master's degree in student personnel administration at Colgate University, I fulfilled a yearlong military assignment as an officer with an infantry division on the 38th parallel in Korea. I used this occasion to study some Korean language, but mostly I traveled throughout South Korea, basically a developing country at that time, and met and interacted with Koreans in a number of contexts.

I returned from Korea to assume a position at Colgate University as director of Upper Class Student Housing. While few international experiences were associated with this program, I did hire an international student from Zimbabwe as an in-residence student assistant. We became good friends, and I learned much about the culture and politics of his country. When he married his Zimbabwean sweetheart, she wore my wife's wedding gown.

After two-years in this position, I returned to graduate school in sociology at the University of Michigan. Once again, my only international experiences entailed interaction with international graduate students and travel to York University in Toronto to visit with my former faculty adviser.

MULTIPLE CAREERS

My first academic position was in the Department of Sociology at the University of Kentucky. There I joined forces with Larry Busch, a fellow sociologist, who had spent several years as a Peace Corps volunteer in Africa. We developed a highly successful collaboration studying the organization, history, politics, research practices, and application of knowledge in US agricultural colleges. This domestic research produced several research articles, book chapters, a few books, and tenure, but little international experience. It wasn't until the 1980s that we took our work overseas, focusing on agricultural research and higher education in India, Sudan, Brazil, and Mexico with support from the US Agency for International Development (USAID), the Indian Council for Agricultural Research, and the Brazilian Agricultural Research Corporation. In both India and Brazil I also led assessments of the impact of USAID's agricultural higher education institution-building efforts.

By the end of the 1980s, our work had received substantial attention and support from the National Science Foundation (NSF), US Department of Agriculture (USDA), USAID, the Ford Foundation, and the Kellogg Foundation. At that time, my department chair suggested that I might want to consider an administrative position in a college of agriculture. I was skeptical, especially since much of my work had taken a hard look at the US system of agricultural research and extension. I did, however, believe that my perspective could provide insights and be value-added in administration, so I began applying for various positions. I interviewed for an assistant research dean/assistant director of the agricultural experiment station position at both the University of Wisconsin and Penn State University. I accepted the Penn State position in 1989.

My work at Penn State involved facilitating and coordinating faculty research in the School of Forest Resources and in the Departments of Food Science and Technology, Nutrition, Agricultural Economics and Rural Sociology, and Agricultural Education in the College of Agricultural Sciences. Once again my involvement in international activities was limited to occasional interactions with visiting international delegations.

Five years later, when the college dean eliminated all four assistant dean positions, I looked for new opportunities. At that time, Cornell University was recruiting for the position of director of Cornell Cooperative Extension and associate dean in the College of Agriculture and the College of Life Sciences and Human Ecology. In 1994 I was selected for this position.

Cornell Cooperative Extension is a large, complex organization with more than 2,500 employees, a $100-million-plus annual budget, and offices in all sixty-seven counties of New York State and the five boroughs of New York City. Its primary goal is to utilize the knowledge generated by Cornell and other land grant universities in New York to enhance and strengthen the quality of life of citizens of the state. While I had never held a formal cooperative extension position, I had studied the system and believed strongly in the importance of extending the knowledge generated by universities for the benefit of society. However, the organization's strong local emphasis afforded me very little opportunity to extend my international research and education experiences. My international activities were limited to short trips to Indonesia, Panama, Honduras, and Costa Rica.

BECOMING AN SIO

In 1998, as I was leaving the extension position and planning to transition to the Department of Development Sociology, a former chancellor of UC Davis stopped by my office with a job announcement for the newly created position of vice provost of University Outreach and International Programs at UC Davis. He noted that he had tried to create this position in the early 1990s, but budget constraints stifled those efforts. At that time, UC Davis had few study abroad programs, virtually no international undergraduate students, and limited, but expanding, international research and development collaborations. However, the institution and its leaders believed that a broad range of international education, research collaboration, and academic outreach and engagement should become increasingly important components of the overall goals of the institution. Over the next several years, a new chancellor and provost were hired and task forces appointed to examine the organization and leadership needs for the campus's international activities. In 1997, the report "Toward a Global University" proposed the creation of an international vice provost with broad responsibilities. For financial and symbolic reasons, the provost decided to combine this proposed position with the existing vice provost for University Outreach, a position recently separated from the Office of Graduate Studies and currently vacant. In 1998 a national search was initiated.

Since this new position combined both the international program area and the outreach and engagement area, the former chancellor was convinced that there would be few candidates with strengths in both areas and that my background would be a good match. He was correct, and I was hired in August 1999, beginning a fifteen-year senior administrative career in international research, education, and outreach.

Location, Location, Location

When I arrived at UC Davis, I found an office comprised of a two-person staff with little international experience and housed in a temporary building on the edge of the campus. Further, multiple programs typically associated with international programs, such as study abroad and services for international students and scholars, reported to the Office of Undergraduate Studies and the Office of Student Affairs, respectively. The vice provost's office was inadequate for hosting campus colleagues, not to mention international delegations. Early in my tenure, meeting with the school and college deans to discuss their international goals and programs was at the top of my priority list. However, when, after visiting my office, one dean informed me that he would never return to such a hovel, I realized that new, strategically located quarters needed to be an equally high priority.

Over the course of my first two years, our office moved three times before I succeeded in acquiring prime, newly renovated space in the central administration building. Our new office was adjacent to the Office of Graduate Studies (approximately a quarter of all graduate students were international) and located in the same building as the offices of the chancellor, provost, Academic Senate, and senior campus leadership for research, undergraduate studies, academic personnel, student affairs, development and alumni affairs, and administration and finance. This enabled both regular formal and informal contacts and meetings with all the relevant leaders of programs related to an expanding international agenda.

At the same time, I was working to consolidate the international programs that were physically and organizationally scattered, seeking adequate space for the study abroad programs and services for international students and scholars, and exploring ways to meet the diverse international program needs of both students and faculty.

Restoring and Expanding the Agenda

After several successful years serving midcareer professionals from developing countries, UC Davis had lost its US Department of State Hubert H. Humphrey Fellowship program due to a combination of factors, including the lack of appropriate campus leadership. By identifying a new director and sending him to Washington, D.C., to meet with the national program leadership, the university was able to get this competitive program reinstated. For the last fifteen years, this has been the only Humphrey program in California.

Simultaneously, recognizing the need to enhance my office's leadership team and to build stronger connections with faculty and with the university's schools and colleges, I created two senior part-time faculty positions: associate vice provost for International Programs and associate vice provost for Outreach and Engagement. During the past fifteen years, highly accomplished full professors and former deans and department chairs from the humanities, physical sciences, environmental sciences, and medicine have occupied these positions and provided invaluable contributions to our agenda and links to a broad network of colleagues and collaborators.

It was clear from the beginning that the goals and agenda of my office had to include more than those of the important international education programs. Internationalizing the campus meant involving all components and functions of the university. Through regular meetings with the chancellor, provost, vice chancellors, vice provosts, and deans, a broad international agenda began to emerge. In the early 2000s I created the Deans and Directors International Programs Advisory Committee. This committee provided a forum for discussing various new programs and for sharing best practices and new developments both on the campus and overseas. When I invited the deans, one influential campus leader indicated he would attend the first meeting but did not expect to attend any subsequent meetings. However, because the meetings were structured to discuss substantive issues and seek their input and advice, this dean and most of the others have continued to participate in these quarterly meetings for a dozen years.

Equally important were annual meetings of me and three or four of my program leaders with selected school and college department chairs and executive councils to introduce our various educational programs and to discuss how to best serve their students, faculty, and visiting scholars. Our office also provided yearly presentations to new faculty on our programs and resources for their international educational, research, and outreach activities. Through these efforts we have helped build a strong international agenda and an important campuswide network.

Faculty Support

I also understood that faculty participation is key to successful campus internationalization. Support and service to faculty was implemented at UC Davis in a variety of ways. During the first year, I negotiated with the provost for a modest start-up program package and devoted $500,000 to a seed grant program for creative, new interdisciplinary, international, and outreach initiatives that had the potential to become self-sustaining. An important component of this program was the involvement of school and college deans and the Office of Research in the review process. After a few years, the initial funds for this program were expended, and I began to use reserves generated in part by my direct report units and from donors. Here the creation of an assistant vice provost for International Alumni and Development was critical. In recent years, lacking sufficient funds, I turned to the school and college deans and the vice chancellor of Research for matching funds. In nearly every case, the deans matched our office funds dollar for dollar for these competitively selected projects. Their support was a measure of the value of this program and the partnerships it generated. Over the dozen years of the program, numerous new international collaborations and partnerships were initiated. Moreover, the 154 faculty projects totaling in excess of $1.5 million have generated nearly $35 million in additional funds.

Our office provided additional support for the faculty international research and education efforts through a funding sources database, a funding opportunities newsletter, and several workshops each year often in conjunction with the Office of Research. These workshops have included presentations by representatives of the NSF, the Fulbright Foundation, the Japanese Society for the Promotion of Science, the Chinese Scholarship Council, Chile's National Council for Scientific and Technological Development (BECAS Chile, the Chilean Ministry of Education's scholarship agency), the Mexican Comision Nacional de Investigacion Scientifica y Technologica, the Brazilian Foundation for the Coordination for the Improvement of Higher Education Personnel (CAPES) and National Council for Scientific and Technological Development (CNPq), the German Academic Exchange Service (DAAD) and Research Foundation, and the British Research Council. To support these programs and services for faculty research, education, and professional development, early in my tenure I created a new analyst position. This position has evolved into a close partnership with the Office of Research and has resulted in many collaborative efforts.

To further involve and support faculty and students, I also turned to faculty-led study abroad programs. I inherited five summer abroad humanities and social science courses being taught in Western Europe and Japan by a few dedicated faculty. By making this a higher priority, assembling a talented staff of professionals and faculty leaders, and promoting these opportunities, today our study abroad program annually involves more than fifty faculty teaching both summer and full quarter programs on six continents, with a third of these programs in engineering and the physical and biological sciences. These programs are complemented by one of the flagship study abroad programs in the country, the University of California Education Abroad Program (UC EAP), which provides both yearlong, full immersion programs and short-term programs at some of the best universities worldwide. I have worked closely with this program and served on a university-wide international task force to review and enhance it, and so I was pleased when my former associate vice provost for International Programs was selected to lead the UC EAP.

These diverse programs have created a cadre of dedicated and committed faculty with current international experiences to share when teaching on campus. These faculty became particularly important when the campus and the Academic Senate tackled a comprehensive revamping of the general education curriculum. The possibility of adding an international component to the requirements, and a fear that this requirement would replace the current domestic diversity requirement, resulted in strong resistance to any change. With strong support from these and other interested and informed faculty, the general education requirements were revamped to include both a domestic diversity and an international component. The international component consists of courses in world cultures that provide students with a global perspective and can be satisfied through study abroad.

However, over the years I have learned that even the most successful and core programs are vulnerable and that their budgets are susceptible to significant cuts. On one occasion, a provost revoked a written budget commitment for our faculty-led quarter abroad programs. Despite the provost's recommendation to terminate this program, we continued it by pooling funds from other programs and restructuring this effort. Today this program offers ten quarter abroad programs, including cultural studies in Cuba, a pre-med curriculum in Mexico, and pharmaceutical chemistry studies in Taiwan.

Senior Leadership

Campus support for internationalization was further enhanced through an annual Chancellor's Fall Conference that focused on this topic. Each year an important topic was selected for this conference, and roughly a hundred campus leaders, including administrators, faculty, students, staff, and alumni, attended a two-day retreat to address the subject. My conversations with the conference planning staff resulted in the 2005 topic being internationalization of the campus. I cochaired the planning committee and in so doing engaged a wide range of professors and staff. This conference greatly strengthened the commitment to internationalizing the campus. It also raised numerous concerns from the supporters of domestic diversity who saw these expanding efforts as competition for limited resources. These concerns led to several productive discussions with colleagues in the international and domestic diversity communities to shape the agenda as complementary and to expand resources for both efforts. At this conference, nineteen specific recommendations emerged across six key areas: internationalizing the undergraduate experience in curriculum; internationalizing the undergraduate experiences abroad; new models of international graduate education; new models of international research collaboration; creating an international community on campus; and expanding the campus's engagement and presence abroad. These recommendations continue to be a valuable framework shaping our goals and priorities; and to ensure that they remain highly visible, a summary is posted on our office's website.

Another important effort was the building of international partnerships and the involvement of the chancellor, provost, and relevant faculty and deans in these efforts. Beginning in 2000 with a trip to China, my office coordinated numerous international trips. I accompanied nearly all of the delegations on trips to Argentina, Australia, Brazil, Chile, China, Egypt, England, Germany, India, Iran, Japan, Korea, Malaysia, Mexico, New Zealand, Philippines, Singapore, Spain, Taiwan, and the United Arab Emirates. These trips involved visits to universities, government agencies, alumni gatherings, and, when possible, UC Davis students studying abroad. Our close working relationship with consulate offices in San Francisco, Sacramento, and Washington, D.C., was often instrumental in successful planning and coordination of these trips. The delegations usually included appropriate key faculty and deans for each country. Often our international hosts were more interested in meeting and interacting with the UC Davis distinguished faculty than with the chancellor. To further facilitate and strengthen achievement of the various goals of these trips, I prepared a one page guideline entitled "UC Davis Senior Leadership Strategic International Meetings and Travel." Among the numerous advantages, such international travel allowed us to strengthen relations with our partners and to discuss several issues and opportunities with campus leadership. It even afforded me the chance to introduce the chancellor and provost to Brazil, Chile, and China.

LEARNING FROM OTHERS

The knowledge and shared experiences gained from professional associations and organizations have been equally valuable parts of the internationalization efforts I've been involved in. Early on I realized that I needed help from colleagues in California, elsewhere in the United States, and abroad. To foster interactions with my colleagues in the University of California system, I founded the UC Senior International Leaders Council of Deans, Directors and Vice Provosts. This group meets twice annually on a UC campus, learns about the specific programs of the host campus, and shares best practices. Unfortunately, the UC system has few international administrators at the senior level and in recent years has even eliminated several positions of this type. This prompted me to turn my attention to national organizations. In the Association of International Education Administrators (AIEA), I found kindred spirits, excellent colleagues, and substantive annual meetings, all of which have been invaluable to me in my work. The Association of Public and Land Grant Universities, the Institute for International Education, and the American Council on Education have also been important sources of useful information and advice. At the international level, the Association of Pacific Rim Universities (APRU) has enabled me to meet and learn from the rectors, presidents, chancellors, and my fellow SIOs from the forty-five leading research universities in Asia, Oceania, and North and South America. As a consequence of my involvement with the APRU presidents and SIOs, I spent 2015 on sabbatical in Australia at Australian National University, the University of Melbourne and the University of New South Wales. Complementing these important sources of advice and counsel have been two Fulbright programs for administrators in Brazil and Japan and a similar program by the German Academic Exchange Service.

COMMUNICATING

Another early effort in my tenure as SIO was centered around communication—providing a platform for sharing information and knowledge on new international education, research, and outreach initiatives and issues; promoting and publicizing the excellent campuswide programs; and building the visibility of the international efforts on and off the UC Davis campus. Although the provost cautioned against a newsletter because of the time and resources it required, I launched *Internationally Engaged* in the fall 2000, to be published twice a year. The lead and feature article in each issue allowed me to address a number of key issues, including: the need to keep our doors and our minds open in the wake of 9/11; the role of international students and scholars in enriching our campus; the importance of academic openness for our national security; the essential aspects of internationalizing the university to meet its vision of excellence and as a gateway to peace; the value of building and rebuilding bridges to the Middle East and Latin America; the importance of expanding academic opportunities while managing risk; and the need for promoting study abroad as academically core, professionally essential, and increasingly affordable. In each issue, discussion of these topics was complemented by ten to twenty articles addressing creative international programs in all of the schools and colleges. This helped strengthen our collaborations across the entire campus.

The web and other social media have also become increasingly important in publicizing key events, such as the study abroad fairs, the International Education Week schedule, talks, demonstrations, guest speakers (such as Shirin Ebadi, the Iranian Nobel Prize recipient, and Allan E. Goodman, president of Institute for International Education), and other activities. Effective and frequent communication has only increased in importance over the last decade.

CHANGING LEADERSHIP

In a decade of building the international programs, I had worked with one chancellor and four different provosts. In 2009 a new UC Davis chancellor was named. Each change brings new challenges and opportunities. Although the new chancellor is international herself, having been raised and educated in Greece before coming to the US for graduate studies, she had not previously worked in the area of international programs. The early meetings and briefings I had with her were important, as was my active participation when she initiated a strategic planning process. The outcome of that process was a vision document identifying six key goals that serve as the framework for campus efforts. Although there was some resistance to emphasizing international research and education, one of the six goals is "Embrace Global Issues," and several of the other goals have strong statements supporting internationalization.

Since the chancellor's arrival, and on the hiring of a new provost, UC Davis's internationalization efforts have increased and flourished. I have continued to assist in international travel with strategic efforts in Europe, South America, and Asia. We negotiated key agreements to support research, education, and student exchanges with Brazil's CAPES and CNPq and with BECAS Chile with critical faculty leadership. Several other important and creative institutional agreements in China with the Chinese Scholarship Council, Hanban (Confucius Institute), and Chinese universities have been jointly led by my director of Asian Programs and me. The Asian Programs director position was made possible through the university's Partners Opportunity Program, which fully supported for three years the spouse of a medical school new faculty hire. In all these instances, a well-informed, native-speaking colleague with country experience was essential. Equally important were my face-to-face meetings with senior leadership in the education and science ministries in Brazil, Chile, and China.

FUND-RAISING

With declining state budget support for higher education, new funding models have been introduced. In California, increasingly our international programs and services are funded with fees and substantial tuition charges. In the last ten years, another important funding source has been gifts from both alumni and friends. To promote this effort, I hired an assistant vice provost for International Alumni and Development, an individual who formerly served as the executive director of Alumni Affairs. A key element in our initial fund-raising effort was the formation of an International Programs Executive Development Council comprised of interested and wealthy regional and international leaders. This group was charged with making a substantial gift and identifying other potential donors. As one might imagine, this effort met with mixed success. I learned quickly that working with this diverse group involved significant management costs, and that fund-raising is a long, arduous endeavor, particularly at a public university that has only just recently launched its first $1 billion initiative. Although we have had limited success, we have built the foundation for several seven-figure donations for four key initiatives: study abroad scholarships, faculty seed grant funds, support for international students and scholars, and a new international center building.

THE CONFUCIUS INSTITUTE

One of my most controversial and difficult program efforts was the creation of a Confucius Institute at UC Davis. The Chinese government launched this program about ten years ago in partnership with Chinese universities and universities around the world with the goal of introducing Chinese language and culture to the partner campuses and surrounding communities. This program now includes approximately 450 institutes worldwide, with more than a hundred of them in the United States. While some partnerships have proven highly successful, the potential for Chinese government censorship and other issues has led to various conflicts and even termination of other partnerships.

With little campus interest and some resistance from the Department of East Asian Language and Culture, I did not initially pursue the possibility of hosting a Confucius Institute at UC Davis. This changed in 2010 when two food experts with strong connections in China, a senior UC Davis professor in food science and a UC Davis alumnus who was a distinguished chef and television celebrity, proposed a Confucius Institute dedicated to Chinese food and beverage culture. Since both UC Davis and our Chinese partner university are regarded as leaders in the fields of food science and viticulture and enology, this proposal had real potential.

I worked with three departments across two colleges and with Jiangnan University to address a number of logistical, budgetary, staffing, and organizational issues, and I traveled to China to present our proposal to the Secretary General of the Confucius Institutes. After two years of planning, we held a highly visible and successful opening with considerable local, national, and international press coverage.

The complexity of this partnership across two universities and several departments and with the Chinese government required substantial time and effort, as well as two more trips to China for face-to-face meetings. Despite the challenges, potential controversy, and extensive efforts on my part, I believe that UC Davis now has a strong foundation for a unique and productive Confucius Institute.

CREATING CENTERS

The nature and opportunities for internationalization have greatly expanded and diversified at UC Davis in recent years. Faculty and deans are bringing new proposals for a variety of programs and for a physical presence overseas on a regular basis. After our office prepared a white paper on the topic of UC Davis Global Centers in 2013, I worked with a new Provost's Global Strategies Workgroup to review the goals and purposes of such physical locations, the issues and challenges, the resources needed, and the tactical locations to consider.

At the same time, the growing need for a substantial physical presence on campus for the various international programs and activities has culminated in the identification of a central location for an International Complex. Ground breaking for the first phase of this complex, an International Center, occurred in the fall of 2014, with completion scheduled for 2016. This 40,000-square-foot, three-story building will provide offices and meeting rooms for the Services for International Students and Scholars, the Education Abroad Center, the Center for International Education of UC Davis Extension programs, and the English as a Second Language program. This effort began over ten years ago, but a lack of funds stalled the plans for several years. Fortunately, after many years of discussions regarding needs, functions, design and location, and the development of a funding partnership with UC Davis Extension, our recommendations became a reality.

OBSERVATIONS AND REFLECTIONS

While reflecting on my expanding international agenda of the past fifteen years, several lessons for successfully internationalizing the campus have emerged.

- Secure full support of the top leadership (chancellor/president, provost) and that your senior leadership team includes a vice provost/vice president devoted to international programs who serves on the chancellor's cabinet.

- Partner with the deans and the department chairs and enhance and maintain regular communication and collaboration.
- Involve all levels of the university in the internationalization efforts, encouraging particular engagement of the faculty and the Faculty Senate.
- Develop close relationships between the vice provost and the staff for international programs and with all the senior academic leadership (research, undergraduate, graduate, academic personnel, and continuing education.
- Work closely with several of the nonacademic senior leaders, particularly those in finance and planning, student affairs, university counsel, alumni affairs, and development, to further the internationalization goals.
- Locate the international office in close proximity to the other relevant senior academic and administrative offices. There is no substitute for location.
- Seek advice and counsel from colleagues across the country and overseas in similar higher education positions and participate in appropriate professional development opportunities (e.g., Fulbright program, German DAAD, AIEA Presidential Fellows).
- Hire talented, motivated, and compatible people at all levels of the organization and give them the resources and latitude to do good work.
- Be flexible. The best-laid plans of mice and men often go astray. This is particularly the case when developing new campus programs and initiatives and when working internationally. Competition for resources, visa and passport issues, changing government regulations and policies, travel advisories, political unrest, cultural misunderstandings, and numerous other challenges may significantly affect plans for international research, education, and outreach.
- Don't take yourself too seriously. Laugh a lot and maintain a good sense of humor.
- Be realistic—but don't stop dreaming. It is important to recognize what is possible under the current conditions and work effectively and strategically to implement programs. However, it is equally important to be a visionary. After all, "the future belongs to those who believe in the beauty of their dreams and strive to realize them."[1]

CHAPTER TWELVE

Whole Person Education in a Whole World Context

International Education and the Liberal Arts

Joseph L. Brockington

I WAS A FIRST-QUARTER, first-year student at what was then Grand Valley State College when I enrolled in a general education course called Liberal Learning, or something of the like. Among the texts for the course were C. P. Snow's *The Two Cultures and a Second Look*, Plato's *The Republic*, and, what has become my favorite and oft-cited touchstone, Mark van Doren's *Liberal Education*. Grand Valley State was, in the fall of 1968, very much a liberal arts college, and this course was a delightful introduction to what would become my philosophy of education and the mission of my current institution, Kalamazoo College.

Located in southwest Michigan, Kalamazoo College was founded in 1833 and is among the hundred oldest institutions of higher education in the United States. Today K, as it's known, has an enrollment of some 1,450 degree-seeking undergraduate students from 40 states and 34 countries, including 22 percent students of color.[1]

The college is widely known for the strength of its academic programs and innovative approaches to experiential and international education. Emerging fifty years ago, the nationally recognized K-Plan combines rigorous on-campus liberal arts coursework with off-campus experiential components in which a substantial proportion of students participate. Every student is required to complete a Senior Individualized Project (SIP), and, historically, over 80 percent of graduates (including 80 percent of science majors) study abroad in the sophomore or junior years for three, six, or nine months. Most Kalamazoo students (about 75 percent) also engage in service learning projects in the local community, and over half of all graduates report having completed at least one career internship.[2] The college has long been passionately liberal arts in nature. Applied courses are an anathema. Indeed, it was fully thirty years after my arrival that the curriculum was expanded enough to allow for the inclusion of a business major.

Mark van Doren describes *Liberal Education* as a peculiar form of education that "makes the person competent, not merely to know or do, but also, and indeed chiefly, to be," a "whole person" education.[3] Marshall Gregory expands on the notion of *being* as the goal of liberal learning as "the last and best—but least understood and least appreciated—mechanism for achieving the fullest development of human potential."[4] The goal of liberal education, he writes, is more moral than intellectual. "It focuses on the development of the individual as moral agents, and it teaches students to reflect both analytically and evaluatively on the fact that the choices we make turn us into the persons we become."

The Kalamazoo Plan, or K-Plan, was discussed and then adopted by the faculty and senior administration during the academic years 1960–1961 and 1961–1962. In an article entitled "Betting the Store" that appeared in the Kalamazoo College alumni magazine *Lux Esto* in 1989, some twenty-five years after the adoption of the K-Plan, Dean Larry Barrett explained that by 1960 the college president, the board of trustees, the faculty, and he had grown increasingly dissatisfied with the very traditional approach the college had taken in delivering a liberal education.[5] By moving from semesters to quarters and by having students use their sophomore and junior summer quarters for on-campus instruction, the Kalamazoo Plan could deliver a liberal arts education that afforded all students a program of intensive on-campus academics, a quarter spent on career service (later career and professional development), one or two quarters of study abroad, and a SIP. A modest endowment for study abroad made it possible that the programs would cost students no more than the price of tuition, room, and board on campus, transportation included. (The college currently continues this tradition, with the exception that transportation is no longer included in the comprehensive fee.)

By leaving space for study abroad in the curricular calendars of each major, the architects of the K-Plan extended the ability to study abroad to every student of every major to go abroad and still graduate in four years. Surveys of alumni have shown that over the past fifty-plus years, graduates have gone on to earn medical and other professional degrees as well as PhDs at a rate that has gained national attention. Kalamazoo College is ranked in the top twenty of all institutions for graduates earning PhDs in chemistry (9th), the life sciences (7th), foreign languages (6th), the physical sciences (17th), economics (18th), English and literature (16th), and psychology (20th).[6] Moreover, since 1962, some 80–85 percent of Kalamazoo graduates have studied abroad, most of them for twenty to twenty-two weeks. This number has greatly influenced the strategic vision of international education at the college.

FROM TEACHER TO SIO

I arrived at Kalamazoo College in the fall of 1979 with a half-finished dissertation to begin a one-year, nonrenewable appointment as lecturer in the Department of German Language and Literature. With time, I completed the dissertation (German expressionist prose), taught courses, and earned tenure, along with getting involved in the college's General Education Program, the Title VI National Resource Center in European Studies (1990–2003), and the vibrant intellectual life at K.

My move from faculty to administration was prompted by the resignation of the Foreign Study Office's long-time director, Joe K. Fugate. Effective October 1992, the office's associate director was appointed director. I had just returned from a wonderful sabbatical year with my family at the University of Hamburg, along with boxes of teaching materials and a mostly-roughed-out book on the *Junge Generation* (emerging German writers who published from war's end in 1945 to the currency reform of 1948). In February 1992 the provost came into my office and offered me the position of associate director in the Foreign Study Office. I had twenty-four hours to make up my mind, and I was not to tell anyone.

Having for the last year luxuriated in German libraries and literary archives and taught a graduate-level seminar on my book topic, I cringed before an imagined future of teaching undergraduate German language classes for the rest of my natural life. I took the job. I figured I could spend four years in the Foreign Study Office and then return to teaching. When, four years later, the president of the college left, and then the provost and the Foreign Study director, it appeared that if Kalamazoo College were to continue to offer study abroad programs and enroll international students, I was the only one left.

RETROSPECTIVE: THE LIBERAL ARTS

In the decade following 1996, as I moved from acting director of the Center for International Programs (CIP, the new designation for the Foreign Study Office) to director to associate provost for International Programs, I took the opportunity to introduce my faculty and staff colleagues to the concepts that underlie comprehensive internationalization: transnational competence, international competence, and global competence.

As the new millennium approached and the national and international conversation moved from international and transnational competence, to global competence and global citizenship, to comprehensive internationalization (also known as internationalization at home), the CIP sought to facilitate a corresponding change in how the college defined *international* and *internationalization*. Because so many Kalamazoo students had participated in study abroad for so long, the college was used to counting these sojourners (and especially noting the participation rate of graduates in study abroad) and then declaring itself "internationalized." For me, Jane Knight's definition of internationalization has been a guiding principle: internationalization of higher education is the "process of integrating an international/intercultural dimension into the teaching, research, and service function of the institution."[7]

One of the chief difficulties I faced in my early years of leadership in the CIP was that my position was really that of study abroad director. Easily 85 percent of my efforts and those of the CIP staff concerned sending Kalamazoo students abroad, 10 percent were related to international students enrolled at the college, and the remainder was devoted to the standard committee work that is the fabric of college administration. This presented me with a problem: I did not want to be a study abroad director, even if that was the only job at hand. It is perhaps because of my training in literature or my fifteen years of teaching that I wanted more for myself, my students, and my institution than my job description provided. So I simply did more. As long as the CIP provided meaningful study abroad experiences for our students, I could do as much "more" as I cared to.

INTERNATIONALIZING STUDY ABROAD AT K

The roles of a senior international officer in US colleges or universities include, among many others, that of diplomat, entrepreneur, educator, leader, and manager—managing up but leading across. Coming into international education administration as a tenured faculty member at the same institution, I was well aware of the suspicion and mistrust that can divide the two groups. Thus, when entrusted with the leadership of the Center for International Programs, I wanted to institute constructive conversation about international education and internationalization at the turn of the new century.

In the late 1990s the International Programs Committee (IPC) was the obvious place to begin the conversation. In addition to reviewing study abroad programs and study abroad learning outcomes, the IPC also reviewed faculty applications for Faculty Study Abroad Grants (FSAG). Early on as an SIO, I allocated $10,000–$15,000 a year from the International Programs budget for FSAGs. Later the budget allocation was replaced by the endowed Isabel Beeler Fund, which funded not only faculty but also student international travel outside of study abroad programs (particularly during the summer for research connected to the Senior Individualized Project).

One of the first collegewide projects that I pursued as SIO was to invite the staff from our study abroad partners and programs to campus for a week-long Resident Director's Conference in July 2000. (Resident directors are usually faculty members at the host institutions where Kalamazoo students do their study abroad.) Since then, the conference has been held on a biannual basis. It not only allows the CIP to update the resident directors about developments in US higher education and on campus, but it also allows the directors to connect with each other and members of the faculty. Over the years, this conference has become both an anticipated element of professional development for the overseas program directors as well as a sought-after opportunity for Kalamazoo College faculty to reconnect with professional collaborations and friendships they developed during program site visits.

Around 2000, the college received a significant grant from the Freeman Foundation to establish an Asian studies department as well as grants from the Mellon Foundation and McGregor Fund to create a pre– and post–study abroad course that we called the Kalamazoo Project in Intercultural Communication (KPIC) Thus, it was logical that in 2002 I was asked by the provost to convene an International Council of the various area studies coordinators, the chair of the IPC, the directors of the International and Area Studies major and KPIC to serve as think tank to consider opportunities for constructive interchange and mutual benefit with regard to three basic questions:

- Where are we with regard to internationalization on and off campus?
- Where do we want to be within three to five years?
- How are we going to get there?

About the same time as I assumed the directorship of the CIP, I began to write an extended essay, more of a personal journal, really (it has never been published), that looked at the place of international education within the liberal arts at the college (parts of which form this chapter). Realizing the imperative of "managing up" and that the unsaid dictum of my job was to make my boss look good, I took great care to keep my provost informed about what I was reading as part of my research with regard to international and transnational competence, internationalization, and globalization. The college and I were fortunate in that the provost at the time, Gregory Mahler, was a history professor with area studies expertise in the Middle East and Canada and a long association with the US Information Agency. In addition, the president of the college, Jimmy Jones, was a committed internationalist. It was, therefore, a comparatively easy task to keep both of these senior administrators informed on developments in international education and to enlist their support for various international projects.

I began to incorporate elements of comprehensive internationalization into presentations I made on campus and at national conferences and also into the design and delivery of the study abroad programs offered at K. In so doing, in addition to earning disciplinary credit for the courses in which students were enrolled abroad, certain programs would also offer experiences and learning opportunities that went beyond the classroom. Since its inception in 1962, study abroad under the K-Plan was not typically directly related to the majors offered. Kalamazoo students, provided they met the language and academic eligibility requirements, could study abroad wherever they chose regardless of major. Pre-meds were just as likely to study in Kenya or Greece as they were to go to Aberdeen, where they could take STEM courses. Spanish majors might study in a Spanish-speaking country or head to Japan. (Indeed, this was cause for frustration when it came to enrollment projections for the programs overseas.)

Because all K students seemed to study abroad everywhere without departmental or program "ownership" of programs, the CIP could begin introducing certain nonmajor foci into the students' experiences abroad. With the collaboration of the college's resident directors abroad (typically host university professors) and on-campus faculty, and recognizing that more than half of the students studied on Kalamazoo-sponsored/-managed programs, we started adding, for example, sustainability instruction (in the form of a course or a project with local students) into programs in Senegal and Costa Rica or an environment course in Ecuador and Thailand. These additions went beyond the typically required "culture" courses that have long been a feature of programs in Europe. Involving both the on-campus faculty and the resident directors abroad in the development of these competency experiences for the students has led to empowerment of both sides when it comes to setting student learning outcomes for their programs abroad.

A further development in the study abroad program along these lines was the Integrative Cultural Project (ICRP) begun in 1993–1994. As described on the CIP website, the ICRP is "a component of the academic program of selected Kalamazoo-sponsored study abroad programs. The primary goal of the ICRP was the integration of students into local cultures, and the development of an ability to appreciate the cultural values around which local people organize their daily tasks."

THE ACE INTERNATIONALIZATION LABORATORY

In the late 1990s and early 2000s, the American Council on Education's (ACE) International Initiatives office undertook a number of efforts in support of colleges and universities seeking more in the way of "international" than what was typically subsumed under "study abroad." The same transition that placed me in the leadership of the college's international office also brought in new senior leadership at K that was very much supportive of the programs and activities of "One DuPont Circle," as President James F. Jones Jr. was fond of calling ACE.

Kalamazoo College's participation in the inaugural ACE Internationalization Laboratory began with an application in 2000 to the ACE Promising Practices competition. That program provided support for "comprehensive campus internationalization." Although the college was not successful in this competition, ACE found itself so overwhelmed with applications that it decided to form the Internationalization Collaborative as a way to bring together campuses of all sizes interested in discussing and sharing ideas and best practices regarding internationalization. (The Internationalization Collaborative is now over ten years old and meets prior to the AIEA annual meeting.) As a result of participation in the early days of the Collaborative, the college was invited to participate in the first cohort of the Internationalization Laboratory.

The ACE Internationalization Laboratory is a fee-based service that "provides institutions with customized guidance and insight as they review their internationalization goals and develop strategic [internationalization] plans."[8] Thanks to the Isabel Beeler Fund, the CIP possessed sufficient unrestricted endowed funds to pay the fee, bring ACE consultants to campus, and provide support for a faculty-staff team to engage in the required Laboratory and Collaborative meetings over the next eighteen months.

The decision that Kalamazoo College should join the ACE International Laboratory was made jointly by Provost Gregory Mahler and me. As Mahler's charge to the review committee indicates, one driving factor was the need to take stock of where the college was after forty years of the K-Plan and to plan for the future. Mahler stated to me on once that "over the past forty-plus years of the K Plan, Kalamazoo College has been a leader in study abroad and has worked hard to add an international and intercultural dimension to our undergraduate education. It's time to take stock. Where are we, where to do we want to go from here in terms of international/intercultural education, and how are we going to get there?"

We used a recent ACE publication, *Internationalizing the Campus: A User's Guide,* as a guiding text for the 2004 review.[9] The process was to be led by a campus leadership team (CLT) made up of administrators, staff, and faculty. (Student input was obtained on an ad hoc basis. In retrospect, I would include students on the team in a full contributing capacity from the outset.) ACE strongly discouraged the SIO from chairing the committee, and so when the provost appointed the group, he appointed a professor of anthropology to cochair the committee with me. The CLT met weekly for two hours, generally over a catered supper.

There was agreement in CLT that the college needed to more clearly define and refine the learning outcomes for the undergraduate program in general and the international portion in particular. Moreover, as the wave of campus internationalization swept US (and international) higher education, it was clear that K would have to reassess itself, its faculty, its curriculum, its student learning goals—indeed, the entire undergraduate experience with regard to both our own definitions of *internationalization* as well as an emerging national consensus on the use and meaning of the term. In the decade that followed, and especially under the leadership of President Eileen B. Wilson-Oyelaran and Provost Michael McDonald, elements of the Internationalization Action Plan that came out of the K Internationalization Laboratory were incorporated first into recommendations for a faculty committee that considered the college's distinctiveness (2007) then into a new strategic plan (2007), and finally into a completely new overhaul of the curriculum, including a bold change in graduation requirements (2009).

LESSONS LEARNED AS TEACHER AND SIO

Now, after almost twenty years as the SIO at Kalamazoo, I continue to fall back on Jane Knight's definition of internationalization as a baseline for the college's strategic vision of international education and internationalization. Through our curricular changes, we have infused the teaching function of the college with international and intercultural perspectives. Likewise, the service functions (both in terms of faculty service to the institution and the institution's service to the local and larger community) have been largely shaped by international and intercultural perspectives. These include, among many others, a curriculum reform in which what is often known as "general education" requirements have been largely eliminated, leaving required the major coursework, foreign language proficiency, three "shared passages" seminars (with a strong focus on international and intercultural issues and including a senior capstone seminar), the Senior Individualized Project, and physical education. New discussions and restatements of the learning outcomes of the college reflect those formulated by the ACE Internationalization Laboratory team, as have new programs adopted by the college, such as the Arcus Center for Social Justice Leadership and the new major in Critical Ethnic Studies. Many of these programs and changes have included money to assist instructors with international travel to develop or revise courses.

In the past several years it has become clear to me, as both a long-time faculty member and the SIO, that internationalization at Kalamazoo College has moved beyond being an end in and of itself to become a means to the various teaching, research, and service goals of the college.[10]

Among the many lessons I've learned over the past twenty-five years, several stand out.

First is a need to recognize and respect institutional traditions, particularly when these involve characterizations of the nature of the institution. In the case of internationalization at Kalamazoo College, I learned this lesson during the effort to move the international characterization of the college from study abroad outputs (expressed in study abroad participation rates) to international education learning outcomes. For more than fifty years the college has based its international reputation on study abroad participation, thus it took several years before people on campus could speak about the international and internationalization in other than numerical terms, and this effort is still not complete.

Second, implementing change within the college is as much about process as product. Like the discussions that underlay the development of the Kalamazoo Plan in the early 1960s, the college's participation in the ACE Internationalization Laboratory was as much about process as product. As Larry Barrett noted with regard to the development of the Kalamazoo Plan,

"Success, I had observed, came less out of what we had planned to do than out of how we had gone about planning it. Our planning, when it worked, had been a growing toward something, an initiation into increasing involvement, a ritual of commitment."[11] As the ACE Laboratory C LT began working its way through *Internationalizing the Campus,* it spent considerable time considering how transformational "deep change" with regard to internationalization could be achieved at K.[12]

Third, there is a need to develop, write down and share (especially with new faculty and administrators to) the institution's story, its history. The CLT quickly came to this conclusion, particularly as we looked at the differing concepts of internationalization from both the ACE and campus viewpoints. In considering the reticence of the college community to let go of study abroad participation as the only measure of internationalization at Kalamazoo, we noted that most of the originators of the K-Plan and other long-time faculty had retired and that we, now the opinion leaders on campus, had not done a particularly good job of introducing new faculty members to the history and traditions of the college. This recognition led the CLT to produce a brief history of Kalamazoo College and a larger work that was written by an alum and former trustee. We also took every subsequent opportunity to (re)define internationalization in terms of strategic vision and not participation numbers.

As the US accrediting agencies have become more insistent that colleges and universities are able to support their assertions about the effectiveness of their educational programs, greater emphasis has been placed on the development of assessment programs and the clear articulation of learning goals. For international educators, this change in the way assessment is conceived has meant a shift away from counting inputs or outputs from particular programs toward measuring progress (or non-progress) in achieving certain student learning goals.

Fourth, gaining the support of all stakeholders at all levels is critical to effecting the kind of deep institutional change that Green and Olsen describe and that will support comprehensive internationalization. The results of what can happen when there is not widespread support became evident only weeks after the CLT began its work. In November 2003, it adopted the following statement:

The goal of comprehensive, transformational internationalization at Kalamazoo College is to place international education at the center of the Kalamazoo College experience. This means that the development of knowledge about international and global dynamics as well as the intercultural skills and attitudes necessary for engaged and responsible citizenship in today's world will be incorporated into all aspects of our curriculum and experiential education programs. This international/intercultural focus will also be clearly evident in our residential life, in our faculty development and reward structures, in our admissions strategies, and in our relationships with alumni, parents and friends of the College.

The provost at the time, who was a member of the CLT, took this statement to the next meeting of the president's staff—where it was roundly criticized. The general consensus of the various members of the president's staff was, "Who are these people to tell us what to do?" While many on the president's staff may have agreed in general with the goals stated, they did not at all agree with the process employed.

At this point the CLT regrouped and began employing a methodology that some team members had learned while working on another ACE project, namely soliciting from individual faculty and administrators as well as from academic and administrative departments answers to two basic questions: "What would a truly internationalized Kalamazoo College campus look like?" and "What would a truly internationalized Kalamazoo College graduate look like?" The answers were collected, sorted, and refined and then sent back out to faculty, administrators, and departments for comment and further refining. After two or three rounds of this, the resulting descriptors (learning outcomes) of an internationalized Kalamazoo College graduate and of an internationalized Kalamazoo College campus were firmly in hand.

As a result of this iterative activity, we learned the value of "name it and claim it." There were (and are) lots of international and internationalizing activities happening on campus. However, until they were collected and identified, there was no widespread recognition of how internationalized the college was.

Using Knight's definition of internationalization, the CLT began looking at the various activities on campus (ranging from athletics to zoology) to see what relationship could be established between the activity and our definition, or what modifications would have to be made to the activity to establish a closer relationship to the definition. One example was the cafeteria. It had the capacity to take individual recipes from international students and adapt them to serve all of the students. Likewise, it should not be that difficult to accommodate demands for Halal meals since vegan options were already standard. We had known from decades of research with our alumni and students that their time at the college "transformed" them (their word). By naming and claiming that transformation as related to international outcomes, we could provide more learning experiences along the same lines.

FINAL THOUGHTS

The story of the comprehensive internationalization of Kalamazoo College during my tenure first as teaching faculty and then as SIO is really the story of the changing nature and definition of internationalization in the United States and around the world. Like so many postsecondary institutions, K has gone from counting inputs and outputs (such as incoming international students, outbound study abroad students, faculty exchange, etc.) to assessing progress in meeting international learning outcomes—from "how many" to "how much." We have seen that participation in study abroad programs is inversely proportional to the racial, ethnic, and economic diversity of the student body, as well as to the number of international and first-generation students enrolled. Also, study abroad participation, which hovered around 85 percent from the early 1960s to about 75 percent in 2012–2013, is also inversely proportional to the college's efforts in comprehensive internationalization, including the Shared Passages seminar series, the incorporation of international learning goals in the faculty's endorsed list of learning outcomes for the college, and, finally, the reflection of internationalization in the college's current strategic plan. Thus, I believe that the more colleges and universities in general, and K in particular, engage in comprehensive internationalization, the less students, families, faculty, staff, and senior administration will rely on the movement of individuals across international borders to achieve international learning outcomes.

Although the internationalization of Kalamazoo College began in earnest five decades ago with the unveiling of the K-Plan and the phenomenal increase in study abroad participation, it is only within the last fifteen years that we have begun to measure international learning outcomes. Both processes have been reflected in the current and former strategic planning and curriculum designs and have been driven by the faculty, supported and funded by senior administration and the board of trustees, and embraced by students and their parents. Known as an "international college" since the inception of the K-Plan, Kalamazoo is currently incorporating international and intercultural elements in the curriculum, the research agendas of faculty, civic engagement of students and faculty, and, of course, study abroad. *This* would seem to meet Knight's definition of internationalization as the "process of integrating an international/intercultural dimension into the teaching, research, and service function of the institution."[13] For a retread German teacher who wanted to be more than just a director of study abroad, that's not a bad career outcome.

The Challenge of Internationalization

Gilbert W. Merkx and Riall W. Nolan

THIS IS A BOOK written *by* senior international officers, but not just for them. It was undertaken with the conviction that such accounts will illuminate what SIOs actually do, what challenges they face, and what their role is as change agents. The larger purpose of this publication is to shed light on the challenge of internationalizing America's colleges and universities. Therefore, it will be of interest not only to SIOs but to all those concerned with the current state and future of higher education in the United States. We hope, in particular, that presidents and chief academic officers will learn more about the challenges of internationalizing their institutions by reading these narratives.

The accounts collected here speak to us at two rather different levels. One level informs our deeper understanding of what it is actually like to do the job. Anyone either intending to become a SIO or intending to appoint one in the near future will learn a great deal about what constrains and enables the work of a senior international officer. Such an understanding can have real implications for institutional change.

At the other level, these essays reveal problems and contradictions in US higher education that relate to more than just internationalization. They touch on our institutional ability to learn and to adapt in response to changing conditions in the world beyond the campus. And here, we feel, there is some cause for alarm. In this final chapter, therefore, we focus on these two aspects of internationalization: the professional lives of those who are leading the effort and the broader question of the impact that their work has had, and can have, on their institutions as a whole.

THE SIO AS PROFESSIONAL

We have seen that SIOs come into the profession from a variety of directions and disciplines. There seems to be no specific form or period of training or apprenticeship for this role, and, indeed, several of our authors appear to have been pushed into it initially by chance and circumstances. Once in place, SIOs seem to learn mainly by doing, and here, it would appear, two factors are determinative: the quality of their relationship with faculty and the presence of a supportive senior leader at the dean, provost, or president level. Absent one or the other, SIOs do not, as a rule, thrive, and several accounts here reflect what happens when one of these key elements—usually the supportive senior leader—disappears.

SIOs, unlike most faculty, are highly dependent on senior institutional leaders for their mandate, their budgets in most cases, and their legitimacy. At the same time, they cannot operate effectively without the support of key members of the faculty, who, when push comes to shove, can ignore senior leadership and its wishes. It is not by chance that the most successful SIOs tend to be those individuals who have solid academic credentials (almost always a PhD) and some record of scholarship.

Many of the qualities that make one an accepted member of the faculty, however, do not necessarily transfer to an administrative job. And so for most new SIOs there is a rather steep learning curve, one which, if they are not careful, may take them further away from their faculty colleagues.

Most SIOS seem to be very aware of the need to steer a careful course here, but administrative arrangements often get in their way. As a generalization, it seems safe to say that SIO appointments that recognize the essentially academic nature of the job will be more supportive than placements within, say, the student affairs unit or the research enterprise. Although we have successful SIOs who operate from these positions, it seems to be harder to promote internationalization effectively from these platforms.

Reporting to the academic affairs side of the university (to the provost in most cases) seems to work well, and an appointment that also includes membership in an academic department allows the SIO a high degree of involvement with colleagues. Positions that report directly to the president, however, run the risk of putting too much distance between the SIO and the faculty while at the same time adding demands that may have little to do with the business of internationalization at the faculty and curricular levels.

As administrators, SIOs serve at the pleasure of the president or provost of the institution. Therefore, unless they also have a tenured appointment within a department, they are extremely vulnerable to changes at the top. Even with such an appointment, basic aspects of an SIO's job—title, breadth of control, budget, and reporting lines—may change with the stroke of a pen. Few SIOs negotiate rights of retreat as a condition of their employment.

Almost by definition, an SIO is usually the only person in charge of international programs on a campus. Although several of our contributors describe moving from the position of director to dean and then to vice president or vice provost, there is not very much room for advancement on most campuses. An upwardly ambitious SIO must therefore contemplate a change of institution in order to substantially change work conditions.

Although several of our contributors describe a career moving from one institution to another, many of them stayed in one place for a considerable amount of time. More typical is the situation in which the SIO remains in place and the upper administration changes. SIOs describe coming to terms with new bosses, new initiatives, and new management styles. In most cases, the frequency with which presidents and provosts change will have negative effects on the longevity of some, if not all, of the internationalization effort, unless care has been taken to build sustainability into financial and programming arrangements.

When institutions measure internationalization, they all tend to measure somewhat different things. Even simple measures, such as the number of students going on study abroad, can be counted quite differently. Numbers alone, of course, say very little about the qualitative changes that may occur as a result of international education programs. And so, in the absence of a clear set of agreed-on metrics to measure change, debate continues as to the real "value" of international education. In part, this is because such changes are notoriously hard to measure. It is also because we are simply not choosing to do so.

Because internationalization is difficult to measure, it is hard to know when one "has arrived." How much internationalization, and of what kind, is "enough," and how will we know? Several of our SIO authors describe a kind of plateau effect, where they felt they had reached a point of diminishing returns at their institution. In most cases, this signals a search for a new position and new challenges. It is unlikely that these SIOs concluded that more could not be done; rather, it appears that the institution's leadership had either changed or lost interest.

These broad patterns appear to have some important implications for SIOs, those seeking to become SIOs, and the national and international organizations to which they belong. First and perhaps foremost, SIOs thrive (or fail to thrive) within a very specific institutional context, or organizational culture, and this culture will vary considerably from one university setting to the next. It is relatively easy to describe, and to understand, why and how institutions and their SIOs fail. It is much more difficult to understand exactly how they achieve success—and, indeed, what success actually means—without detailed knowledge of the specific case at hand. SIOs, whatever their other attributes, must possess a high degree of awareness, nimbleness, and flexibility if they expect to thrive and survive.

Second, no matter how skilled the SIO may be, larger forces are always at work, and in many cases these are determinant. SIOs share this feature of their jobs with other senior administrators—presidents and provosts come to mind—whose best efforts are often undone by events having little, if anything, to do with their job performance. It is equally true, however, that SIOs who are in the right place at the right time can on occasion take advantage of shifts of circumstance.

As noted, SIOs occupy an intercalary position between faculty on the one hand and administration on the other. Although presidents and provosts would be fairly comfortable dealing with an SIO from a nonacademic background, it's fair to say that most nonacademic SIOs face an uphill road in establishing good working relations with faculty at most of our institutions. Although this fact does not reflect particularly well on faculty, it is a fact of life nonetheless, and one that needs to be kept in mind during searches. We have just one example in this collection of an SIO who did not come from the academic side of things, but all of us are familiar with SIOs from the ranks of business, the diplomatic corps, or the nonprofit sector. And although some of these appointments have been successful, most have not. The Delphi study of thirty or so successful SIOs, which we mention in our opening chapters, listed academic experience as one of the most important attributes for an SIO.

This raises another, and related, issue, that of the PhD as a qualification for the job. Here again, although we have examples of successful SIOs who do not hold PhDs, none appear in this book, and they are relatively few across the profession. It appears that although the doctorate is not a sufficient condition for success, it is, in most cases, a necessary one. This has the effect of creating a glass ceiling for people working in the international programs office, many of whom have no intention of obtaining a PhD. So it appears that we have a two-tiered system in international education, where only one pathway can realistically be expected to lead to an SIO position. And since many of our universities make the possibility of appointment with tenure a condition of hiring an SIO in the first place, opportunities for non-PhD holders are not likely to increase in the near future.

THE INSTITUTIONAL CONTEXT

Our ten authors narrate their experiences as SIOs at a diverse set of twenty-two colleges and universities across the United States, which is only a small sample of the approximately four thousand not-for-profit institutions of higher education in the country. From these stories some patterns emerge, nonetheless, with sufficient clarity to warrant discussion, particularly with respect to two central questions: Is American higher education becoming more international? Is it preparing students to live in a globalized world?

In their essays, the authors describe a number of their own successes in promoting these goals. All of them expanded participation in study abroad programs. Likewise, they played a supportive role in the recruitment of foreign students. They improved services for foreign students and scholars and grew the number of faculty with foreign language skills and foreign area expertise. They introduced new certificates, major, or minors with an international focus and established partnerships with foreign universities. And they incorporated internationalization as a goal in university strategic plans or mission statements.

Recognition of these accomplishments must be tempered, however, by several factors. First, they were of direct benefit to only a minority of students. Second, changes in senior personnel or institutional priorities on occasion halted or even reversed progress on internationalization. Third, it proved difficult and sometimes impossible to overcome the organizational balkanization of international activities found at most institutions. And finally, perhaps most important of all, in no case was the internationalization effort successful in revising the core undergraduate curriculum to make it more global and less Eurocentric in character.

These collective failures have little to do with the energy and talents of senior international officers as agents of change. However, they do speak volumes about the institutional character of American higher education. Several features of US colleges and universities make internationalization difficult.

Despite their organizational complexity, colleges and universities are top-down institutions when it comes to the appointment of key administrators. Boards of trustees or regents can choose and remove the president, the president can choose and remove the provost, the provost can choose and or remove the deans, and the deans can choose or remove department chairs. Everyone serves at the pleasure of those above, and the removal of any individual in the line of authority will affect all those below. Senior faculty members usually have tenure, but administrators have no such job security.

The average length of service of a sitting college or university president in 2012 was 7 years. Presidents of community colleges averaged 7.2 years of service and presidents of independent colleges 7.1 years. Presidents of private doctoral-granting institutions had shorter terms of 6.8 years. The shortest tenure in office was of presidents of public doctoral institutions, averaging 6 years.[1] These averages were skewed by a small number of individuals with many years of service, so the median length of service, not reported, was almost certainly significantly lower. The tenure of provosts and deans is almost certainly shorter still. In sum, the chief international officer is likely to experience every five to six years a change of president and provost that will have significant impact on his mandate.

The situation with respect to faculty is quite different. Tenured faculty members turn over slowly, defend the interests of their department, and have long memories. The rise or fall of a department is linked to course enrollments, and those enrollments are linked to the requirements of the core curriculum. Once a department has succeeded in making some of its courses into requirements, they will fight to keep those requirements. Requirements are usually defended in terms of lofty principles, but they are actually a matter of self-interest in most cases. As a result, the rare revisions of the general curriculum are lengthy and conflict-ridden processes that usually end with compromise and often result in little more than minor change. The only notable exception in the last half-century was the widespread removal of language requirements in the 1960s, from which foreign language enrollments never recovered. Except for the loss of language requirements, the undergraduate curriculum today differs little from what students encountered half a century ago.

Another factor impeding internationalization is that departments are intellectually defined by their disciplines. Most disciplines are not cognizant of geography or culture. The obvious exceptions are geography and anthropology, which are inherently comparative. Some subfields of other disciplines are international in orientation, such as world history and comparative politics, but these are not the dominant subfields in their disciplines. History, political science, political science, sociology, psychology, and the humanities are dominated by Americanists.

Moreover, the disciplines tend to denigrate interdisciplinary research as not meeting their standards. This is particularly challenging for research on global issues, which often requires interdisciplinary approaches. Institutions that establish interdisciplinary centers for foreign area studies or research on global topics may find that departments are unwilling to reward their faculty for collaborating with such units. In fact, departments are likely to look on international service of any kind with disfavor when it comes to tenure, promotion, and salary decisions.

The professional schools add yet another layer of balkanization. These have considerable autonomy, a reflection of the fact that they have their own revenue streams. Until the 1980s the professional schools were almost entirely uninterested in internationalization. However, the steady advance of globalization over the last three decades and the growth of research in the STEM fields overseas has led to increasing international activity in business, medicine, nursing, engineering, law, architecture, and public policy. These activities are generally not coordinated with other aspects of a university's internationalization effort, but they are targets of opportunity for collaboration and coordination.

FORCES FOR CHANGE

In the quarter-century following the end of the Cold War, global integration has accelerated with a rapidity described as "hyperglobalization."[2] Rather than the Pax Americana and end of ideology predicted in the 1980s, the dominance of the United States has declined and conflicts framed in ideological or religious terms have multiplied. This phase of globalization has also been marked by the expansion of economic outsourcing and offshoring, what has been termed the rise of "global value chains."[3] Academic research has experienced a similar globalization; more research is being published overseas than in American journals, and the number of foreign authors publishing in American research journals is also growing. The globalization of economic and scientific production is paralleled by the growth of transactional networks in other fields, such as health, law, film, music, and labor markets.

The expansion of transnational networks not only drives globalization but also exerts continuing pressure for the internationalization of higher education. All the academic disciplines and professional schools are becoming more international both in content and personnel. Even English has had to move beyond the Anglo-American canon, inasmuch as English is now a world language with a transnational literature and there are more English speakers outside than within Britain and the United States. As a result, faculty members in American colleges and universities are inevitably, if gradually and sometimes reluctantly, becoming more internationally oriented.

Likewise, students are aware of the global character of modern society and are interested in developing global skills. A 2008 survey released by the American Council on Education found that 81 percent of entering students were planning to study abroad (55%) or wanted to study abroad (26%).[4] Unfortunately, these hopes were more likely to be dashed than honored.

In 2012–2013, American students studying abroad constituted only about 1 percent of all students enrolled in US colleges and universities. Some colleges, however, have outstanding participation rates, and this has worked well for them. For example, in 2005 Goucher College announced that study abroad would be a graduation requirement for all students entering in 2006 and beyond. The result was a flood of applications, doubling previous rates. Other colleges with very high rates of study abroad participation make a point of advertising their success and have strong application pools.

Study abroad is only one aspect of international education. Other forms of overseas student experience, such as participation in overseas research projects, internships, or other service learning experiences, are also valuable. However, overseas experiences are vastly enriched by other dimensions of education, such as learning foreign languages, gaining deeper knowledge of the histories and cultures of other societies, understanding the various dimensions of globalization, and developing the ability to interact successfully with people of different backgrounds. These dimensions should be part of every student's education, not just as preparation for an undergraduate experience overseas but as preparation for living in a globalized world.

Four thousand institutions of higher education in the United States are competing for funding and enrollment. International education is a target of opportunity for each of them. Inevitably, in some of the institutions the alignments are favorable, and they come closer to offering a genuine international education to all students. When such an institution gets it right, as Goucher College did, recognition can be swift.

International education is now a big business, as a look at any AIEA or NAFSA conference program will quickly confirm. For-profit groups have realized that there is money in study abroad, and they are jostling for market share. Some of these providers are first-rate, others less so. All of them would like universities to let them manage study abroad for their students. Another trend is the appearance of international student recruitment firms, which offer an alternative to the university's own efforts to identify and attract international students. These service providers, in both study abroad and student recruitment, offer a quick shortcut to certain aspects of internationalization. However, they may come at the cost of lost opportunities to build faculty capacity and motivation, as well as lost revenue from an institution's own study abroad programs and recruitment efforts.

FINAL REFLECTIONS

In higher education—as elsewhere in life—nothing stays the same for very long. The accounts of SIO careers presented here have been, perforce, largely retrospective. At the same time, however, they provide valuable guideposts for what may lie ahead for many institutions at a time when the landscape of higher education, and particularly that of international higher education, is changing quickly.

The senior international officer is both an agent of the central administration and an advocate for those faculty and staff committed to international education. Navigating between these two roles is both an opportunity and a challenge. To be successful, the SIO must persuade both sets of players that internationalization is a win-win game from which all can benefit. The professional and interpersonal skills that make this kind agency possible provide much of the substance of the narratives in this book.

The success of an SIO is not, however, purely a matter of agency. Every SIO must confront contingencies over which they have no control. A supportive president or provost may leave. The institution may adopt or have forced on it a new set of priorities. The economy may take a sharp downturn leading to budget cuts. The devaluation or appreciation of the dollar or of a foreign currency may lead to cancellation of an overseas activity. Political upheavals, terrorism, epidemics, and natural disasters may also be disruptive.

This relationship between agency and contingency was the subject of Niccoló Machiavelli's famous discourse on the relationship between *virtú* and *fortuna*. Machiavelli used the term *virtú* to describe not moral virtue but the force of character and the skills necessary for effective action. Machiavelli used *fortuna* to refer to events that affect the context within which the leader must act but that the leader cannot anticipate. These events may be favorable, but they may also be calamitous. Machiavelli observed that it does little good to have good fortuna if one does not have the virtú to take advantage of the situation. If anything, it is better to have virtú than fortuna, because at least one will have the talent to deal effectively with adversity. But when fortuna and virtue coincide, the possibility for effective action is maximized.

As SIOs, all of our authors have experienced periods in which both the central administration and the campus community were excited by the prospect of becoming more international. These are periods of institutional transformation when great strides are made. These favorable conjunctures may be short-lived or long lasting, but each one can leave some indelible mark on the institution.

The larger historic conjuncture we're experiencing now is one of enormous potential for US higher education. The consequences of globalization are more obvious than ever. The American academy faces growing pressure from students and parents to become more international. Faculty in both the disciplines and the professional schools are increasingly receptive to internationalization. The position of senior international officer has become well established. All this suggests that the time is right for a transformative internationalization process.

The transformation of any educational institution, however, requires that the SIO as change agent enjoy both fortuna and virtú. The narratives in this volume make clear that their authors were not short of virtú in their SIO roles. Whatever skills they initially lacked, they learned on the job, and sometimes on two or three jobs. What they also establish is that their talents were only effective when they had fortuna, and that the fortuna that mattered was nothing less than administrative support at the top of the institution as provided by the provost and president.

We view this conclusion as both significant and positive for the challenge of adapting US higher education to a globalized world. The president or provost who chooses to make their institution more international can easily establish the favorable conjunction required for transformative change, first by bringing on board an effective SIO and then by backing that person. Given sufficient time and support from the top, and favorable external circumstances, any good SIO has the virtú required to take her institution to the next level. What the SIO cannot provide, however, is institutional fortuna. This kind of support can only be provided by the top level of academic leadership at an institution. Given this, the internationalization of American higher education is a challenge that requires leadership by the presidents and provosts of US colleges and universities.

Notes

Chapter 1

1. Campbell Stewart, "The Place of Higher Education in a Changing Society," in *The American College*, ed. Nevitt Sanford (New York: Wiley, 1962), 908.
2. Frederick Rudolph, *The American College and University: A History* (New York: Knopf, 1962).
3. National Center for Education Statistics, *Digest of Education Statistics: 2012* (Washington, DC: National Center for Education Statistics, 2012), chap. 3.
4. Some were later declassified and published after the war. The most famous of these was the anthropologist Ruth Benedict's study of Japanese national character, which became both an anthropology classic and a best seller in Japan. Ruth Benedict, *The Chrysanthemum and the Sword: Patterns of Japanese Culture* (Boston: Houghton Mifflin, 1946).
5. Richard D. Lambert, Elinor G. Barber, Eleanor Jorden, Margaret B. Merrill, and Leon I. Twarog, *Beyond Growth: The Next Stage in Language and Area Studies* (Washington, DC: Association of American Universities, 1984), 4–10.
6. Stephen A. Freeman, "Undergraduate Study Abroad," in *International Education: Past, Present, Problems and Prospects* (Washington, DC: Government Printing Office, 1966), 397.
7. The NDEA point man for this legislation was Eliot Richardson, the assistant secretary for education in the Department of Health, Education, and Welfare. Richardson later served as secretary of defense and attorney general under President Nixon.
8. Richard D. Scarfo, "History of Title VI/Fulbright Hays," in *International Education in the New Global Era*, ed. John N. Hawkins, Carlos Manuel Haro, Miriam A. Kazanjian, Gilbert W. Merkx, and David Wiley (Los Angeles: International Studies and Overseas Programs, UCLA, 1998), 23–25.
9. The legislative history of development assistance is discussed in detail in Vernon Ruttan, *United States Development Assistance Policy: The Domestic Politics of Foreign Economic Aid* (Baltimore: Johns Hopkins University Press, 1996), esp. 49–58, 70–79, 210–211.
10. Freeman, "Undergraduate Study Abroad," 387–392.
11. An early assessment of the foreign student presence in US institution is provided in "The Foreign Student: Whom Shall We Welcome? A Report of The EWA Study Committee on Foreign Student Affairs," in *International Education: Past, Present, Problems and Prospects,* 327–330. A more contemporary overview is provided by Richard Lambert in "Foreign Student Flows and the Internationalization of American Higher Education," in *Language and International Studies: A Richard Lambert Perspective*, ed. Sara Jane Moore and Christine A. Morfit (Washington, DC: National Foreign Language Center Monograph Series, 1993), 206–236.

12. For an excellent firsthand account of the impact of such programs at Michigan State University, see Ralph Smuckler, *A University Turns to the World* (East Lansing: Michigan State University Press, 2003).

13. Gilbert W. Merkx, "Foreign Language and Area Studies Through Title VI: Assessing Supply and Demand," in *Language Policy and Pedagogy*, ed. Richard D. Lambert and Elana Shohamy (Philadelphia: John Benjamins, 2000), 93–110.

14. Burkart Holzner and Matthew Harmon, "Intellectual and Organizational Challenges for International Education in the United States: A Knowledge System Perspective," in Hawkins et al., *International Education in the New Global Era*, 31–65.

15. This issue was identified by Richard D. Lambert, "Domains and Issues in International Studies," *International Education Forum* 16, no. 1 (1966): 1–19.

16. See Weber's discussion of class, status, and party in Hans Gerth and C. Wright Mills, ed. and trans., *From Max Weber: Essays in Sociology* (New York: Oxford University Press, 1946),180–195.

17. I am using these terms in a manner analogous to Pierre Bourdieu's concepts of economic capital (wealth), social capital (vertical prestige), and cultural capital (academic prestige).

18. It is, to be sure, possible for a faculty member to translate academic prestige into above-average salary increases as well as discretionary power over budgets through grants for sponsored research or through appointment to a position of administrative authority. Power and vertical prestige do not, however, translate back into academic prestige. Once an individual has traded academic prestige for power, the demands on time of administration make the maintenance of individual academic prestige (which requires an active research agenda) increasingly problematic. This translates to the hypothesis that the longer a person is in administration, the lower their academic prestige.

19. Limits on presidential budgetary and discretionary authority over lower institutional levels can be quite functional for the university president by reducing the parade of supplicants and appeals that otherwise surge from below. Trustees and faculty alike expect the president to be successful in extracting resources from private donors or, in public institutions, from the legislature, which is difficult to achieve if the president's time is occupied with institutional matters. Unfortunately, insulation from discretionary authority also makes it difficult for the president to shape institutional development.

20. The athletic director, for example, may control a very large budget and staff and be a person of high prestige in the surrounding community while at the same time on campus be the target of faculty and student animosity.

21. The department chair, like the shop foreman, is caught between higher authority and her constituents. If the chair is motivated by vertical prestige, pleasing the administration may lead to administrative advancement. If the chair is motivated by academic prestige, then there is every reason to be tenacious in defense of the department's quest for academic quality at the expense of being a thorn in the side of the administration.

22. There are some differences in the resources available to the provost and the A&S dean. The provost has greater vertical prestige than the dean and has direct authority over the dean. The provost also controls the allocation of funding increases, should they exist. However, in other respects the dean has more discretionary power than the provost, both in terms of

the number of direct subordinates (often twenty or more chairs) and in terms of discretionary authority over appointments, salaries, promotions, and tenure decisions affecting of hundreds of faculty.

Chapter 2

1. *Investing in Human Capital: Leadership for the Challenges of the 21st Century* (New York: Institute for International Education, 1995), 8.
2. Sue Estroff, "Who Are You? Why Are You Here? Anthropology and Human Suffering," *Human Organization* 43, no. 4 (1984): 368–370.
3. Jane Knight, "Updated Definition of Internationalization," *International Higher Education* 33 (Fall 2003): 2.
4. *College-Bound Students' Interests in Study Abroad and Other International Learning Activities* (Washington, DC: American Council on Education, 2008). 1.
5. Susan Lambert, Riall Nolan, Norman Peterson, and Deborah Pierce, *Critical Skills and Knowledge for Senior Campus International Leaders* (Washington, DC: NAFSA, Association of International Educators, 2007).
6. Wendell Berry, *The Gift of Good Land: Further Essays Cultural and Agricultural* (San Francisco: North Point), 134–148.

Chapter 4

1. This topic is explored in John D. Heyl and Danny Damron, "Should I Stay or Should I Go? Career Dilemmas for International Educators," *International Educator* 23 (September/October 2014): 50–53.
2. Jim Collins, *Good to Great and the Social Sectors* (New York: HarperCollins, 2005).
3. Maurice Harrari, "The Internationalization of the Curriculum," in *Bridges to the Future: Strategies for Internationalizing Higher Education,* ed. C. Klasek (Carbondale, IL: AIEA, 1992), 71.

Chapter 8

1. Cooperative Institutional Research Program, "Cooperative Institutional Research Program College Senior Survey," 2013, http://www.heri.ucla.edu (hereafter cited as CIRP-CSS).
2. See Uliana Gabara, "Faculty Seminar Abroad: Cornerstone of Comprehensive Internationalization at the University of Richmond" (manuscript submitted for review), which offers an extensive analysis and history of the Seminar as well as a handbook for creating your own version of it.
3. *Internationalizing Higher Education Through the Faculty* (Washington, DC: National Association of State Universities and Land Grant Colleges, 1993); J. D. Heyl, *The Senior International Officer (SIO) as Change Agent* (Durham, NC: Association of International Education Administrators, 2007); National Association of State Universities and Land Grant Colleges. (1993).   J. K Hudzik, *Comprehensive Internationalization: From Concept to Action* (Washington, DC: NAFSA, Association of International Education, 2011); J. Knight, *Higher Education in Turmoil: The Changing World of Internationalization,* Vol. 13: *Global Perspectives on Higher Education* (Rotterdam, the Netherlands: Sense, 2008).
4. On the numbers of undergraduate internationals, see Open Doors, *Report on International*

Educational Exchange (New York: Institute of International Education, 2014), published annually.

5. CIRP-CSS.

Chapter 10

1. Donald Shön, *The Reflective Practitioner: How Professionals Think in Action* (New York: Basic Books, 1983).

2. Edgar H. Schein, *Organizational Culture and Leadership,* 3rd ed. (San Francisco, Jossey-Bass, 2004).

Chapter 11

1. Eleanor Roosevelt, http://www.brainyquote.com/quotes/quotes/e/eleanorroo100940.html.

Chapter 12

1. See https://reason.kzoo.edu/diversity/.

2. Kalamazoo College Office of Institutional Research, http://www.kzoo.edu/college/?p= fastfacts.

3. Mark Van Doren, *Liberal Education* (Boston: Beacon Press, 1959), 67.

4. Marshall Gregory, "A Liberal Education Is Not a Luxury," Chronicle of Higher Education, September 12, 2003, http://chronicle.com/weekly/v50/i03/03b01601.htm.

5. Larry Barrett, "Betting the Store," *Lux Esto: The Magazine of Kalamazoo College* (Spring 2005): 7–13 (originally published in *Lux Esto* in 1989).

6. See http://www.kzoo.edu/college/?p=fastfacts.

7. Jane Knight, *Internationalisation: Elements and Checkpoints* (Ottawa: Canadian Bureau for International Education, 1994), 3.

8. See American Council on Education, "Internationalization Laboratory," 2015, http://www.acenet.edu/news-room/Pages/ACE-Internationalization-Laboratory.aspx.

9. Madeline Green and Christa Olson, *Internationalizing the Campus: A User's Guide* (Washington, DC: American Council on Education, 2003).

10. Uwe Brandenburg and Hans de Wit, "The End of Internationalization," *International Higher Education* 62 (Winter 2011): 15–17.

11. Barrett, "Betting the Store," 7–13.

12. Green and Olsen, *Internationalizing the Campus,* 21.

13. Knight, *Internationalisation,* 3.

Conclusion

1. Wei Song and Harold V. Hartley, *A Study of Presidents of Colleges and Universities* (Washington, DC: Council of Independent Colleges, 2013), 8.

2. Arvid Subramanian and Martin Kessler, "The Hyperglobalization of Trade and Its Future" (Working Paper 3, Global Citizen Foundation, London, June 2013).

3. Gary Gereffi, "Global Value Chains in a Post–Washington Consensus World," *Review of International Political Economy* 21, no. 1 (2014): 9–37.

4. *College-Bound Students' Interests in Study Abroad and Other International Learning Activities* (Washington, DC: American Council on Education, 2008).

Acknowledgments

This book is the result of collaboration among many people. The editors and the authors of its chapters are closest to the project, but its subject matter reflects the cumulative wisdom of countless conferences, workshops, and discussions among senior international officers of US colleges and universities over the last quarter-century. The great French sociologist Emile Durkheim wrote, "Collective representations are the result of an immense co-operation, which stretches out not only into space but into time as well; to make them, a multitude of minds have associated, united, and combined their ideas and sentiments." This book is precisely such a collective representation.

The Association of International Education Administrators (AIEA) has been the focal point for many of these discussions. All twelve authors have been closely associated with AIEA. We are particularly grateful to Jack Van de Water, the second president of AIEA and the first author to submit his chapter for this book; to John Heyl, another past president of AIEA and the second author to submit; and to Howard Rollins, the third author to submit. Their chapters inspired those who followed. We are also grateful to the executive director of AIEA, Darla Deardorff, and her staff, under whose stewardship AIEA has grown and prospered without losing its essential character as a forum for the exchange of ideas and informal networking.

Douglas Clayton, executive director of the Harvard Education Publishing Group, has been consistent in his support of this project from the very beginning, as well as tolerant of our delays. We are grateful for his encouragement. We also thank the very efficient staff of HEPG, including Chris Leonesio, editorial and production director, and Laura Cutone, marketing manager.

About the Editors

Gilbert W. Merkx is Professor of the Practice of Sociology at Duke University, where he served as vice provost for International Affairs from 2001 to 2010. He received his BA from Harvard and MA and PhD from Yale.

Merkx was born in Maracaibo, Venezuela. He has been a Fulbright scholar in anthropology at the University of Huamanga in Perú and a visiting scholar at the Instituto Di Tella in Buenos Aires and at the Latin American Institute of the University of Stockholm. He has taught on the faculties of Yale University, Göteborg University (Sweden), and the University of New Mexico, where he was director of the Latin American and Iberian Institute from 1980 to 2001. At Duke University he has been director of the Center for International Studies, the Center for Latin American and Caribbean Studies, and the Center for Islamic Studies. He served as director of International and Area Studies from 2010 to 2015.

His research has focused on public policy formation, international education, and social networks. He has done field research in Peru, Argentina, Sweden, Mexico, Chile, and Uruguay. His books include *The Jewish Experience in Latin America* (with Judith Elkin, Allen & Unwin, 1987), *International Education in the New Global Era* (with John Hawkins et al., International Studies and Overseas Programs, UCLA, 1997), and *Constructal Theory of Social Dynamics* (with Adrian Bejan, Springer, 2007).

Merkx served as editor of the *Latin American Research Review* from 1982 to 2002. He is also past president of the Association of International Education Administrators (AIEA) and serves on its board and those of Venice International University and the Scholars at Risk Network.

Riall W. Nolan is professor of Anthropology at Purdue University, where, until 2009, he served as associate provost and dean of International Programs. Nolan earned his PhD in social anthropology from Sussex University in 1975.

At the start of his career, Nolan worked overseas for nearly twenty years in the field of international development, as a project designer, manager, and evaluator. He has lived and worked in Senegal, Tunisia, Papua New Guinea, and Sri Lanka. His work included grass-roots community projects with the Peace Corps, project design and management with USAID, and policy analysis with the World Bank. He has also participated in numerous consulting assignments for both bilateral agencies and NGOs.

Prior to coming to Purdue in 2003, Nolan managed international programs at the University of Pittsburgh, Golden Gate University, and the University of Cincinnati. He is the past chair of NAFSA's task force on International Education Leadership and a past board member of both AIEA and the Society for Applied Anthropology. He presently serves on the national board of Engineers Without Borders and on the editorial board for the UK-based journal *Anthropology in Action*. He has been a Fulbright scholar, a Foreign Area fellow, and a Ford-Rockefeller fellow, and he has won teaching awards at both Pitt and Purdue. He writes, consults, and presents frequently on issues of international development, cross-cultural adaptation, and applied anthropology.

About the Contributors

Joseph Brockington is associate provost for International Programs and professor of German language and literature at Kalamazoo College. He has served as a member of the founding board of the Forum on Education Abroad, AIEA's executive committee, and the national team of the International Education Leadership Knowledge Committee of NAFSA. Brockington has published and presented on topics in education abroad, international programs administration, campus internationalization, and legal and risk management issues in education abroad.

Uliana Gabara led successive stages of comprehensive internationalization at the University of Richmond for twenty-six years, including the Faculty Seminar Abroad, curriculum internationalization, university partnerships, equal access to study abroad (resulting in 60 percent participation), a 12 percent international student population, and a purpose-built International Center. Her initiatives include collaborative online teaching and a cultures and languages across the curriculum program. Gabara earned a PhD in Slavic languages and literatures from the University of Virginia, and an MA in English philology at the University of Warsaw.

John Heyl is the founder and editor of IELeaders.net, a website devoted to the senior international educator. Previously he served as the senior international officer at the University of Missouri–Columbia and at Old Dominion University. Heyl is a former president of AIEA (2000–2001), the author of *The Senior International Officer (SIO) as Change Agent* (AIEA, 2007*),* and a coeditor (with Darla Deardorff, Hans de Wit, and Tony Adams) of *The SAGE Handbook of International Higher Education* (Sage, 2012*).* He earned a doctorate in European history from Washington University–St. Louis.

Maria Carmen Sada Krane has directed international programs at Nebraska Wesleyan, Agnes Scott College, and Creighton University. Before becoming a senior international officer, she taught linguistics and foreign languages in the United States and in her native Brazil. She has presented her research on various facets of internationalization at conferences worldwide. Krane's most recent publication, for ACE, focuses on Brazilian student-scholar mobility. Her service to the profession includes membership on the TOEFL and International Student Exchange Programs Boards and a term as president of AIEA in 2003–2004.

William Lacy is professor of sociology in the Department of Human Ecology at the University of California, Davis. From 1999 to 2014 he was vice provost for University Outreach and International Programs at Davis and was responsible for leadership of all campus international initiatives. Lacy has a PhD in sociology/social psychology from the University of Michigan. He is a fellow of the American Association for the Advancement of Science, a recipient of two Fulbright awards, and president of AIEA in 2010–2011.

Howard Rollins recently retired after forty-five years of service to Emory University and Georgia Tech. At Emory, he was the founding director of the Center for International Programs Abroad, providing leadership for study abroad. In 2003 he became associate vice provost of International Programs at Georgia Tech, where he led the development of the campuswide International Plan, an initiative that won several national awards for excellence, including the Senator Paul Simon Award. Rollins earned a PhD in psychology from the University of California, Los Angeles.

Joseph Tullbane is founder and president of the I-Quad Group, an international education consultancy. Until 2013 he directed international education at St. Norbert College. He now serves as vice president for strategy at Initiative-One, a national leadership firm. His education includes degrees in architecture from Rice University; a MA in international relations from American University; and a PhD in Russian-area studies from Georgetown University. In 2009 Tullbane received the Timothy Rutenber Award for outstanding service to AIEA.

David Ward, an urban geographer, is a native of Manchester, England. He has an MA from Leeds University and a PhD from the University of Wisconsin–Madison (UWM). After teaching at Carleton University and the University of British Columbia, he returned to UWM in 1966, where he served as provost from 1989 to 1993 and as chancellor from 1993 to 2001. From 2001 to 2008 Ward was president of the American Council on Education. From 2011 to 2013 he served as interim chancellor of the University of New Mexico.

Jack Van de Water holds a PhD in comparative education from Syracuse University, where from 1968 to 1976 he served as associate director of International Programs. From 1976 to 2003 he managed international activities at Oregon State University, first as director and then as dean, working as a program developer and administrator, fund raiser, grant writer, and change agent. He was also an assistant vice chancellor for the Oregon University system. Van de Water served as AIEA's president from 1985 to 1986.

Index

academic affairs, SIO's role in, 147–149
academic departments, 45, 48, 88, 90, 91, 94–95, 101, 124, 219
administration. *See* central administrators/ administration
administrative experience, 129–130
administrative philosophy, 40, 42
advisory council, 124
agency, 85, 222
Agnes Scott College, 116–118, 122–124
agreements, 177–179
agricultural assistance programs, 17–18, 19, 183
allies, 83
American Council on Education (ACE), 6, 43, 206–207
Amherst College, 12
area studies, 94–95
Army Specialized Training Program (ASTP), 15–16
Arthur, Tom, 96
Asian languages, 13
assessment, 143–145, 209
Association of International Education Administrators (AIEA), 2, 7, 43, 55, 73–74, 78, 115, 136, 146, 193
Association of International Educators, 7
Association of Pacific Rim Universities (APRU), 193
audit culture, 30

Board for Food and International Development (BIFAD), 16, 18
branch campuses, 102, 105–106, 179
Bright, Dave, 93

budget challenges, 45, 47, 138–143, 191, 195–196
Bundy, McGeorge, 16

Cambridge University, 10–11
campus culture. *See* institutional culture
campus policy, 25
capacity building, 176–177
career development, 39–40
career trajectories, 7, 49–51, 53–63, 65–85, 87–109, 111–122, 128–129, 151–153, 169–172, 183–192, 201–202
Carol Weinstein International Center, 143
cathedrals, 10–11
CEA Global Education, 59–60
Center for International Programs Abroad (CIPA), 90–93
central administrators/administration, 19–20, 22, 84
    changes in, 46–47, 107–108, 118–119, 125–126, 136–138, 180, 194–195, 215, 218
    faculty and, 123–124, 174, 203
    philosophy of, 40
    relationships with, 61
    SIO and, 122–123, 147–149
    strategic partnerships with, 34
    support from, 92, 103–104, 109, 114, 125, 174, 191–192, 197–198, 209–210, 214
centralized approach, to internationalization, 133–136
CEO relations, 61
chief financial officer, 174
China, 118, 196–197

choices, 84
classical curriculum, 12–13
Coalition for International Education, 74
co-degrees, 94–95, 100
Colgate University, 184–185
collaboration, 94–95, 173, 198
Collaborative Online International
    Learning (COIL), 148
college-business community partnership,
    153–154
college education, 11–12
colleges. *See also* higher education;
    universities
    independent, 11
    residential, 10–11
Columbia University, 11
communication, 193–194
community outreach, 116, 163–164
community partnerships, 153–154
Confucius Institute, 196–197
continental model, 11–12
contingency, 84, 85, 222
Cornell University, 184, 186
Council for International Education and
    Exchange, 7
Council of National Resource Center
    Directors (CNRC), 73, 74, 78
Council on International Educational
    Exchange (CIEE), 140
Council on Student Travel, 7
Creekmore, Marion, 95–96
Creighton University, 118–122
cultural narratives, 34–35
Cultures and Languages Across the
    Curriculum (CLAC), 148
curriculum
    classical, 12–13
    educational process and, 48
    internationalization of, 129. *see also*
        internationalization
    reform, 25, 44, 208, 219
    transformation of, 12–14

Davis, William E., 71–72, 75
deans, 20–21, 22, 48, 103, 175, 218
department heads, 48–49, 92–93
direct enrollment, 139–140
disciplines, 219
Domenici, Pete, 74
donor funding, 142–143, 204
drinking age, 93
Duke University, 76–82, 85

educational institutions. *See also*
    institutions; universities
    comparison of US, 14–15
Emory University, 88–98
engagement, 173–174
English as a second language (ESL)
    programs, 5, 113, 163
English language, 220
European Association for International
    Education, 7
European languages, 13
exchange programs, 139–141. *See also* study
    abroad programs
external champions, 47, 49
external funding, 142–143

faculty
    administrators and, 123–124, 174, 203
    development, 145
    incentives for, 29–30
    interests of, 35
    international, 1, 183
    international experience for, 129, 145
    involvement of, 92–93, 103, 109, 123,
        129, 131–132, 154–155, 159, 189–191
    prestige of, 20
    relationships, 5, 34, 41, 48–49, 83, 123,
        158–159, 179
    role of, 48
    support from, 174, 189–191, 214
    turnover, 180, 219
Faculty Study Abroad Grants (FSAG), 203

financial aid, 138–139, 140
food shortages, 17–18
Foreign Assistance Act, 16
foreign languages, 1, 118, 147–148
Foreign Language Teaching Assistants (FLTAs), 118
foreign student enrollments, 17–19, 21. *See also* international students
Forum on Education Abroad, 7
Freeman Foundation, 204
Fulbright Act, 16–17
Fulbright-Hays Act, 16–17
Fulbright Program, 16–17, 67–68
funding, 29, 42, 45, 47, 73, 91–92, 138–143, 195–196, 204
fund-raising, 195–196

general education, 208, 219
Georgia Institute of Technology, 97–108
German model, 11
global challenges, 24
global citizenship, 202
globalization, 13, 24, 133, 220–221, 223
global skills, 220–221
goals, 41, 156–157
Golden Gate University, 171–172, 174, 179
Göteborg University, 70–71
graduate school, 12, 15
grants, 204
GT Lorraine, 102–103

Harvard University, 11, 67
higher education
    curriculum, 12–14
    European model of, 11
    history of, 9–12
    purpose of, 24
    state support for, 45
    in US. *see* US higher education
hubris, 35, 180
human resources, 51
Hunter, Howard, 96–97

IELeaders.net, 60
ignorance, 180
Illinois Wesleyan University (IWU), 54, 60
incentives, 29–30
India, 105
information sharing, 193–194
Institute for International Education of Students (IES), 140
Institute of Comparative and International Studies (ICIS), 94–97
Institute of International Education (IIE), 144
institutional character, 5
institutional context, 217–220
institutional culture, 6, 41, 47, 129, 172–173, 179–181, 216, 217–220
institutional funding, 138–141
institutional learning, 36
institutional politics, 19–21
institutional strategy, 137–138
institutional traditions, 208
institutions
    comparison of educational, 14–15
    history of, 130–132
    private, 14
    public, 14, 19, 100
    research, 10, 11, 15, 19, 20
    social, 20
    transformations of, 131–132
Integrative Cultural Project (ICRP), 205
Intensive English Language Institute (IELI), 119–122
interdisciplinary research, 219
international advisory council, 124
International Affairs Committee (IAC), 77, 80
International Affairs Group (IAG), 80
international committees, 49
international connections, 176–179
International Cultural Service Program (ICSP), 45
International Degree, 44–45

international education
activities, 9
assessment in, 143–145, 209
budget issues, 138–143, 191
business of, 221
challenges of, 15
different perspectives on, 19
federal support of, 85
field of, 3, 159
growth of, 7, 183
leadership, 37–52, 87–109
liberal arts and, 199–212
in the US, 9–22
international educators, 2
international experience, 83, 121, 129, 145, 184, 221
international faculty, 1, 183
internationalization
administrative coordination of, 1–2
approaches to, 35
building blocks of, 28–33, 35–36
capacity building for, 176–177
centralized approach to, 133–136
challenges of, 14, 155–158, 213–223
educating about, 125
faculty support for, 189–191
forces for change and, 220–221
forms of, 182
high-level support for, 6, 125
history of, 3
indicators of, 26
institutional culture and, 6, 47, 129, 172–173, 179–181, 216–220
institutional strategy and, 137–138
leadership support for, 191–192
levels of, 25–26
meaning of, 24–25, 202, 207, 210–211
metrics of, 215
motivation for, 175
need for, 1, 23–24, 131–132
planning for, 34, 136–138
policy support for, 176, 177

as process, 208–209
progress toward, 26–28
promotion of, 84
reasons for, 132–133
resources for, 176
routes to, 1–2
SIO's role in, 33–35
support for, 47–49
WWII and, 15–19
Internationalization Collaborative, 6
Internationalization Laboratory (ACE), 206–209
Internationally Engaged, 193–194
international office, services of, 42–43
international partnerships, 177–179, 192
International Programs Committee (IPC), 203
International Student Exchange Program (ISEP), 115, 117, 121
international students, 1, 17–19, 116, 183
assessment of issues related to, 144–145
growth in, 141–142
interaction between US and, 101–102, 104–105, 134–135, 139
needs of, 164
number of, 143–144
recruitment of, 106, 119–120, 125, 164, 166–167
international studies, 1
introspection, 130

Jordan, 118

Kalamazoo College, 199–212
Kalamazoo Project in Intercultural Communication (KPIC), 204
Kiesler, Charles, 56

languages, 13, 147–148, 220
language services, 163–164
Latin American Institute (LAI), 71–76

leadership
  changes in, 107–108, 118–119, 125–126,
    136–138, 180, 194–195, 215, 218
  confidence in, 157
  experiences of, 151–167
  international education, 37–52, 87–109
  pathways to, 87–109
  senior, 191–192, 197–198
  from the side, 61–62
legal commitments, 178
liberal education, 11–12, 133, 199–212

Machiavelli, 222
Marshall Plan, 16
McGregor Fund, 204
Mellon Foundation, 204
Miami-Dade Community College, 18
Mississippi State University (MSU), 113
monasteries, 11–12

National Association of Foreign Student
  Administrators, 7
National Defense Education Act (NDEA),
  16, 17, 19, 38, 70
Nebraska Wesleyan University (NWU),
  114–116, 122–123, 124
networking, 48–49, 121

Office of International Programs, 45–46
Office of International Research and
  Development (OIRD), 46
Office of Strategic Services (OSS), 15
Old Dominion University (ODU), 57–59
online learning, 148
Open Doors report, 144
opinion leaders, 173, 209
Oregon State University (OSU), 37,
  "39–48
organizational change, 21
organizational culture. *See* institutional
  culture
outsourcing, 220

overseas campuses, 102, 105–106, 179
Oxford University, 10–11

parochial interests, 95
partnerships, 25, 34, 42, 176–179, 192, 198
Penn State University, 186
PhD qualification, 217
planning, 28–29, 136–138, 179
Point Four Program, 16, 18
policy support, 176, 177
politics, institutional, 19–21
power, 20
president, 20, 84, 137–138, 174, 175, 180,
  215, 218
prestige, 20–21
Princeton University, 11
private institutions, 14
professional development, 43, 51, 167–168,
  192–193
professional organizations, 146–147,
  192–193
professional schools, 12, 15, 219–220
promotions, 49–50
provost, 20–21, 22, 84, 174, 175, 214–215,
  218
public institutions, 14, 19, 100
Purdue University, 172, 179–180, 181

Quality Enhancement Plan (QEP), 102,
  103, 104

Reagan, Ronald, 73
relationship building, 34, 41, 48–49, 61,
  83, 121, 179, 182, 198
research institutions, 10, 11, 15, 19, 20
residential colleges, 10–11
resources, 176
revenue generation, 119
Rudolph, Frederick, 13

sabbaticals, 89
Sanderson, Steve, 93–94

School for International Training (SIT),
140
self-knowledge, 128–130
senior international officer (SIO), 2
  academic affairs and, 147–149
  in administrative structure, 50–51,
    214–217
  advice for new, 48–52
  attributes of successful, 30–31
  career trajectories, 7, 49–51, 53–63,
    65–85, 87–109, 111–122, 128–129,
    151–153, 169–172, 183–192,
    201–202
  as change advocate, 23–36, 41, 223
  experiences of, 151–167
  goals of, 41, 156–157
  hiring of, 30–33
  influence of, 44, 48
  as itinerant professional, 53–63
  leadership by, 4, 37–52, 61–62
  learning from, 35–36
  lessons for, 60–63, 82–84, 127–149,
    181–182, 197–198, 207–211
  off-campus work of, 145–147
  on-campus presence of, 124–125
  past experiences of, 128–130, 181–182
  position of, 122–124, 223
  as professional, 214–217
  role of, 4, 21–22, 33–35, 123, 169–182,
    203, 222
senior leadership, 191–192, 197–198.
    See also central administrators/
    administration
Singapore, 105–106
SIO. See senior international officer
    (SIO)
social capital, 83
social institutions, 20
social media, 194
Soviet Union, 17
space program, 17
Sputnik, 17
staffing, 138, 141–142, 157, 198

stakeholders, 83, 84, 173, 175, 176, 178,
    209
Stewart, Norman, 68
Stimson, Henry, 16
St. Norbert College, 151–167
strategic conversations, 174–176, 178, 179
strategic partnerships, 34, 42
strategic planning, 28–29, 136–138, 179–
    181, 183
students
  international, 1, 17–19, 101–102, 104–
    106, 116, 119–120, 125, 134–135, 139,
    164, 166–167, 183
  US, 27–28, 101–102, 134–135
study abroad programs, 1, 12, 13, 21, 38–39
  assessment of, 144
  demand for, 220–221
  developing, 50, 88–89, 153–154, 205
  direct enrollment, 139–140
  expansion of, 115–118, 141, 183
  faculty involvement in, 92–93, 103
  faculty-led, 190–191
  financial aid for, 138–139, 140
  Fulbright Program, 16–17
  funding of, 91–92
  impact of, 89
  internationalization of, 203–205
  International Student Exchange Program
    (ISEP), 115, 117, 121
  justifications for, 133
  longer term, 101, 102
  participation in, 27, 90–91, 101, 120–121,
    131, 221
  semester-long, 139, 162–163, 179–180
  structure for, 139–140

technology, 49, 148
technology-transfer programs, 1
tenure, 49–50, 219
Texas Women's University (TWA), 113–114
Third Lateran Council, 11
Title VI funding, 73, 79, 114–115, 142
trustees, 175

UC Davis Global Centers, 197
universities. *See also specific universities*
  institutional politics, 19–21
  origins of, 9–12
  overseas campuses of, 102, 105–106
  private, 14
  public, 14, 19, 100
  research, 10, 11, 15, 19, 20
University College London (UCL),
  88, 89
University of California, Davis, 186–198
University of California Education
  Abroad Program (UC EAP), 190
University of Cincinnati, 172, 174, 179
University of Huamanga, 68
University of Kentucky, 185
University of Missouri-Columbia (MU),
  55–57, 60, 62
University of New Mexico, 70, 71–76, 85
University of Pennsylvania, 11
University of Pittsburgh, 181
University of Richmond, 130–132,
  136–143
US Agency for International Development
  (USAID), 185

US higher education
  budget challenges in, 47
  comparison of institutions, 14–15
  curriculum, 12–14
  early history of, 11–12
  exceptionalism of, 9–12
  institutional politics, 19–21
  international education in, 9–22
  WWII and, 15–19
US military, 15–16
US students, 27–28, 101–102,
  134–135

V-12 Navy College Training Program,
  15–16

Wakeman, Frederick, 16
whole person education, 199–212
William and Mary University, 11
win-win strategy, 84
World War II, internationalization and,
  15–19

Yale Report (1828), 12
Yale University, 11, 12, 69